Christian Zeidler

Mobile Support in Customer Loyalty Management

GABLER EDITION WISSENSCHAFT

Mobile Computing

Herausgegeben von Univ.-Prof. Dr. Otto Petrovic

Mobilfunkdienste haben Wirtschaft und Gesellschaft in den letzten Jahren nachhaltig verändert. Noch nie hat sich eine Technologie so rasch weltweit verbreitet – auch nicht das PC-basierte Internet. Neben Sprachdiensten gewinnen Datendienste zunehmend an Bedeutung und viele sehen das Mobiltelefon bereits als den Massencomputer der Zukunft an.

Die Schriftenreihe publiziert hervorragende Forschungsarbeiten aus dem Gebiet des Mobile Computing. Diese untersuchen Phänomene wissenschaftlich fundiert und geben somit wichtige Impulse für Entscheidungsträger in Unternehmen. Besonderer Wert wird auf eine integrierte Betrachtung von Technologie, Wirtschaftlichkeit und Anwenderakzeptanz gelegt.

Christian Zeidler

Mobile Support in Customer Loyalty Management

An Architectural Framework

With a foreword by Univ.-Prof. Dr. Otto Petrovic

GABLER EDITION WISSENSCHAFT

Bibliographic information published by the Deutsche Nationalbibliothek
The Deutsche Nationalbibliothek lists this publication in the Deutsche Nationalbibliografie;
detailed bibliographic data are available in the Internet at http://dnb.d-nb.de.

Dissertation Karl Franzens Universität Graz, 2008

Veröffentlicht mit Unterstützung der evolaris next level Privatstiftung im Rahmen des graduate
research opportunity program (GROP).

1st Edition 2009

Editorial Office: Claudia Jeske / Anita Wilke

Gabler is part of the specialist publishing group Springer Science+Business Media.
www.gabler.de

Cover design: Regine Zimmer, Dipl.-Designerin, Frankfurt/Main
Printed on acid-free paper
Printed in Germany

ISBN 978-3-8349-1436-1

Foreword

Companies are increasingly faced with the fact that the communication habits of their customers have changed sustainably – not only through the use of the Internet, but even more through the use of mobile services. Traditional marketing and communication instruments are increasingly being supplemented or even replaced by the direct, personalized address of the customer. The most powerful tool for this kind of communication is the mobile phone. It provides a direct and interactive communication channel to the customer. For numerous people, the mobile phone is no longer simply perceived as another medium, but rather as an indispensable part of daily life, even as part of their personality. At the same time, it is not only used for telephony, but also as a central communication and information hub. While the Internet is increasingly leaving the traditional personal computer, and conquering the mobile phone, the sending of messages via mobile phone has been a standard way of communicating, not only for young audiences.

This suggests the assumption that the direct communication channel will be used strongly by marketers in the near future in order to attract new customers and provide extended services to existing ones. Since it is such a powerful tool, its use represents a particular challenge for companies – as it represents the direct, sensitive connection to the heart and mind of the customer. The presented work thus examines the question of how existing loyalty programs can be supported by mobile services to adapt to the customers' true worlds of communication.

The author combines the technological potential of current and future mobile services with the requirements of the Relationship Marketing to answer these questions. A key result of this work is the presented reference model for mobile supported loyalty. Based on the reference model, the current business models in the area of loyalty programs and possible transformations through the integration of mobile services are discussed. In the final step the author describes the evaluation process of the results through the application of the model within case studies from the fields of banking, retail and multi-partner programs.

Through this integrated perspective, based on a sound technological basis as well as economic considerations, a result emerged that provides a scientific investigation into a real phenomenon within the selected area of work, and develops practical solutions in the application field. The largest challenge now remains the sustainable transformation of the real value system in which loyalty programs are embedded. Only then can these programs live up to the evolving worlds of communication of their members.

Prof. Dr. Otto Petrovic

Preface

At this point, I would like to take the opportunity to thank all those who have supported and encouraged me in the last few years, and have made possible the presented work.

In this context, first and foremost, I want to thank my supervisor, Univ.-Prof. Dr. Otto Petrovic, for his numerous suggestions during the development of the research question and support in methodological issues. Univ.-Prof. Dr. Reinhard Haberfellner deserves my thankfulness for the willingness to conduct the second assessment and to take on the related effort.

Furthermore, I would like to thank my colleagues at the evolaris research lab, particularly Mrs. Corrina Höll, Dr. Christian Kittl, Mr. Kurt Köstenbauer, and Mr. Hans Jörg Peyha who continuously supported me in all problems of the workday life of a research project.

Special thanks belong to my partner Barbara, my parents, my sister, and all my relatives for their constant support and motivation. Therefore, I would like to dedicate this work to my family.

Dr. Christian Zeidler

Contents

List of figures

List of tables

1 Introduction and problem frame

For a customer communication strategy to be successful in the sense of building a loyal customer base that will recurrently generate revenue with a business, a range of influential factors must be considered: customer satisfaction or the familiarity with, and appeal of the brand are mainly product related while the relationship oriented factors driving loyalty are trust, perceived quality of the interaction or relationship and the expected utility from the relationship over time.

Mobile technology, when used correctly, can help achieve and deepen some these factors. While it is clear that it will not be able to replace the traditional channels entirely in a close future, it will rather offer another, much closer, channel to the customer that will enable businesses that leverage this advantage to establish a more attached customer base. The question is for the ideal complementary use of traditional and mobile communication channels and their integration with one another. Mobile technology offers potential when it comes to being close to the customer in a sense of location, but also temporally, and communicating, a maybe even customized, message. Mobile offers the opportunity of efficiently keeping relationships through more frequent, direct contact with added services and personalised dialogues.

The goal is to integrate the new technology in the customer's shopping experience in order to offer better services and communication possibilities that reflect today's technical possibilities, but above all, the expectations of today's customers.

1.1 Background and setting of the research topic

Mobile technology has evolved in a tremendously fast way from a niche position as an exclusive wireless voice transmission technology to a multimedia enabled mass market product. Roughly everybody, today, caries their mobile phone with them throughout the whole day. Businesses that succeed in integrating their customer communication and loyalty schemes with the ubiquitous advantages of the mobile-enabled consumer base will be well positioned to realize the potential and capability of mobile-based loyalty initiatives. Key to seizing this opportunity will be a company's capability to develop and offer new services that can be used to reach and serve the greatest possible number of customers.

The idea of applying digital mobile technology to marketing purposes has spread quickly following the success of mobile telecommunication. The advantages of this most direct communication channel to the customer are apparent, the ability of direct interaction with the customer builds the centre, further, the imminence of innovations concerning location based or context aware services, mobile ad-hoc networks and the ever increasing attractiveness of data based messaging formats open up even more potentials for interaction of suppliers, prospective suppliers, and their customers.

First experiences with mobile marketing have been made in practice and the academic community has started treating the topic from a range of different perspectives (Dickinger et al. 2004, Lehner et al. 2004, McManus and Scornavacca 2005). Motivation for an application in the context of loyalty schemes has been given in a range of publications mainly from the background of practical applications (Impaq Group 2005). Loyalty schemes, as they are mainly found in customer communication programs, offer an interesting topic for research in this context because of mainly two facts. On the one side, loyalty schemes involve many features that can well be provided by applications on mobile devices by using available communications technologies, while on the other side, classical loyalty schemes are facing a range of problems that show the need for new concepts, mechanics and business models.

Today's loyalty schemes are often based on membership cards equipped with barcodes, magnetic stripes or memory chips. A number of different loyalty program types can be identified: Membership programs offer the customer a consistent discount on all products purchased by the member. Simple repeat programs offer rewards based on basic transactional behaviour. Rewards and points programs offer a more complex compensation for a customer's behaviour and can act as a tracking and segmentation service for the provider. The expected return from the operation of such schemes is often argued to be higher revenues generated by more loyal customers who are offered incentives to stick with the supplier through his customer loyalty scheme. The increased profitability is thought to be generated by reducing the required servicing costs, less price sensitivity, increased spending and favourable recommendations passed on to other potential customers by loyal buyers (Uncles et al. 1997).

A series of recent studies have shown that classical card-based loyalty schemes are most often not generating the expected results. A study conducted in Austria has shown that 17% of the population aged 15 or older hold a loyalty card from only one vendor, while 51% hold cards from different vendors (Market 2005). In the UK, 41% of the population are found to have a high loyalty card usage while having a low affinity with the supplier (Impaq Group 2005). These findings support the idea of a pre-dominant polygamous loyalty, customers are happy to join a loyalty program, but be-ing involved with one supplier will not keep them from signing up with other sup-plier's schemes. For business travellers a study conducted in the early 1990s has al-ready shown that 80% of them are members of more than one airline loyalty scheme (Dowling and Uncles 1998).

A higher standard of more personalised service needs to be achieved in order to utilize the unique advantages of mobile technology. The ability to respond to individual situa-tions and requirements is something that can set a business apart from the others. In-troducing mobile technology into the retail cycle enables the business to increase per-sonalisation by focusing on customers individually. First experience with porting tradi-tional concepts like couponing to mobile technology has shown success, voucher re-demption in mobile programs is dramatically different to paper-based schemes. Higher redemption rates are achieved, and customers are more involved (Kavassalis et al. 2002 or Schwarz 2001). The major challenge for mobile applications consists in creat-ing services that bring benefit to customer's everyday lives. New applications will not just be games and fun ones, many new applications will be developed with the aim of enabling the mobilisation of existing services or enhancements of offers from other channels.

1.1.1   Research question and expected results

It is the goal of this research to identify the potential that mobile services offer regard-ing the management of customer relationships and to develop a framework that pro-vides an infrastructure capable of leveraging these advantages through a service deliv-ery platform that can be made accessible to marketers in order to enable the integration of the mobile channel into the traditional marketing mix.

How can the characteristics of the mobile communication channel be employed in order to contribute to customer loyalty? How must applications and services using the mobile channel be designed as to provide an efficient tool that can contribute to loy-alty marketing?

Table 1: Research question

The expected outcome of the research was defined as an applicable artefact consisting of a definition for the system architecture of a mobile information system supporting retail loyalty schemes with respect to most recent knowledge on factors driving the adoption and acceptance as well as leveraging the potential of mobile to the full extent. The system architecture is to be developed in the form of a reference model that can be adapted to various application scenarios through configuration of the developed elements (Brocke and Buddendick 2004).

The objective of this research is to counter the methodological deficit in the design of mobile services, as well as addressing the lack of a holistic view on the role of interactive media in marketing and offering a framework for evaluation and application.

1.1.2 Relevance and contribution of the work

The current state-of-the-art in mobile application development is characterized by the evolution of personal information management applications – like the access to e-mail, contact, or calendar data – or mobile entertainment, like games, and the provisioning of music or the download of ringtones and wallpapers. In the marketing domain the use of on-pack and couponing campaigns have emerged to be valuable extensions to traditional advertising. While enabling technologies like mobile payment and advanced data-services are evolving, the full potential for mobile services has yet not been leveraged.

This research work contributes to the marketing domain with respect to the application of mobile information systems for customer communication as a loyalty-supporting toolset, contributing to the discussion of the role of a continuous relationship between businesses and their customers.

In the information systems domain, the conception of mobile-enabled information systems poses challenges towards a range of topics. Next to the treatment of enabling, infrastructure-oriented topics surrounding networks, devices and protocols, a design process for mobile services as an adoption of traditional software processes with respect to the ubiquitous and interactive characteristics of the media has not yet been presented, but is a major success factor for building accepted mobile information systems.

1.2 Practical problem frame

The desire to address customers most appropriately in a large number of potential situations makes a multi-channel communication concept indispensable. Historically, marketing communication systems are often print-output oriented and do not support the integration of different communication channels. The delivery via Internet technologies like e-mail and the World Wide Web is gaining ground as they offer extensive cost-saving potential for the sender, and a clear advantage in delivery speed. The mobile channel although, has, until now, remained mostly unused with only a small number of companies using mainly the most basic application possibility of SMS-messages in their customer communications and not targeting them in the highly personalised manner that the dialogue marketing concept, as the most advanced model of relationship oriented marketing, proposes (Kalyanam and Zweben 2005).

1.3 Theoretical problem frame

A number of theoretical approaches to customer loyalty exist. These theories often approach the topic from the customer's point of view in order to explain customer behaviour and then, based on the findings, derive activities to be implemented by companies in order to actively manage customer loyalty.

The theories that aim to describe the relationship based approach to marketing can be classified into three principal categories, theories of the *neoclassical paradigm*, theories of the *neo-institutional paradigm* and theories of the *neo-behavioural paradigm*. Within the behavioural paradigm, two subcategories can be identified. Theories based on a *psychological* approach and theories following a *psycho-sociological* approach.

Paradigm	Theory
Neoclassic	Value theory
	Profit theory
Non-Institutional	Information economics
	Transaction cost theory
	Principal-agent theory
Neo-Behavioural	**Psychological Theories**
	Learning theory
	Risk theory
	Cognitive dissonance theory
	Socio-Psychological Theories
	Interaction/ Network approaches
	Social exchange theory
	Social penetration theory

Table 2: Relationship marketing theories

The design of information systems has been discussed intensively in previous research, and the ongoing standardisation in modelling techniques as a mean to describe information systems supports the evaluation of proposed artefacts with a general audience before implementation. The creation of reference models for specific application domains that constitute a solution for a recurring information systems design question has evolved as an accepted means of research in order to provide generic solution approached to defined problems. Reference models are conceptual models that define the core concepts of an application domain (Frank 2007). The model defines functional concepts of the targeted application domain, without paying attention to the technical part of implementation as a specific software-based information system. Reference models are not only a description of reality, but also include prescriptive elements that contribute new aspects to the domain.

1.4 Research methodology and classification of the thesis

The proposed research follows a highly interdisciplinary approach. For the development of mobile services, it is exceptionally important to examine the characteristics of the mobile system and to understand the constraints that are imposed on existing mobile services while fulfilling the user's real needs and expectations. From the point of view of mobile information systems design, this allows for an application oriented use of latest technologies. For the business and marketing community, new tools are being created based on real requirements rather than the pure application of today's technical feasibility. The objectives of the research project consist in the development of a comprehensive architecture for a mobile information system supporting the traditional functions of customer relationship management systems or specifically, card-based loyalty programs, by extending them with the features provided by the mobile communications channel as well as the development and analysis of the related business models.

1.4.1   Research concept

This thesis is to be attributed to the research domain of *management information systems*. *Management information systems* is to be considered as an applied science. Applied sciences follow certain specific characteristics: The research questions emerge from practice, multidisciplinary approaches are required, and the aim of the research is to construct artefacts as parts of reality. The statements are prescriptive and normative. The criteria of quality for the research are the ability of the results to solve the problems identified in the practical application (Ulrich 1984).

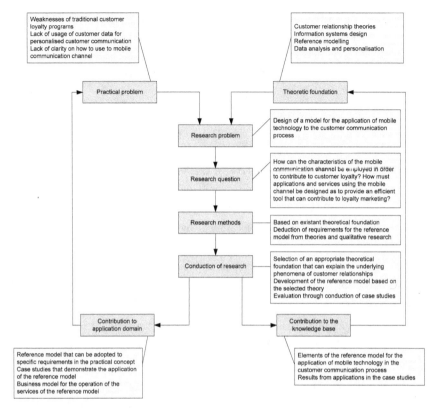

Figure 1: The research process

1.4.2 Methodological approach

The proposed research follows the design science paradigm which in this context consists of the application of kernel theories and well-tried methods to the design and development of information systems for applications in innovative, not yet resolved or presently emerging fields or the development of new application methods (Hevner et al. 2004). The design science paradigm envisages an iteration of build-and-evaluate loops during the design process in order to achieve a final design artefact of highest possible quality with respect to underlying theory as well as feedback from practical application. The business need derived from the application domain as described above builds the basis for the relevance of the proposed research. Hevner et al. define design science as to address research through the "building and evaluation of artefacts designed to meet the identified business need". The differentiation of design science and routine design is provided by the selection of problems and topics treated in respect to their uniqueness, innovativeness and most important their potential to contribute to the "archival knowledge base of foundations and methodologies". The artefacts proposed for design in the course of this research are the architectural model for the reference model for mobile customer communication as well as according business models.

The methodological framework for the evaluation of the proposed system is based on a stakeholder-centred design process, involving all potential actors concerned with the use of a mobile information system for mobile customer communication. Testing of components in real application contexts is conducted iteratively through case study research, and results will be evaluated according to emerging findings. The design incorporates a perspective on how to conduct system integration of the new components from the reference model into existing loyalty frameworks or information technology infrastructures.

Based on the created reference model, the applicability of the identified elements is tested in different contexts and the results are incorporated into the reference model based on the iterative design process that is being followed.

Through the conduction of case studies, the customer acceptance of the proposed mobile services can be analysed, and the success of the communication channel can be evaluated in comparison to other communication means.

User experience design of the services is evaluated according to the prevalent technology acceptance models of Davis (1989), Nielsen (1993) and Rogers (1995). While Davis describes usefulness and ease of use as central determinants of the acceptance of technical innovations, Nielsen extends Davis' model with the aspects of cost, compatibility and reliability of an innovation. Rogers replaces usefulness and ease of use by the precondition of a "relative advantage" and further identifies the factors of possible trial and the perceptibility of an innovation.

The first stage to be approached is the explorative design of a mobile loyalty system with respect to the described mobile particularities. In a classical rewards and points loyalty program, there are four major consumer-facing elements: earning points, tracking points, spending points and receiving information. These functions will build the core of the system for the first design iteration to be continuingly extended through the course of the research based on the selected relationship theory and results from application in the case studies.

In order to follow a rigorous approach in the construction of the reference model for mobile customer communication, a defined process model for the construction of the reference models has been identified and applied. The employed model is based on the definition of Schütte (1998), it consists of five phases: Problem definition, construction of the framework for the reference model, construction of the structure of the reference model, model construction and application.

Within the first phase of problem definition, it must be defined which specific problem is to be solved through the application of the reference model and what the major elements of the problem are. The domain for which the reference model is valid is defined in this phase, as well as the future applicants of the model. The next phase consists of the definition of the framework for the reference model. The framework serves the intention to make the model understandable to future applicants and provides an overview of the elements and interfaces of the reference model. In the third phase, construction of the structure of the reference model, the model's level of abstraction is defined, as well as the applied modelling techniques. Further, the elements of the reference model are defined. In the model construction phase, the model is specified in detail by defining the functions of each identified element. And the last phase consists of the application of the created reference model in a specific context of the individual application domain.

In a parallel process to the system design effort, according business models for the use of the proposed mobile loyalty scheme are developed. The positioning of the different stake-holders in the value network encompassing infrastructure providers, service companies, mobile network operators, aggregators, vendors and consumers are modelled and analysed in order to provide a basis for the development of different application scenarios for the system. The different scenarios will be evaluated with regards to the value generation, the associated revenue flows and the strategic impact for each of the stakeholders. One major question in this section is in witch terms the use of the mobile as a new channel to the customer influences currently existing business models around traditional loyalty schemes. With new players from a new technical background entering the industry and offering systems for the support of loyalty schemes via the mobile channel, a question that has remained unanswered until now, is how they can position themselves within the industry with respect to the fear of vendors for a loss of their competitive advantage with the rapid dissemination of innovative loyalty strategies and associated systems in between their closest competitors.

1.4.3   Structural approach

The first section of this thesis illustrates the relevance of the respective research topic and introduces the applied methodology as well as an overview of the theoretical background of the identified problem frame.

The second section examines customer relationship as a marketing paradigm. The development of marketing paradigms, from transaction orientation to relationship orientation is analysed. The characteristics of customer relationship marketing, dialogue marketing, computer support in marketing and marketing and campaign management form the foundation for an in depth analysis of loyalty marketing and the role of interactive media in marketing. Functions of the target framework will be derived from the relationship marketing foundations discussed in this section.

In the following section, mobile technologies and their marketing-oriented applications are presented and structured in order to provide a two-tiered view of the technology side of the topic. The components of mobile communication: networks, devices, software and services constitute the first tier, representing the infrastructure. A study of the characteristics of mobile services, their role in interactive communication, the classification of mobile marketing applications and research concerning its effectiveness constitutes the second, domain specific, tier of the analysis.

In the third section, the framework for the mobile-supported customer loyalty scheme as a reference model for mobile customer communication is presented. The adopted design process with respect to the characteristics of the development of mobile services based on the user centred design paradigm is described. Following the design process description, the results consisting of the identified functional and non-functional requirements and the architectural framework is discussed.

The fourth section deals with the analysis of business models for the mobile-supported customer loyalty scheme. After a brief introduction including the definition of the term business model and the theory of business model design. A look at the common business models in mobile and information technology infrastructure and related value creation represents the foundation for the evaluation of alternatives.

In the fifth section, an empirical evaluation and analysis of case-studies relating to the research topic is presented. Success factors in mobile customer communication are identified. The relevance of adoption and network effects and the relevance of user-centric design and usability are specified.

In the final section an overview of the results of the presented research is given and the results are set in a practical context in order to derive tangible recommendations for practitioners from both the represented domains, information systems and marketing.

2 Requirements derived from relationship marketing and customer loyalty

Together with the next section on mobile technology and mobile services, that provides the mobile infrastructure perspective on the framework for mobile supported loyalty schemes, this section constitutes the foundation for the design of the framework for the mobile-supported customer loyalty system.

In order to provide an in-depth domain analysis that will allow capturing the functional and non-functional requirements for the target system. The relevant characteristics of relationship marketing and loyalty theory will be elaborated in detail with respect to related theory and application. A look at how relationship marketing evolved from the long dominating transaction oriented view on marketing and how it developed over time clearly shows the importance of technological, mainly information system related, innovation as an influential factor on how marketing is conducted within companies. The current trends in relationship marketing, namely one-to-one and dialogue marketing, as well as the influence of advances in information systems are treated individually. The mechanisms and features of loyalty marketing as it must be supported by the framework are derived from loyalty marketing efforts in place today. Finally, the findings will be reviewed in the context of mobile and interactive communication as new marketing channels.

2.1 The aim and emergence of marketing paradigms

When marketing evolved as an academic discipline in the beginning of the 20th century, it overlapped with the emergence of distribution oriented intermediaries on the markets of the industrial era. The topics of interest for the emerging discipline consisted of the analysis of relationships between the sales process and the divisions of the firm performing production and distribution oriented tasks (Bartels 1976). Marketing researchers therefore had, unlike the approach of mainstream economists of that time, a highly operational perspective of markets and firms. The research interest of the early marketing discipline was focussed on the analysis of the efficiency of marketing channels and the services performed by them in distributing goods from the producers to the consumers. The process of marketing was understood as generating additional forms of customer value based on time and location utilities (Sheth and Parvatiyar 1995).

The institutional school of marketing thought of the mid 20th century still viewed the phenomena of value determination as strongly linked to the exchange of goods supported by the actions of appearing intermediates. Marketing theory further evolved by considering organizational dynamics and was also influenced by other social sciences, such as psychology and sociology. But exchange remained a central principle of marketing (Kotler 1972).

By the end of the 20th century, critics of the transactional exchange paradigm, supported by empirical evidence, of growing relational engagement of buyers and sellers, initiated a change in focus from value exchanges to value creating relationships. Cooperative and interdependent relationships were seen to be of greater value than transactions based relationships (Kalwani and Narayandas 1995). This concept of relationship marketing is very similar to the marketing practices of the pre-industrial era in which producers and consumers interacted directly with each other and developed emotional and structural links as a means to reducing uncertainty and risk in their economic market (Sheth and Parvatiyar, 1995).

2.1.1   Roots of relationship marketing

Although the history of marketing as an academic discipline only dates back to the early 20th century (Bartels 1976), marketing practices were shown to have existed in history from far earlier on: The pre-industrial economy was mainly based on agriculture and the trade of related artefacts and tools. The producer traditionally acted as both, manufacturer and retailer of his products. Producers and consumers developed relationships based on the previous experiences with each other. This knowledge reduced uncertainty and risk, and enabled production of customized products for each customer. (Sheth and Parvatiyar, 1995)

Cooperation between producers was also quite common, motivated by the need to do business with partners that could be trusted. Trade relationships, based on trust among the partners, were a major element of business practices in the pre-industrial era where ownership was closely linked with the management of business (Staehle 1999).

Branding of goods, a still common marketing practice today, evolved at that time. In order to build trust and influence repeat purchases, producers marked their goods with their own family names. In this way, they provided a means of identification of products, and provided a sign of quality guaranty and to promote loyalty to that certain brand (Room 1987).

During the time of early industrialisation, marketing remained customized and relationship oriented. Customised products were manufactured for individuals and industrial customers. There were no inventories of finished products that were manufactured for an anonymous market. Rather, products were produced for which the demand already existed. Advertising or price competition among suppliers was therefore not required, but relationships among customers and suppliers were essential. Branding as a means of marketing became very popular during this period and producers attached their names to products as a proof of personal warranty of quality.

2.1.2   The evolution and dominance of the transactional approach

A more transactional approach to marketing emerged with the beginning of mass production and equivalent mass consumption. Industrialisation led to a range of effects supporting this development: the population moved into industrial towns and needed retailers to supply basic services like food, housing and clothing (Cundiff 1988). Manufacturers were motivated to produce in mass quantities and distribute through numerous channels given the associated economies of scale. On the one hand, economies of scale in lowered the cost of producing goods. Consequently prices of the products they sold were lower. On the other hand, it increased the pressure on producers to indentify markets on which to sell their products.

The transition from direct exchange to industrial mass production led to a higher separation of offer and demand, as production was no longer closely related to the demand of known and related customers. This effect led to a phenomenon that was not known until this time, producers now had stocks of their finished products that needed to be placed on the market. This new effect was one of the reasons that led to the emergence of marketing and distribution intermediaries that would take over the risk of inventory and the role of the distributor. These intermediaries stored the surplus production of manufacturers, and took over the responsibility of locating new buyers for the manufacturer's product.

The focus on sales and promotion of goods and the decoupling of production and distribution led to the emergence of transaction orientation. And with the emergence of this transactional approach to the selling of goods, the value of building relationships decreased. With the need to support the industrial mass production, the products needed to be sold as they were produced, and mass consumption was promoted. The measures that were developed for marketing performance, sales numbers, volume, and market share, reflected the transactional approach and the desire to maximize profits in the short term as a consequence of uncertainties towards the future.

In the later phase of the industrial period, new marketing concepts emerged. Marketing practitioners discovered the value of repeat purchases, making it valuable to develop brands and gain loyal customers (Sheth and Parvatiyar, 1995). The tools and practices that emerged at that time are still common today and still represent important parts of loyalty programs and relationship marketing efforts. Market segmentation and targeting evolved as tools allowing retailers to focus on specific customer groups and offering them a specific portfolio of goods reflecting their needs and requirements. The strategic option of product differentiation and price discrimination also dates back to this period, following the discovery that the focus on serving specific needs in an individual way was a means to set a company apart from others and make it attractive to customers.

This progress represented a new emergence of a relationship approach to marketing during the end of the industrial era. Direct customer communication and the build-up of relationships with customers gained new importance. The majority of retailers although remained focussed on a transactional approach in an environment characterised by strong competition.

2.1.3   The emergence of modern relationship marketing

With the transition to the post-industrial era, substantial development toward relationship marketing has emerged, both in practice and from an academic perspective.

As products became more and more complex, systems selling became apparent as customers needed to be supplied with parts, supplies and services related to the products and good they purchased. From the demand side, companies introduced new concepts like single supplier contracts forcing the development of key account management programs at the vendor's side (Shapiro and Wyman 1981). These effects of course led to stronger relationships among buyers and sellers. Key account programs were a sign of commitment of sellers towards their most important customers. The emerging relationships were the foundations of what has evolved as relationship marketing (Anderson and Narus 1991). Business-to-business markets led the development of relationship marketing, and it was only until performing information systems allowed retailers with large amounts of anonymous customers to follow this trend.

A range of environmental and organizational developments of the post-industrial era supported the re-emergence of the relationship oriented approach by encouraging more direct interactions between producers and customers of both, services and goods. The rapid technological advancements of this era, especially in information technology, that led to the ability of recording transactional data and identifying relevant customers. The trend towards total quality programs which required close integration of supplier and buyer. The emergence and growth of the service economy based upon products that can only be supplied upon an existing relationship. And the increase in competitive intensity, leading to concerns about customer retention which was soon found to be an important source of revenue (Sheth and Parvatiyar 1995).

The technological innovations around information and communication technology have made it easier for producers to interact with customers directly, and as a consequence gain knowledge about their customers by creating data on transactions, preferences and behaviour. The role of intermediary is sustainably challenged, as customers are willing to switch to direct ordering and producers are introducing systems that allow for just in time production and delivery. Mass customisation as a result of flexible production processes, and deep customer knowledge is one other source of value from relationship enabled through information technology.

The trend towards total quality programs which had a deep impact on companies' perspectives regarding quality and production cost led to another type of closer integration and collaboration of suppliers. As the total quality movements demanded an integrated perspective on the whole value chain, close relationships where established among customers and suppliers along the value chain.

The emergence of the service and information economies, in which the good is typically produced and delivered by the same organisation, made relationship marketing an important driver of revenues in this sector. Many services gain efficiency by being based on a relationship and building upon previous cooperation. Maintaining the relationship is therefore an important aspect of the service and information economies. The notion of relationships in service marketing has therefore evolved both in practice and in academic research (Crosby et al. 1990). As competitive pressure increased with the intensity of competition, producers where concerned with customer retention to a greater extent. It was soon argued that retaining a customer would cost less than acquiring a new one (Rosenberg and Czepiel 1984).

2.1.4   The institutionalisation of customer relationship management

The concept of relationship marketing attempts to achieve involvement and integration of customers and suppliers, resulting in a close and interactive relationship with them (McKenna 1991). One fundamental purpose of relationship marketing is to increase marketing productivity by realising higher efficiency and effectiveness (Sheth and Sisodia 1995).

A number of different factors support the achievement of higher efficiency, a higher rate of customer retention, more efficient consumer service and insight on customer behaviour based on purchase histories allowing analysis of purchase frequency, product preferences and supporting segmentation. Based on this data, individualized marketing and the adoption of mass customisation processes becomes possible and sellers can better address the needs of each individual customer, making marketing more effective. The numerous advantages of relationship approaches and the evolving evidence of a strong economical impact of successful relationship marketing (see section 5.1.1) have led to strong position in the marketing domain for relationship oriented approaches, from the practical as well as from the economic perspective.

2.2   Relationship marketing theories as a foundation for the mobile supported loyalty scheme

In order to derive a functional design for the proposed system for mobile customer interaction, a theoretical foundation is required that explains the effects of the interactive system's supported functionalities within the definition of a theoretical framework of relationship marketing.

Consequently, in order to identify an appropriate theoretical framework for use as the foundation to the design for the mobile customer interaction features, an analysis of the most common theories in relationship marketing has been conducted. The analysis follows the approach by Bruhn (2003) in comparing the proposed theories by examining whether the major requirements needed for an explanation of the effects of an interactive mobile communication channel can be covered by those theories.

Relationship marketing, as an interdisciplinary research area, has theoretical foundations in a range of different fields. Within the area of relationship marketing itself, three major marketing paradigms can be identified that allow single theories to be grouped: The *neoclassical paradigm*, the *neo-institutional paradigm* and the *neobehavioural paradigm* (Kaas 2000).

The *neoclassical* and the *neo-institutional paradigms* originate from the field of microeconomics. The *neoclassical paradigm* is founded on the extremely simplified assumptions of complete information and perfect rationality. The *neo-institutional paradigm*, in return, applies more realistic underlying assumptions like information asymmetry or limited rationality.

Within the *neo-behavioural paradigm* a more interdisciplinary approach is followed. Disciplines represented within this paradigm include psychology, sociology or socio-psychology (Bruhn 2000). The empirical-positivistic approach of this paradigm supports the development of hypotheses with relevance to the theories' application base.

	Theory	Reference	Description
Neoclassic	Value theory		Significance of quality, customer satisfaction, perceived value, and relationship quality within relationship marketing.
	Profit theory	Blattberg and Deighton 1996	Analysis of the value of customer relationships from a corporate perspective.
Non-Institutional	Information economics	Klee 2000	Explanation of interaction uncertainties and derivation of strategies to reduce uncertainty.
		Ahlert, Kenning and Petermann 2001	Trust as success factor for service based corporations.
	Transaction cost theory	Klee 2000	Pre-conditions for an advantageous initiation of customer relationships.
		Grönroos 1994	Profitability of long-term business relationships.
	Principal-agent theory	Jensen and Meckling 1976	Elucidation of customer and employee behaviour within customer relationships.
		Bergen et al. 1992	
Neo-Behavioural	**Psychological Theories**		
	Learning theory	Seth and Parvatiyar 1995	Clarification and influencing factors for the emergence of customer relationships.
	Risk theory	Seth and Parvatiyar 1995	Clarification and influencing factors for the emergence of customer relationships.
		Fischer and Tewes 2001	Trust and commitment as intermediary variables for service processes.

Cognitive disso- nance theory	Seth and Parvatiyar 1995	Clarification and influencing factors for the emergence of customer relationships.
Socio-Psychological Theories		
Interaction/ Net- work approaches	Grönroos 1994	Structuring of interaction processes.
Social exchange theory	Houston and Gassenheimer 1987	Emergence and maintenance of customer relationships; evaluation, long-duration, and stability of customer relationships.
Social penetration theory	Altman and Taylor 1973	Emergence and development of customer relationships.

Table 3: Overview of relationship marketing theories (adapted from Bruhn 2003)

2.2.1   Evaluation criteria for theory selection for the mobile supported loyalty scheme

In order to evaluate the applicability of the theories within the construction of the mobile supported loyalty schemes, these are assessed according to six requirements for their application to relationship marketing as defined by Bruhn (2003):

Theoretical requirements
The theory must be able to explain the different forms and types of customer relationships.
The theory should support the ability to explain the different customer relationship phases, from build-up to termination.
The processes for the emergence of customer relationships must be analysed.
The dynamic aspects of customer relationships, how the transition between phases occurs, must be explained by the theory.
The conditions for the emergence and maintenance of customer relationships should be explained.
It should be feasible to express the point of view of both, the buyer and the seller regarding the customer relation.

Table 4: Requirements towards theories (adapted from Bruhn 2003)

2.2.2   Theories of the neo-institutional paradigm

Following theories of the *neo-institutional paradigm* can be considered as to provide a theoretical approach to relationship marketing: Information economics, the principal-agent theory and the transaction cost theory.

Compared to the theories of the *neoclassical paradigm*, the *neo-institutional* theories are based on more realistic assumptions concerning the behaviour of actors. The still very abstract perspectives on the topics however make it difficult to extract a view on a process of relationship management as will be shown in the following discussion.

Information economics

The *theory of information economics* explains interactions along three quality dimensions: Search qualities, experience qualities and credence qualities. Search qualities can be judged by the customer prior to the purchase, experience qualities can be judged only after the purchase, and credence qualities cannot be evaluated, even after the purchase.

According to information economics, the seller can actively define the three quality dimensions when offering his product on the market. Beyond that, the seller posses complete information on all three quality dimensions. The seller can adapt these qualities according to the phase of any customer relationship. For early phases of the customer relation, it is meaningful to provide high search qualities. In the course of the progress of the relationship, these can be enhanced with experience and credence qualities.

From the perspective of the customer, the qualities of the product change in the course of the relationship. Experience and credence qualities are more important at the beginning of a relationship, while the proportion of search qualities increase with the experiences that a customer makes with a specific seller. The insecurity of the buyer is therefore reduced in the course of the relationship (Klee 2000).

Signalling and *Screening* are the two measures that can be taken by sellers and buyers in order to address the uncertainty of information according to the *theory of information economics*.

Perspective \ Action	Signalling Transmission of information	Screening Search of Information
Seller	I More Informed of own capabilities • Depiction of own potential • Reference customers	III Less informed of external factors • Credit rating for loan request
Buyer	II More Informed of external factors • Disclosure of specific data on customisation needs	IV Less informed of seller's potential • Comparison of several offers

Figure 2: Information activities of buyers and sellers (Bruhn 2003)

While *Screening* refers to the search of information by the party with an information deficit, *signalling* represents activities related to the transmission of information from the more informed party to the less informed.

Based on the evaluation requirements defined in the introduction to this section, the *information economics* approach to relationship marketing does provide a possibility to differentiate between the types and forms of relationships as these are defined by the search, experience and credential qualities. The different phases of customer relationships and their transitions are not explained by information economics. An explanation of the process of relationship management is provided by the changing role of signalling and screening activities. Both perspectives the buyer's and the seller's are considered by the approach.

Agency theory based approaches

The *agency theory* encompasses information asymmetry, uncertainty and risk awareness of parties for the description of economic relationships (Jensen and Meckling 1976). Traditionally, the *principal* represents the role that is the contract issuer, demanding certain effort and behaviour from the opposite party. The *agent*, the contract recipient, decides on whether to accept or reject the contract and on the performed effort level. For the application in relationship marketing, a clear allocation of the roles of principals and agents to the buyer or seller is not generally feasible (Bruhn 2003) as they are in a state of interdependence.

A more detailed look at the common forms of information asymmetry allows for identification of the roles within the relationship. Three types of uncertainties are generally considered (Spremann 1990).

Hidden characteristics, a type of information asymmetry concerning the characteristics of a product or service offered. It this case, the characteristics are well known to the seller, but not to the buyer. The buyer must act on incomplete information in his purchasing choice or invest into strategies to reveal the characteristics of the product.

Hidden action is a type of uncertainty where the contract issuing party cannot take effect on the execution of the contract, as it might be to time or cost-intensive to control the executing party. This describes the situation in which a buyer, contracting a seller to execute a specific task does not have the possibility to fully evaluate the quality of the service or product delivered by the seller.

Hidden intention, the third type of relationship uncertainty, describes an information asymmetry concerning the intentions of the relationship partner. This situation would occur when the agent signs the contract with the prevailing intention to act at a low effort level.

The negative consequences of the uncertainties caused by the described types of information asymmetry have been shown to be relevant only in the short run. Hence in the course of an ongoing relationship, whether *hidden characteristics*, nor *hidden actions* or *hidden intentions* should occur (Kumar, Scheer and Steenkamp 1995).

When evaluating the *agency theory approach* as a foundation for an operational process of relationship marketing that can constitute a basis to the mobile elements of a loyalty scheme, following observations can be made: While the theory explains different types of relationship by attributing them to the general types of information asymmetry described above and provides perspectives for buyers and sellers within the relationship by analysing the different roles within every type of uncertainty, it does not provide a view on the development process of customer relations, nor on the dynamic aspect of such relations.

The transaction cost theory

The *transaction cost theory* by Coase (1937) and Williamson (1975) describes economic relationships by examining the role of the costs of initialisation, handling, control and termination of business relationships in terms of contracts as well as encompassing opportunity costs.

Uncertainty, specificity and frequency of the transactions increase these transaction costs according to *transaction cost theory*, transaction within long term relationships are therefore assumed to lead to lower average coordination costs. This argumentation benefits long term relationships as they are said to reduce the cost of coordinating the procurement process. The higher the uncertainties of the transaction and the specificity of the resources and the greater the frequency of the transaction, the more advantage can be gained from a well defined buyer-seller relationship.

Looking at *transaction cost theory* as a method for supporting the development of the mobile supported loyalty scheme, following points must be considered: As transaction costs are encountered by both sides of a relationship according to *transaction cost theory*, it can be argued that both perspectives, that of the seller and that of the buyer are considered. The occurrence of relationships can be explained by the profit optimising target of transaction cost minimisation. Concerning the types and forms of relationships, *transaction cost theory* is limited to contractual relationships that induce all the costs encompassed by the theory. Phases or a clear process of relationship management is not provided by the transaction cost theory.

2.2.3   Theories of the neo-behavioural paradigm

The theories of the *neo-behavioural paradigm* can be grouped into theories belonging to the *psychological* or *socio-psychological theories*. *Psychological theories* are based on knowledge of human behaviour, cognitive processes, like perception or learning, and human emotions. Socio-psychology deals with the human behaviour in a social context. It deals with the behaviour of groups, communication, social cognition, social roles and interaction (Kroeber-Riel and Weinberg 2003).

Theories with psychological foundations

Psychological theories relevant to relationship marketing according to Bruhn (2003) are selected *theories of learning*, the *risk theory* and the *cognitive dissonance theory*.

The risk theory

The *risk theory* describes the phenomenon of action with the motivation of risk minimisation. The risk that can be assessed by the individual, according to the theory, is a subjective risk based on the perceived probability of misjudgement. Perceived risk has to be considered as a multidimensional phenomenon constituted by performance, physical, financial, psychological and social risk (Kaplan, Szybillo and Tocoby, 1974). Repeat purchases, which build the foundation of a customer relationship, can be explained by this theoretical approach as the repetition of transactions with the same partner eliminates uncertainties and therefore minimises the involved risk (Dittrich 2000, Heitmann and Aschmoneit 2003).

The impact of the perceived risk on the behaviour of the customer depends on a number of different personality characteristics (Bänsch 1995). The vigour of the behavioural impact is a function of the perceive probability of a negative outcome and expected consequences of a negative outcome.

One rather obvious strategy for risk minimisation is the enlargement of the informational base of the customer. A perceived risk is therefore said to motivate a customer to further gather information for his purchasing decision. The motivation to search for supplementary information is stronger, the higher the risk perceived by the customer (Kroeber-Riel and Weinberg 2003).

Brand loyalty can be explained by an intensified behavioural pattern of risk minimisation through the regular use of the same supplier for which the information base provides enough positive aspects to reduce the risk perceived as compared to switching the supplier.

The cognitive dissonance theory

The *cognitive dissonance theory* builds on the assumption that individuals attempt to maintain a balance within their cognitive system (Nieschlag et al. 2002). In the case of existing dissonance, actions are taken to restore balance. Following a purchase, a consumer will show behaviour that reduces potential dissonances. These behaviours can include the re-evaluation of the purchasing process, enhancement of the process or suppression of the information on the purchase. If the reduction of *cognitive dissonances* can be achieved by repeating a purchase within the same setting, long term buyer-seller relationships can be explained by the factor in which they reduce cognitive dissonances.

For the customer relationship management, a range of design issues can be drawn from the *cognitive dissonance theory*. Generally, a supplier must beware not to cause *cognitive dissonances* among his or her customers. Beyond that, many elements of traditional customer relationship processes do support the rebalancing of *cognitive dissonances* after a misbalance has occurred.

The role of learning theories

The *learning theory* relevant to the establishment of customer relationships is the *theory of learning through the principle of reinforcement* (Kroeber-Riel and Weinberg 2003). It is based on the cognitive process of information reception. The theory proposes that behaviour that has generated high value and utility in the past will be maintained. Behaviour that has only been redeemed with small utility will lead to a change in that behaviour (Wilkie 1994). In terms of customer relationships, high value through satisfaction and quality can therefore lead to long lasting relationships.

Beyond the traditional learning theories based on the principle of reinforcement, forms of more complex learning have been analysed. These often go further than only analysing the storage of information, but include the learning and internalisation of behavioural aspects (Trommsdorff 1998).

The *theory of contingency-based learning,* for example, states that behaviours will be adopted faster the stronger the attitude was that can be associated to the behaviour. *Imitational learning* describes a type of learning where the observation of certain behaviour leads to an adaptation of that behaviour by the observer. Whether the behaviour is adopted by the observer or not heavily depends on the model person that is being observed. *Expectancy learning* is dependent on the height of the gratification offered, and the probability that the gratification will occur. In *learning based on comparison*, the value of a reward or punishment is compared to earlier rewards or punishments. In *consistency based learning*, the coherences of the behaviours are analysed according to their consistence, through this mechanism, inconsistent behaviours are eliminated.

How these theoretical approaches to learning can serve as a theoretical foundation for the framework of the mobile supported loyalty scheme will be discussed below.

Evaluation of psychological theories for application as a foundation of the mobile supported loyalty scheme

Based on the evaluation requirements defined in the introduction to this section, the approach of *psychological theories* to relationship marketing does not provide a possibility to differentiate between the types and forms of relationships. Neither the different phases of customer relationships, nor their transitions are explained. The *psychological theories* allow for an explanation of the maintenance and emergence of customer relationships, this makes it possible to extract criteria for the build-up of a relationship. The perspective considered by the *psychological theories* is, however only the one of the consumer, as *psychological theories* cannot be applied to organisations or companies in general.

Socio-psychological theories

Socio-psychological theories relevant to relationship marketing according to Bruhn (2003) are theories based on interaction and network approaches, the *social exchange theory* and the *social penetration theory*.

Interaction and network theory based approaches

Interaction theories cover the examination of different form of interaction, often dived into four specific groups of interaction types depending on the number and form of interacting entities: *Dyadic-person* and *dyadic-organisational* theories for interactions between two entities, and multi-person or multi-organisational theories for interactions between more than two entities.

The *network theories* build upon the organisational approaches of the *interaction theories*. These can be used to explain buyer-seller relationships. *Network theory* supports an analysis of direct and indirect relationships between entities within a specific network, and the dynamics of these relationships by examining their links, frequencies of interaction, intensity and substance.

The goal of *network theories* consists in describing the optimal allocation of limited resource between entities within the network by making use of exchange mechanisms that profit all entities involved. *Network theories* therefore offer a framework for the analysis of corporate relationships, but do not provide more than a high-level overview that remains descriptive rather than analytical.

When analysing the *interaction and network theories* for application as a theoretical foundation for the architecture of the mobile supported loyalty schemes, following remarks must be made: Both perspectives, the buyer and the seller are taken into account by the theories, they also explain the emergence and maintenance of customer relationships. However, there is no theoretical explanation of the phases or dynamic aspects of relationship management. The interaction and network theories can therefore not serve as a theoretic foundation for the architecture of the mobile supported loyalty scheme, as it requires a process oriented view of relationship marketing.

Social exchange theory

The *social exchange theory* deals with the analytics of the appearance and maintenance of any social relationships. The theory has been applied to customer relationships. The most fundamental element of the *social exchange theory* is the mutual exchange of values (Houston and Gassenheimer 1987). The mutual exchange of values indicates that any supply of value by one exchange-entity will be compensated by the provisioning of a value by the other exchange-entity. Drawn for the mutual exchange of values, the goal of equality is the foundation of the exchange process. Any entity involved in an exchange therefore tries to attain this equality between the exchanging-entities.

The restricted exchange process is the most basic type of exchange that is distinguished by the *social exchange theory*. It involves two exchange parties: each of them delivers and receives something in the exchange process. The generalised exchange process involves at least three exchange entities. These are aligned along a value chain in which they transfer the value along to the next partner in the chain while the exchange value is delivered back along the chain. Complex exchange processes take place in more complex networks involving at least three entities. In contrast to the generalised exchange process it is possible within the complex exchange process to have direct exchanges between all members of the network.

Next to the exchange processes, the exchange theory also provides a model of different types of exchange based on two core types: the value exchange and the symbolic exchange. Within a value exchange, the value of the exchanged goods is economically equal. Within a symbolic exchange, one party receives value from a symbolic perception of the good. These types of symbolic exchange play an important role in relationship marketing when considering brand or product loyalty.

The *social exchange theory* also provides a means to explain the emergence and the maintenance of customer relationships. The customer's behaviour within the relationship is explained by the factor of relationship judgement. The judgement of the customer is based on the expected net outcome of the next transaction. This net outcome is the difference between the good's value and the exchange value, or the price to be paid.

On the level of the relationship, relationship cost and value are determined and compared. If the expected net outcome is higher than the net relationship value, the exchange leads to a satisfied customer. The net relationship value depends on prior experiences of the customer with the same or similar types of sellers. Relationship alternatives are also considered in the decision process according to the *social exchange theory*.

An evaluation of the *social exchange theory* as a theoretical foundation for the mobile customer loyalty scheme framework shows that the theory is capable of differentiating among the types and forms of customer relationships along the patterns of the restricted, generalised or complex exchanges. The emergence of customer relationships is partly explained, but cannot be followed and explained on a detailed level. Different phases within the buyer-seller relationship and their transitions are not considered by the social exchange theory. This makes the *social exchange theory* as only partly applicable as the theoretical foundation of the framework to be constructed within this thesis.

The social penetration theory

The *social penetration theory* explains the emergence and maintenance of social relationships by explaining the development of a relationship through an analysis of the interactions of the relationship entities.

According to the *social penetration theory*, a social relationship develops through interactions that let the relationship entities discover new elements of the counterpart's personality. The personality elements that get shared among the relationship parties are structured in two dimensions, the personality breadth and the personality depth (Altman and Taylor, 1973)

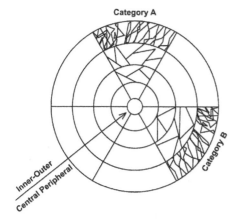

Figure 3: Personality model according to the social penetration theory (Altman and Taylor 1973)

The breadth of the personality has two further sub dimensions, the categories and the frequencies of interaction. The categories are the topics treated during the continuation of the relationships. The frequency states the number of interactions within such a category. The requirements of the customer and the product categories offered by sellers can be such categories in the representation of the parties' personalities.

The depth of the personality represents a layering of elements within an entity's personality. The outer layers of the personality have more elements, these are however more superficial. The inner layers are more personal and fewer where the central characteristics of one's personality are found according to the social penetration theory. The disclosure of elements of higher personality depth gets more difficult with further advancement as these inner elements are better protected and a disclosure can be associated with risk. Personality depth, from the perspective of a customer relationship, is the knowledge a company can acquire on a customer over the period of an ongoing relationship. The same progress of disclosure of personality elements takes place for the customer concerning his knowledge on the company. Increasing numbers of interaction disclose elements of the company.

The process that takes places as two parties continuously interact and incessantly disclose deeper elements of their personalities to each other is referred to as the social penetration process, it is characterised in eight dimensions as defined in the following table (Altman and Taylor, 1973).

Dimension	Description
Interaction diversity	In the course of the relationship, interactions gain in diversity. There is an increase in the discussed topics that represent personality breadth over the course of the contact. Concerning the types of interaction there can also be an increase in diversity, as for example the use of non-verbal communication among relationship parties.
Interaction uniqueness	Interaction uniqueness describes the creation of rituals unique to the relationship. This can include knowledge on preferences and behaviours of the customer or supplier.
Replaceability and equivalence	Information within an interaction can be communicated in different ways that are equivalent. This is possible based on the deep knowledge of the relationship parties and their experience with each other.
Openness	With a deepening relationship in terms of the social penetration theory, and the associated trust, relationship parties can be increasingly open to each other on the topics common to them.
Understanding of roles	A better understanding of the roles taken by the relationship parties is gained in the course of the relationship. Based on the repetition of tasks within the partnership and an increased knowledge on the competences of the partner.

Informality	Informality increases with the deepening of the relationship and again, the knowledge of the respective party allows acting on a less formal level.
Possibility and acceptance of criticism	With an increasing importance of the relationship, the parties will increasingly adopt criticism by the other relationship party. Because the parties are important business partners, the comments and proposals by the partner will be treated as an opportunity to strengthen the relationship.
Exchange efficiency	The knowledge of the relationship parties finally leads to higher exchange efficiency in terms of an economic advantage of a deep integration of a supplier and a buyer.

Table 5: Dimensions of the social penetration process

As the intensity of the relationship increases, the dimensions of the social penetration process become more and more effective. The increase in customer knowledge has a positive effect of the interaction of the relationship parties as it drives trust.

Another element of the *social penetration theory* is the process model of follow-on interactions. This process model allows the analysis of subsequent transactions and the reasons why they occur. In order to achieve this analysis, the social penetrations theory draws back on the *social exchange theory* and adapts the notion of comparison levels. Based on past interactions and exchanges, the customer predicts future outcomes of exchanges and decides on whether to continue interacting or terminate the relationship.

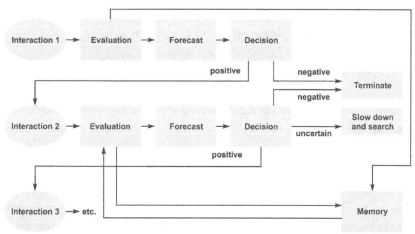

Figure 4: Social penetration theory's interaction model (Bruhn 2003)

The information of the customer on past transactions and his prediction of further outcomes constitute the link of the transaction sphere and the relationship sphere according to the social penetration theory.

The analysis of the *social penetration theory* shows that it fulfils all requirements in order to act as the theoretical foundation for the functional framework of the mobile supported loyalty scheme. It provides a possibility of differentiation between the different types and forms of the relationships, by providing the notions of personality breadth and personality depth. The theory provides an explanation of the different phases of relationships. The relationship's progress is explained by the dimensions of the social penetration process as presented in the table above. The *social penetration theory* provides a process model that describes the dynamic character and the transition from on phase to the other. By integrating elements of the *social exchange theory*, the emergence and development of relationships can be explained. And both the perspectives of the supplier and of the buyer are accounted for in the theoretical framework.

The *social penetration theory* will therefore serve as the theoretical foundation for the development of the functional requirements of the mobile elements supporting loyalty schemes as developed in the form of a generic framework in this thesis.

2.2.4   Neoclassic relationship marketing theories

The *neoclassical paradigm* of marketing research originates from the field of microeconomics. Within this paradigm, decisions of households and corporations are being analysed under predefined initial conditions. These conditions tend to be rather simplified, as the assumption of complete information or perfect rationality.

The *value theory* provides an explanation of the buyer perspective of the buyer-seller relationship. It explains the customer's behaviour related to the seller's products and services. The *value theory* is based on the concept of utility maximisation. Consequently, a customer will engage in a relationship when it represents value and therefore utility to him. This utility can originate from the quality of the relationship, the customer's prior satisfaction or the perceived value.

The *profit theory* in turn tries to provide an explanation of the seller perspective regarding the buyer-seller relationship. Following the assumption of profit maximisation, companies chose their actions according to an economic evaluation of the alternatives. The initialisation of mechanisms targeted to enhance customer relationships would therefore be a consequence of profit maximisation and contribute to it. Customer lifetime value models (see section 5.1.1) are a classical example of the application of the *profit theory*. Customer lifetime value refers to the customer's net present value to a seller (Berger and Nasr 1998). Based on the results of the customer lifetime value analysis, marketing budgets can be targeted to the customers with the highest value potential.

When evaluating the theories of the *neoclassical paradigm* for application in the context of the mobile supported loyalty scheme, it must be noted that the theories do not explain different forms and types of customer relationships. Additionally, neither different phases, nor the processes of customer relationships are explained. The emergence and maintenance of a customer relationship can be explained by the value and profit theories, and through the two different approaches the perspectives of the buyer and the seller are both taken into account.

2.2.5   Evaluation of theories for the mobile supported loyalty scheme

In order to provide a comprehensible result of the analysis of the major theories in the field of relationship marketing, the evaluation results are discussed here next to each other and an argumentation for the selection of the *social penetration theory* as the theoretical foundation for the development of the framework for mobile supported loyalty schemes is presented.

Theory	Discussion
Information economics	Based on the evaluation requirements defined in the introduction to this section, the *Information economics* approach to relationship marketing does provide a possibility to differentiate between the types and forms of relationships as these are defined by the search, experience and credential qualities. The different phases of customer relationships and their transitions are not explained by information economics. An explanation of the process of relationship management is provided by the changing role of *signalling* and *screening* activities. And both perspectives the buyer's and the seller's are considered by the approach.
Agency theory	When evaluating the *agency theory* approach as a foundation for an operational process of relationship marketing that can constitute a basis to the mobile elements of a loyalty scheme, following observations can be made: While the theory explains different types of relationship by attributing them to the general types of information asymmetry described above and provides perspectives for buyers and sellers within the relationship by analysing the different roles within every type of

	uncertainty, it does not provide a view on the development process of customer relations, nor on the dynamic aspect of such relations.
Transaction cost theory	Looking at the *transaction cost theory* as a method for supporting the development of the mobile supported loyalty scheme, following points must be considered: As transaction costs are encountered by both sides of a relationship according to transaction cost theory, it can be argued that both perspectives, that of the seller and that of the buyer are considered. The occurrence of relationships can be explained by the profit optimising target of transaction cost minimisation. Concerning the types and forms of relationships, transaction cost theory is limited to contractual relationships that induce all the costs encompassed by the theory. Phases or a clear process of relationship management is not provided by the transaction cost theory.
Psychological theories	Based on the evaluation requirements defined in the introduction to this section, the approach of *psychological theories* to relationship marketing does not provide a possibility to differentiate between the types and forms of relationships. Neither the different phases of customer relationships, nor their transitions are explained. The psychological theories allow for an explanation of the maintenance and emergence of customer relationships, this makes it possible to extract criteria for the build-up of a relationship. The perspective considered by the psychological theories is, however only the one of the consumer, as psychological theories do not apply to organisations or companies in general.
Interaction and network theories	When analysing the *interaction and network theories* for application as a theoretical foundation for the architecture of the mobile supported loyalty schemes, following remarks must be made: Both perspectives, the buyer and the seller are taken into account by the theories, they also explain the emergence and maintenance of customer relationships. However, there is no theoretical explanation of the phases or dynamic aspects of relationship management. The interaction and network theories can therefore not serve as a theoretic foundation for the architecture of the mobile supported loyalty scheme, as it requires a process oriented view of relationship marketing.

Social exchange theory	An evaluation of the *social exchange theory* as a theoretical foundation for the mobile customer loyalty scheme framework shows that the theory is capable of differentiating among the types and forms of customer relationships along the patterns of the restricted, generalised or complex exchanges. The emergence of customer relationships is partly explained, but cannot be followed and explained on a detailed level. Different phases within the buyer-seller relationship and their transitions are not considered by the social exchange theory. This makes the social exchange theory as only partly applicable as the theoretical foundation of the framework to be constructed within this thesis.
Social penetration theory	The analysis of the *social penetration theory* shows that it fulfils all requirements in order to act as the theoretical foundation for the functional framework of the mobile supported loyalty scheme. It provides a possibility of differentiation between the different types and forms of the relationships, by providing the notions of personality breadth and personality depth. The theory provides an explanation of the different phases of relationships. The relationship's progress is explained by the dimensions of the social penetration process as presented in the table above. The *social penetration theory* provides a process model that describes the dynamic character and the transition from on phase to the other. By integrating elements of the social exchange theory, the emergence and development of relationships can be explained. And both the perspectives of the supplier and of the buyer are accounted for in the theoretical framework.
Neoclassical theories	When evaluating the theories of the *neoclassical theories* for application in the context of the mobile supported loyalty scheme, it must be noted that the theories do not explain different forms and types of customer relationships. Additionally, neither different phases, nor the processes of customer relationships are explained. The emergence and maintenance of a customer relationship can be explained by the value and profit theories, and through the two different approaches the perspectives of the buyer and the seller are both taken into account.

Table 6: Evaluation of relationship marketing theories

2.2.6   Theory derived functions for the mobile supported loyalty scheme

As the analysis has shown that the *social penetration theory provides* the most complete representation of the aspects of relationship marketing, functions must now be derived from the theory that build the foundations of the framework to be constructed.

In the next section, relevant elements that can be operationalised into a software platform will be extracted from the theory and matched with potential implementation strategies. The selection and detailed specification of the implementation will follow in the later section on the technical implementation.

Relevant elements of the social penetration theory and realisation strategies

Based on the detailed presentation of the social penetration theory above, the elements relevant to the design of the framework will be discussed here and consequently this section will provide the connection between the theory itself and the architecture of the framework that encompasses its foundations.

Modelling of the personality breadth and depth

The model of the *personality breadth and depth* must constitute the fundamental data model for the mobile loyalty framework. Modelling the customer entity according to the elements of its personality allows to support the social penetration process along all its dimensions and to control communication between buyer and seller.

For a functioning operationalisation of the elements of the social penetration theory, the elements of the theory's personality model must be extended by traditional elements of customer data, like address, age and other socio-demographic parameters.

The breadth and depth of the personality can be implemented as categories of interaction and via specific frequency and relevance measures. The breadth can be represented by categories according to the products or services provided by the company, these therefore need to be defined as part of the system configuration. The depth dimension can be represented by frequency measures on the interactions or by evaluation specific relevance measures that can be extracted from the interaction information. The measures can include the evaluation of the communication channels selected to interact on a special topic. Some channels may represent a deeper depth than other more formal channels, e.g. the use of self-service terminals versus being served by sales personnel. These factors also must be configurable by the operators of the program. A generic function and the configuration interface, however must be provided by the framework.

The dimensions of the social penetration process

The dimensions of the social penetration process can be grouped into certain categories according to the factors that drive their value. This consequently makes it easier to analyse how they can be represented within the target framework. These are the dimensions of the process; they have been defined in more detail in the presentation of the theory above:

Dimensions	Drivers for increase in dimension value		
	Trust	Personalisation of the relationship	Multichannel communication
Interaction diversity			
Interaction uniqueness			
Replaceability and equivalence			
Openness			
Understanding of roles			
Informality			
Possibility and acceptance of criticism			
Exchange efficiency			

Table 7: Dimensions and drivers of the social penetration process

Trust among the exchanging parties is an important factor for a number of dimensions of the social penetration process. Openness, informality, criticism and exchange efficiency are all driven by trust. Generating trust cannot be a factor of the framework alone, actually it is that factor that can be least influenced by the communication infrastructure as provided within the mobile loyalty scheme. The system can not directly act with a positive influence on trust, but it can be designed to not deteriorate trust that has been built up within the relationship. Deterioration of trust occur trough inappropriate communication per means of timing or content or through missing information or service quality.

Personalisation is a major factor within the socialisation process of the social penetration theory. It drives the uniqueness of interactions, replaceability and equivalence, the understanding of roles, and exchange efficiency. Personalisation is an element that needs to be considered profoundly when designing the technological framework for the mobile customer loyalty system, the enabler of personalisation is information technology, in order to provide a personalised service, the required technical features must be considered when designing the data model, the processes and the interaction interfaces of the system.

Multichannel communication supports the process' dimension of interaction diversity by supporting the ability to adapt the communication channel to the customers' requirements. It also supports the notion of replaceability and equivalence of interactions by providing interfaces and a channel selection adapted to the needs and custom habits of the customer. Informality is also supported by the free choice of interaction channels in the mobile supported framework as well as the dimension of exchange efficiency.

The dynamics of the social penetration process

The process model of the social penetration theory, consisting of evaluation, forecast, decision loops taking place after each interaction and alternatively leading to the termination or continuation of the relationship represents the dynamic character of the relationship.

The process model for the interactions must be reflected within the framework and must be able to predict the evaluation, forecast, and decision steps of the customer. In order to achieve this integration of the process model into the system, the interactions with the customer must closely be monitored via advanced analytics and actions taken by the system must be in accordance with the previous feedback and interactions of the customer. Again the notion of personalisation plays an important role as it is through the use of personalisation techniques for the communication and interaction actions that the dynamic notion of the customer interaction process is supported.

Encompassing elements of the social exchange theory explaining the emergence and maintenance of the customer relationship

The emergence and maintenance of the customer relationship is explained in the social penetration theory based on the two respective process models, the social penetration process and the process model for interactions.

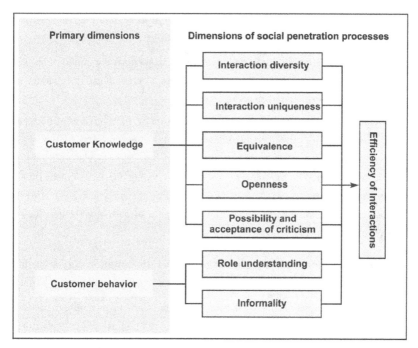

Figure 5: The social penetration process (Bruhn 2003, Georgi 2000)

The process model for interactions describes how the relationship emerges and evolves with each interaction between the relationship parties. Its logic describes the dynamics of the social penetration theory as described above. As the dynamic evolves, the relationship strength is dependent on the results of the customers' evaluation process. The process model will be represented in the system to enable the tracking of the dynamics. Therefore the data is also available for the monitoring of the emergence and maintenance of the customer relationships.

The social penetration process and its dimensions will also be modelled into the framework. The data captured from the execution of the process can be employed in order to create monitoring and reporting functions on the emergence and maintenance of the customer relationship. These reports can either be used by the interaction system to enhance the relationship as needed or can be displayed in reports for managers to derive required actions.

Analysis of the different roles within the relationship process from the perspective of the social penetration theory

The framework for the mobile supported loyalty system supports the notion of separating the different actors clearly by being positioned as a communications channel between the two roles of seller and customer.

As the social penetration theory provides an explanation of the behaviour of both parties of the relationship it can support the development of the framework by describing the processes that occur on each side of the relationship. The processes on the customer side are supported by the framework's customer facing interfaces via the mobile and other channels. The company's side is supported by the analytical features of the framework and the features supporting the management of customer relationships in the interest of the company.

2.3 Customer relationship management as the operationalisation of relationship marketing

The development of relationship marketing as a new marketing paradigm resulting from a less transactional approach in the buyer-seller relation as well as the theories aiming to explain the emergence and the processes of relationship marketing have been elaborated in the preceding sections. Beyond this abstract approach to the marketing paradigm of relationship marketing, it is important for this thesis to also consider the practical applications based on the implementation of the relationship marketing approach within corporate environments.

This practical application of relationship marketing is often referred to as the management of customer relationships, or customer relationship management (CRM). The acronym CRM is also often used when referring to information systems that support the processes of relationship marketing. As is widely agreed upon, the implementation of information systems alone do not enable a company to follow the relationship marketing approach comprehensively. A more holistic approach is required when wanting to establish customer relationship marketing within the company. Internal processes beyond those of the marketing department must be adapted and newly oriented towards the customer. While high-quality customer relationship systems support this holistic approach, their implementation can be difficult, time consuming and therefore is often highly costly.

Customer relationship management therefore consists of both, the implementation of a performing information system and the adaptation of internal and external processes towards a customer centric approach. This is also valid for loyalty systems, which represent a special form of customer relationship marketing systems by encompassing both, analytical and operational features.

Instruments of relationship marketing can be divided into two major types of instruments: Instruments for phase-driven relationship management and instruments for phase-independent management of relationships.

- The phase-driven instruments of relationship marketing act along three distinct phases of relationship marketing. The customer acquisition phase, the customer retention phase and the customer recovery phase (Bruhn 2003).

- The phase-independent instruments for relationship marketing consist of quality management instruments, complaint management instruments and internal customer orientation instruments. These instruments restructure the traditional marketing mix of product, promotion, price and place according to the requirements of a more relationship oriented approach to customer interaction.

Through the instruments of relationship marketing, the traditional marketing mix is applied depending on the customer relationship life-cycle and therefore yields higher efficiency.

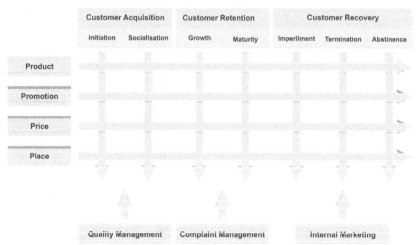

Figure 6: Operational instruments of relationship marketing (Bruhn 2003)

2.3.1 Customer relationship instruments for the acquisition phase

The first phase in the customer life-cycle, the acquisition phase, can be divided into to further sub-phases. The initiation phase and the socialisation phase.

In the initial situation to the initiation phase the company and the customer have not yet had any contact. It is the company's goal to establish a contact with the customer and win him in order to establish a new customer relationship. Two tasks are associated with this early phase of the customer lifecycle: The persuasion of the customer and the stimulation for the first purchase.

The customer persuasion must be achieved through the demonstration of the ability to satisfy customer needs by the company. It is closely related to the management of customer expectations. Customers expectations can actively be managed by the use of pull and push promotions. Push promotion refers to the traditional advertising oriented promotion where the company provides information to the customer via the advertising channel. Pull promotion provides information to the customer if and when it is requested. This approach actively supports the management of customer expectations. Assurances and recommendations by third parties play another major role in persuading the customer, as they limit risk (Kumar and Reinartz 2006).

In the next step, an instrument must be put in place to stimulate the use of the product and service. Short-term stimulation can be achieved by sales promotions at the point-of-sale. These short-term stimulations can be used to generate single transactions. Strategies for long-term stimulation are more efficient for building real relationships between the company and the customer. This can be achieved by actively stimulating the repeated purchase by a customer or stimulating the use of multiple products of that company by offering bundles.

The socialisation phase starts with the first contact between the company and the potential customer. The customer must be familiarised with the offering of the company, its products and services, as the foundation for the relationship is set at this stage (Bruhn 2005).

The required acclimatisation can be achieved either directly through the characteristics of the product, or indirectly through company characteristics which are not related to the product consumed by the customer. When seeking to achieve acclimatisation directly through the product, this can be achieved by providing customer training for the product, a special platform for customer service or a very special product quality. Indirect acclimatisation is enforced by characteristics like the provisioning of direct and single contact persons or a strong brand.

2.3.2   Customer relationship instruments for retention management

Customer retention must be managed along the customer relationship lifecycle phases of growth and maturity.

Within the growth phase, the customisation of products according to the requirements and wishes of the customer can provide an important instrument to enter an ongoing relationship with the customer and gain advantage over competitors lacking the personal customer information needed for the personalisation of the goods. By keeping the production system and products flexible, the customers' feedback can also be introduced into an ongoing innovation process which will lead to more market oriented products and services.

The offering of value-added services can be another instrument of managing the growth phase and keeping the customer from changing the supplier. Different types of value-added services can be offered to the customer. They can be materialistic, e.g. the provisioning of complementary goods, or non-materialistic like training related to the purchased good. The value added services can be offered with or without charging an extra price.

An important instrument for supporting growth is cross selling, the intentional management of sales activity to raise the customer's sales level by either selling related products to the customer or raising the purchasing frequency. Cross selling can be closely related to the measure of customisation.

In the maturity phase, new instruments for the management of the customer relation are needed. The maturity phase is characterised by a saturated customer and a marginal cost of selling additional goods to that customer that does not justify the effort. In this phase, the economic potential of the relationship must be leveraged to the full extent with minimal effort. This can be achieved by building switching barriers and developing efficiency improvements. Switching barriers can consist of contractual-, economic- or functional switching barriers (Shapiro and Varian 1999). Efficiency improvements can be achieved through cost reduction by standardisation, unit cost reduction through increased sales quantities and taking full advantage of the customer's willingness to pay.

2.3.3   Customer relationship instruments for recovery management

The imperilment phase of the customer lifecycle usually occurs recurrently throughout a customer relationship. It is the phase where a customer considers to possibly defect and to eventually terminate the relationship. Often, the triggers for the imperilment phase are errors and failures in the products, services or interactions of the company with the customer. Possible instruments to respond to this status are the rectification of eventual errors and restitution of possible mistakes. Promotion and pricing policies can be tools to provide rectification and restitution.

The dissolution and abstinence phases follow a non-averted imperilment phase. The relationship with the company has been terminated. There is only room for a reactivation of the customer relationship with instruments similar to those of the initiation phase: customer persuasion and customer stimulation. The instruments can be adapted to the type of defection that is encountered. Different types of defections must be considered: company induced defection, competitor induced defection, or customer induced defection.

2.3.4 Further instruments of relationship management

Independently of the phases of the customer life-cycle referred to above, there are instruments for customer relationship management that are valid along all the phases of the customer life-cycle. These consist of product and service oriented instruments: Product quality management, complaint and support management as well as the internal customer orientation.

Quality management instruments are usually implemented along three phases: the strategic planning of quality management, the implementation of quality measures and the phase of ongoing quality control (Reichheld 1996). Strategic quality planning aligns the goals of quality management with the overall strategic goals of the company and develops quality guidelines for the major production and service processes. The goal of the quality implementation is the accomplishment of the developed quality strategy. The measures for quality assurance must therefore be implemented along all internal and external processes. Quality control consists of the controlling activities that are introduces in order to assure a constant level of service and product quality.

The role of complaint and support management is often required when quality management cannot avoid shortcomings in the product or service quality. A well managed support operation can have positive effects on the whole organisation (Stewart 1998). If complaints are resolved to the customer's satisfaction, the organisation can raise the chance of keeping the involved customer's relationship going. The main target of complaint management within an organisation is to ensure reinstated satisfaction in any case of expressed dissatisfaction. This is achieved by implementing a customer oriented corporate strategy, avoiding reactions from dissatisfied customers, achieving additional acquisition and retention effects and gaining information on product deficiencies (Strauss and Seidel 2005).

Internal customer orientation is an important factor for the customer's perception of product or service quality. This is demonstrated by the gap-model of service quality (Parasuraman et al. 1991). The gaps identified are: the gap between the customer's expectation and the management's perception of these expectations, the gap between the target quality and the specified product or service specifications, the gap between the specified quality and the delivered quality and the gap between the actual product or service delivered and the quality communicated externally.

2.4   One-to-one dialogue oriented marketing approaches and loyalty schemes

The one-to-one marketing approach is characterized by the wish to interact individually with the most valuable customers of the company. By targeting this segment specifically, the spending on marketing campaigns can be employed in the most efficient manner, as only high potential customers are approached. The communication is further personalised by capturing the needs and requirements of the most profitable customers and responding to those requirements.

Several types of information system and marketing activities are indispensable to operationalise this goal. From the information perspective, two categories of data are crucial to gain knowledge about the behaviour of individual customers: The variety of needs the customer is trying to satisfy through use of the company's products or services. And the value of the distribution of the profits current customers generate for the company (Gillenson et al. 1999).

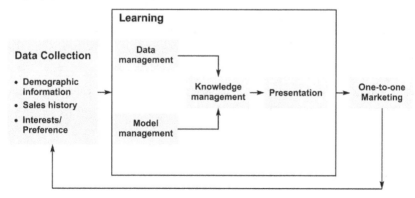

Figure 7: Learning from data in one-to-one marketing systems (Gillerson et al. 1999)

Human behaviour is predominantly based on repetition and the formation of habits therefore making behaviour predictable (Koebler-Riel 2003). This is the foundation of the use of past actions and behaviour to predict further value of a customer and personalise the marketing strategy towards this customer. It is said that "there is no greater predictor of future behaviour than past behaviour" (Kahan 1998). Therefore behavioural analysis is the foundation of one-to-one marketing communication.

An accompanying approach can consists in conducting a cognitive analysis of customer data by including demographic information like age, income, presence of children and psychographic information as lifestyle and interests from third party sources and trying to identify characteristic values for groups of customers. The identification of these parameters can help in approaching the correct group of non-customers with a marketing campaign targeted to gain them as customers. As the profile of the approached group is similar to the profiles of the existing customers, the chance is high that they are confronted with the equal needs and wants that can be covered accordingly by the company approaching them.

2.4.1   Recency, frequency, and monetary customer value indicator

A mathematical computation that is known under the acronym of RFM (recency, frequency, and monetary value) was created based on the knowledge gained on behavioural habits of the consumer population.

RFM is one of the most widely adapted behavioural analysis techniques especially where customer pools tend to be very large as is the case with many loyalty schemes. It is a methodology that is relatively easy to implement on top of customer purchasing history records. (Clark and Clark 2006) The process requires that each customer record has been assigned a unique identifier, such as a unique account or customer number. Hence, each transaction is stored with the unique identifier for the respective customer conducting that purchase.

Based on the collected information, a summary of the customers' purchasing history can be created individually, allowing different sorting and segmentation possibilities.

- Sorting by the date of the last or most recent purchase
- Sorting by the total number or frequency of purchases
- Sorting by the average amount spent per order

The RFM analysis now builds upon the score that each customer has achieved in the three rankings by conducting following steps:

- Sorting the customers by purchase dates in reverse chronological order
- Dividing the customer list into quintiles
- Assigning the customers a score according to the quintile they are in. The customers with the most recent purchase are therefore assigned a score of 1 the customers with the least recent purchase receive a score of 5.

Next, the customers are sorted by the number of orders and the total spending amount and the same methodology is applied.

This total 3-digit score now represents the value of a customer in terms of recency, frequency, and monetary value. It is often used to target top-tier customers with special advertising and marketing campaigns as these customers are assumed to be most reactive to the campaigns.

2.5 Loyalty scheme mechanisms and components

The loyalty programs in place today implement a wide variety of mechanisms and customer interfaces through the functions that they provide to their users. A central element of every customer loyalty program are the means of communication that exist towards the customer, each possible communication channel brings along advantages and disadvantages for the achievement of the goals of the loyalty program. The communication features of current loyalty schemes are discussed in the first section of this chapter. Rewards represent another important feature of loyalty programs, functioning and properties of rewards in the context of loyalty schemes are discussed in the second section. The data collected through the loyalty scheme represents an important asset for the operation company. The third section will present current data collection methods and present how the data gathered through the loyalty scheme is used within the operation companies.

2.5.1   Customer communication in current loyalty schemes

The range of available channels for businesses to communicate with their current and prospective customers is as vast as the marketing domain itself. They range from the traditional media like newspapers, direct mail, the telephone and TV to new media channels as e-mail, web sites, instant messaging or their mobile counterparts being sms, mms or mobile Internet portals.

Each of these channels must be used in accordance with the customer's expectations towards the communication with the company and poses a distinctive set of challenges and opportunities. These challenges and a comparison of key attributes for the communication channels shall be analysed in the following section with special respect to the role of new-media and mobile communication channels and their role and contribution in expanding a company's communication strategy beyond the traditional marketing communication channels.

Direct mail

Direct mail represents an important media for customer communication, both in terms of spread and effect. Studies show that response rates are currently increasing and readership of postal direct mailings is strong across all demographic clusters (Clark and Clark 2006). One advantage of direct mail over the digital media marketing channels is the relatively low barriers, both in terms of customer acceptance and legal issues.

Although postal mailings represent a very traditional marketing channel that does not seem related to the interactive and multimedia-rich marketing channels of the new media. Its ongoing success is still built on the advance and intensive use of information technology. Therefore, a lot can be learned from the practices of successful direct mailing in terms of target group selection, content and message composition and response management.

The success of direct mail even in times of the availability of more advanced, intelligent and interactive communication channels must be attributed to a set of very specific factors that are unique in a certain way to the direct mailing. The first factor is that a mailing is rather inviting than intrusive, it allows for the recipient to decide when or whether they consume the information. The second factor is that it works well together with new media by pointing customers to offers on the Internet or other more interactive channels. And the third factor is that the recipients have a haptic experience when receiving and consuming the message. Although these factors seem unique to the direct mail they can be adapted by other media and be accounted for when designing the communication experience with other media.

The targeting of direct mail is one of the most essential elements for a successful campaign. Untargeted direct mails lead to high costs for massive numbers of mails being sent to the recipients outside the target group, and might even lead to image damage as inappropriate offers are communicated to customers. As a result targeting must be conducted precisely in order to achieve maximum return on investment.

The second important factor of successful direct mailing campaigns is the content. Based on input from CRM systems or one-to-one marketing databases the customer base can be analysed and augmented with external demographic data to select content and marketing messages more appropriately for every single recipient. Marketing messages that respect personal preferences and the customer's current products in use will make a more professional appeal and lead to higher response and reaction rates.

In order to achieve a superior return on investment from direct mailing campaigns, high-quality processes, methods and tools are required as a means to fulfil the aspects described above. This best practice that is well treated in marketing literature for postal direct marketing (e.g. Bell et al. 2006) can be valuable for other media, as mobile or the web, when adapted accordingly.

The generic best practice process for direct mail communication (Jaffe et al. 1992) consists of three distinct phases. The first phase consists of building an understanding of customers segments and their purchasing behaviours. Based on the business goals the most attractive customer segments must be identified and the most effective way of reaching them must be selected. In order to time messages ideally, so that they reach a potential customer when he can be most effectively influenced, it is essential to understand the product's purchasing cycle and contact the customer close to his next potential purchasing decision.

The second phase of the best practice process for direct marketing campaigns is based on the factors that influence the purchasing decision directly. These are the purchase timing, the product value and the customer's emotional involvement. Understanding purchase timing allows proper prediction of purchases, dependent on this knowledge different strategies for communication must be chosen. For unpredictable purchase cycles the communication must support, brand and relationship building measures. For low purchase frequencies but good predictability of purchases, the communication can focus on instant selling. When the frequency of purchases is high, a mixed strategy must be followed. Building the brand and relationship but at the same time facilitating immediate sales. The product value influences communication strategy by requiring an information and value based communication approach for high value goods and a more sales and reaction oriented approach for goods of lower value. The customer's emotional involvement decides upon whether the brand and its core values are communicated for a high emotional involvement, or product information and benefits are communicated with a stronger push towards an immediate sale for goods with less emotional involvement by the customer.

The third phase of the design process for direct marketing campaigns consists in setting the correct marketing goal based on the factors evaluated in the previous phases. A set of seven goal categories can be identified (Clark and Clark 2006):

- Build brand awareness for market entry, product introduction or brand repositioning.
- Generate qualified leads followed by lead conversion and services.
- Generate trial for high frequency purchase with low emotional involvement.
- Increase purchase frequency among existing customers in high frequency markets.
- Cross-selling and up-selling in high margin, low frequency markets.
- Maximise short term sales for product of the well predictable purchasing cycle category.
- Customer retention and win-back for customers at-risk or lost.

Current developments in web based customer communication

With the rapid diffusion of the Internet and the successes of many e-commerce sites, the web has gained importance as a customer communications channel. A corporate website today must provide more than a simple company presentation online. The corporate website must encompass appropriate e-commerce operations, presentation of products, description and handling of services and must serve as an active communication channel towards the customer.

For loyalty programs, the website can represent a very valuable interface. It can support the loyalty program by giving customers the ability to manage their personal details and preferences online, view their status and points balance, redeem points for rewards from an online catalogue or interact with other customers involved in the loyalty program.

Online communities represent one of the currently most interesting trends in the use of the Internet as a channel for customer interaction. In the most basic definition (Heitmann and Aschmoneit 2003, Rösger et al. 2007) is a website that provides an infrastructure to a group of people to communicate, share information, build networks and exchange and discuss ideas.

One of the most valuable assets of an online community is the emotional and mental commitment of its users to the community. Through this commitment, added value is provided to all members of the community as people are empowered to share their knowledge and experience, therefore helping other users in proving information they might require.

The creation of a community as a marketing strategy can be highly complicated, especially if the aspect of new media communication is not close to the core business of the company. The need to reach a critical mass of users and the constant call for care and maintenance make the establishment of a community an effort with high uncertainty. Another strategy for leveraging the power of communities is the participation in communities that already exist, thus well established communities can be used for the own marketing purposes.

Further trends on the web include the increased use of multimedia, especially within video- or image sharing sites that can also build strong communities, or the use of podcasts or blogs in order to transport marketing messages. The conduction of surveys via corporate websites or online service providers for surveys provides one of the most efficient forms of gathering market information and customer opinion. A number of factors must be anticipated when using the Internet as a source for market insight and research. The business goal of the survey must be well defined, including a clear definition of its purpose and the potential action steps to be taken on the results. The survey has to be well designed, following the principles of questionnaire design, usability and web-design. And the sample has to be well selected in a manner that the results drawn from the survey be representative.

Email

Email as a marketing channel is suffering heavily under the problem of ever increasing amounts of spam that make users restrain from accepting this channel as an essential source of information under certain circumstances. Still, email is a perfect channel for targeted communication with customers whose profiles are known and who can be provided with relevant information.

Besides the creation and maintenance of own newsletters, external mailing lists can offer advertising space with an often very targeted audience that allows a company to select an appropriate list that fits their target group, and advertise within the content of that external newsletter.

Concerning the customer reaction, an incoming message can either, be rejected by the user and deleted from his inbox, or can be treated as relevant and lead to an action by the recipient. One of the most valuable actions that can be taken by the user is to forward the message among his peers, leading to a viral distribution of the marketing message.

As mentioned in the introduction to this section, non-solicited email, or spam, does have great impact on email as a marketing communication channel. Many consumers are unwilling to provide their email addresses in fear of receiving such unsolicited mails. It is important to note that while the legal framework concerning spam mails has evolved and created clear rules concerning the use of marketing emails, consumers might still perceive emails as spam just because they do not feel that the content is relevant to them, even though the message complies with all legal regulations. Spam, not in legal terms, but as it is perceived by users must therefore be divided into two categories. First the messages that often have offensive context and are sent through insecure mail servers to address lists that have been collected illegally and secondly the messages that are being sent in accordance with legal standards, but are unwanted by the user. This second category poses a threat to every company making use of email as a marketing channel as the unwanted email relates directly to the company and might negatively impact the customer relation with the user receiving the message.

Another major problem that affects email as a professional communication channel among companies and their customers is the insecurity of the messaging protocol in place for email itself. By common means, it is not possible today to authenticate with certitude the sender of an email message. Even though digital signatures or other technical means for identification exist and could reduce this problem, they are not widely used, and average users do not have access to these technologies. For the banking industry the abuse of email for phishing attacks by hackers has made the email channel an absolutely untrustworthy channel that must be avoided in corporate communications.

The most common method for ensuring that a user is willing to receive email from a company is an appropriate opt-in procedure. The most common today is the double opt-in procedure, that consists in submitting an email address through a web form or similar, and then receiving a welcome message with a link to click on in order to confirm the subscription. This procedure ensures that the user entering the address in the web form also has access to the email account he is submitting. Opt-outs can also be designed as a single or double procedure and will mostly be selected depending on the impact of the opt-out.

Email marketing can have an important positive impact when conducted in a high-quality form. It generally induces only low cost, while generating sales opportunities and driving the customer relationship (Clark and Clark 2006). Targeting and well conducted analytics are the key drivers of email marketing success (Jupiter Research 2005). Targeting and personalisation have to go beyond basic personalisation tactics that do not make the messages relevant to the recipient.

Call centres

Within the modern communication mix, call centres take an important role. Customers expect to be able to reach a company and be able to talk to a knowledgeable representative within a matter of minutes. Whether to provide this service or not will heavily depend on the type of market the respective company acts upon. Within a high cost goods markets, such a service will be more expected by the customer than within a low cost mass market. Providing high quality call centre support, and scaling the service nationally or even internationally can be a large cost factor that needs to be taken into account when evaluation the efficiency of a call centre.

Call centres can provide effective communication with customers and potential customers in terms of service delivery, information responses or even sales. Two major trends dominate call centre developments. The consolidation and the outsourcing of call centre operations.

Consolidation of call centre operations implies locating a single call centre to handle the incoming calls for a range of geographical locations. Outsourcing leads to externalisation of the operation of the call centre to contractors that provide the service.

While both means reduce cost of call centre operation, it is unsure whether the quality of the service provided can remain at level.

Beyond the telephone, a number of new client facing technologies to enhance call centre operations have evolved with the spread of digital media. Web-based interfaces allow a more batch oriented processing of customer requests and therefore allow call centre staffing to be more flexible. Mobile messaging as well is attractive for time critical customer notifications like pick-up notifications. Email and interactive voice response systems (IVR) constitute further interaction possibilities that can enhance the service provided by the call centre.

The role of multichannel

Today's corporate marketing communication must satisfy the needs and expectations of their customers to a full extent. Many companies are confronted not only with one specific category of customers but must serve a whole range of different segments.

These segments often will favour much different communication channels for conducting daily business with the company. Multichannel communication therefore today is a request that is imposed by the market a company is acting upon.

Customers also heavily integrate channels. Studies show that 50% of shoppers consult the Internet before they shop at a physical store (CMO Counsil 2005). These shoppers also research products and alternatives online. Retailers on their side seek new delivery possibilities to reach more customers. This need led from the catalogue channel to the use of interactive channels.

For customer loyalty, this should not have a fundamental impact, it must only be assured that the quality of the service and products be of equal value among the channels. Loyalty must be based on value towards the product and brand rather than towards the channel.

It is important for companies that provide multi channel access to their services that a customer is served according to his accustomed way across all channels, this includes the acceptance of loyalty cards and gift vouchers among all channels, the consistent offering of offers and pricing and the ability to claim service via a different channel than the one the sale was conducted.

2.5.2   The role of customer rewards in loyalty schemes

By influencing cognitive processes, rewards can be said to be able to drive individual's behaviour. The rewarded activities tend to be amplified by individuals following a rather basic learning scheme based on the amplification principle which build on the theory of conditioning (Kroeber-Riel and Weinberg 2003). This is the cognitive process that reward elements in loyalty programs are built on. They mean to amplify the positive purchasing behaviour by closely linking it to the reception of a certain reward, be it by collecting points for later redemption, or receiving an immediate cash discount on certain goods purchased. Of course, the selection and promotion of the reward that will be able to drive the behaviour of customers must be rightly in line with the customer's expectations and needs and must closely fit to the desires of the defined target group.

Value of rewards

The reward itself, as a driver for customer participation in a loyalty scheme, plays an important role in shaping the attractiveness of the program. Understandably, the real and perceived values of the reward will have major influence on customers' behaviour towards and within the program.

It has been shown (Sharp and Sharp 1997) that higher value rewards reinforced the desired behaviour better than lower value rewards. When the rewards where stopped though, those you had received higher value rewards were more likely to return to the previous pattern of behaviour than those who had received the lower value reward. It can be learned that the perceived or real withdrawal of valuable privileges can easily lead to an opposed behaviour than anticipated.

For the reward to have any effect at all, it must be attractive enough to truly stimulate a change in behaviour among customers. The offered value must be in close accordance with the needs and desires of the addressed target group. Rewards are said to be most effective when they are closely related to the brand or product they are intending to promote. A trend can be identified towards rewards that offer higher convenience to loyal customers rather than simple give-aways (Kopalle and Neslin 2003).

Following the amplification theory presented in the beginning of this chapter, it can be said that interaction frequency will drive program efficiency. Frequent interaction, may it be mentally or emotionally, must be sought by the program. Simple handling of a card at the point of sale, or the regular reception of a statement, is not a significant emotional program interaction. A higher level of interaction is to be sought in order to drive program efficiency.

Concerning the offered reward value, it must reflect the value of the customer to the program and it must meet the customers' expectations while remaining affordable for the provider and allowing configuration flexibility. A number of general points can be stated, that have to be considered when selecting the value-level of a respective reward (Clark and Clark 2006):

- The reward is attractive enough to draw the customer to participate
- The reward is not so big that the customer becomes loyal to the reward and not to the business or brand
- The reward is not so expensive that it makes the program uneconomical
- The reward is structured so that it can be altered, reduced or even withdrawn without alienating too many best customers
- The reward is able to attract new customers of "best customer" profile
- The reward encourages the customer to interact with the program frequently

A loyalty program's benefit cannot consist in the gift, discount or reward alone. It is rather the improved service and the stronger relationship, based on the usage of the information that the loyalty program generates that will provide value to the operator of the program.

Function of rewards

Rewards offered within loyalty programs must be selected and designed in order to serve a range of concrete functions.

Firstly, the reward should support both, the retention of existing customers and the attraction of new customers. Generally, it must provide a compelling reason to partici- pate in the program. For the attraction of new customers the program can be designed to offer a sign-up bonus, it is important though, not to create the appearance that the new customers get a higher value treatment than existing customers. The retention of existing customers can be supported by offering soft rewards as product or brand re- lated privileges. Service alone tends to drive retention, acting as a reward without a strict loyalty program around it.

The reward should drive the function of encouraging customers to modify their behav- iour. The careful selection of rewards and the respective thresholds that need to be reached in order to qualify for the reward can support the aimed purchasing behaviour. The collection of complete customer data, supplied by the customer at registration, along with the identification of the customer at each transaction are further functions that need to be motivated by the reward.

The increase of purchase size and frequency along with the goal to move customers up through the segments are further functions supported by the reward offered within the loyalty program. Again, soft rewards within the loyalty program can play an important role in reaching these goals.

Properties of good rewards

In order to optimally serve its functions within the loyalty program and show optimal efficiency, the reward should be selected with a number of specific properties in mind.

The reward must be flexible enough to cope with changes in and around the loyalty program. The program can develop in terms of scale, and the reward must be able to adapt to such new situation. The conditions can also change with modified needs and preferences of the customers. As the reward influences consumer behaviour, it must be adapted to new environmental conditions regularly in order to reach the defined goals sustainably.

Affordability of the reward is an important property when it comes to examining overall program profitability. The reward must be attractive enough for the customer to make him change his behaviour, though the total spending on rewards cannot exceed the total returns from the program. One strategy that is often encountered in practice solves this problem in a very smart way. Rewards are often drawn from existing spare capacity of the program provider (Singh et al. 2007). In this way, a potentially wasted resource can efficiently be used as a reward for a valued customer. This practice is for example encountered within airline loyalty programs, where empty first class seats are offered to customers with lower-class tickets as an upgrade for some amount of collected bonus miles.

As has been discussed above, the loyalty program must offer value to its customers. If this value is to be reached via a reward, this reward must be attractive enough to be desired by the selected target group.

The reward can represent an important source of differentiation from competitors. In order to achieve this, it must fulfil two criteria: it must be imaginative and unique. An imaginative reward will capture the customers' attention, and a unique reward will support the lock-in notion of the loyalty program.

It is also important that the reward is seen to be attainable within the program. This means that the required threshold to obtain the reward can be reached by a large number of customers when they adapt their purchasing behaviour only slightly. Only when the relation of purchasing behaviour and reward is clear to the customer, will he be able to adapt his purchasing behaviour as desired by the loyalty program. Previous research has shown that the attainability of rewards plays an important role in influencing customers' affinity and regular usage with loyalty programs (Crank 2007).

It is important to assure, when defining the properties of the reward for a loyalty program, that the profile of the reward matches the profile of the company that runs the program. If a wrong type of reward is selected, it will attract the wrong type of customers, and might even push off the desired customers. Further, a reward must be compelling enough to persuade customers to redeem it once they reach the required threshold. Previous research in the United Kingdom has shown that many program participants do not claim their earned rewards. In 2003 there was more than 400 million pounds worth of rewards that had not been claimed within loyalty programs (Clark and Clark 2006). The same is true for airline miles, were there are said to be non-redeemed stocks worth the equivalent of up to 700 billion dollars (Economist 2005).

Well selected rewards will encourage continuous interaction with the program. One of the best ways to achieve this is to give rewards directly at the point of purchase. This strongly links the feeling of receiving a reward to the transaction. Straight discount programs often fail to achieve this direct interaction.

Getting value from the reward

In order to obtain value from offering a loyalty program and rewards to customers, the benefits obtained from customers' participation in the program must be higher than the cost associated with the operation of the program and the provisioning of the rewards and benefits.

When the cost of providing the reward, including its direct cost, the cost of fulfilment, the cost of handling and storing and the expected amount that will be redeemed, is known, the required uplift in sales from the loyalty program can be calculated. Many loyalty programs offer a 1% reward on sales. Each Euro spend would equal the collection of one point worth 0.01 Euro in redemptions. In practice, as not all customers are taking part in the program, and not all of them will redeem their points, the cost of the program will be less than 1%.

Types of reward

Rewards offered to customers within loyalty programs can vary a lot. But generally they can be classified in "hard rewards" like discounts or points and "soft rewards" like privileges and benefits. The right type of reward needs to be selected for the specified target group and goals that the program should achieve. Lower tier customers are often given hard rewards, while top tier customers are given soft rewards as a means for recognition.

Discounts

Discounts are often a motivating factor for participation in loyalty programs. According to research among loyalty program participants, 66% of customers name discounts as their main reason for joining a loyalty program. Their behaviour though shows that when it comes to redeeming their points, most customers do not go for discounts, but rather choose gifts or cash back options (Clark and Clark 2006).

When discussing discounts it must be differentiated between untargeted and targeted discounts. While untargeted discounts are offered to all customers, targeted discounts are offered to selected customers only via the means of the loyalty program.

Untargeted discounts bring along a range of disadvantages that need to be considered when choosing a reward strategy. Generally, building a business based on discounting alone is very vulnerable to competition. Products can be dangerously devalued, and profits margins are eroded (Aaker 2001). When the discount is discontinued, and the price is brought back to the normal level, customers might perceive that as an increase in prices. The biggest advantages of untargeted discounts though, are the cross-selling opportunities they can offer, and of course they a very easy to implement.

Targeted discounts are offered to certain customers only. This can be handled by the communication means of the loyalty program. Traditionally that would involve sending a letter and including a coupon or registering the customer for this specific discount in the loyalty system for the next purchase controlled by a loyalty card. In the mobile loyalty system, the interactive mobile communication channel can support the transmission of this information faster and in a more personal manner. Regular discounts closely linked to the loyalty program offer a range of advantages. The customers perceive a real advantage from being members in the loyalty program when they receive targeted discounts. And, when presenting the members' discounts to all customers, this feature can attract new members to the program. Disadvantages of targeted discounts include the complexity involved in offering different prices to different customers, and a potential resistance by customers to the fact that different people pay different prices for the same good (Clark and Clark 2006).

Loyalty program points

Loyalty programs based on points are generally very versatile. The collected points can be redeemed as discounts, privileges, or cash back. Often, rewards can also be redeemed from partner companies rather than from the issuer of the points alone.

One advantage of point based schemes is the flexibility they offer. The rewards can be continuously changed without affecting the collection mechanisms and can therefore be adapted to the customers' requirements easily. Single-company loyalty programs also often face the challenge of not being able to allow their participants to build up enough points to obtain a reward. In a points based program, integration of partner companies is easy as points can be spend and collected at any partner's location.

Soft rewards, exceptional services, and privileges

Rewarding customers with a more personal and service oriented experience can be a very effective means of recompensing loyal customers. The soft rewards are those that are often well remembered by customers. Rather than a pure and simple price discount, an exceptional service experience will be remembered and discussed with others.

This is true of course for all companies that constantly provide exceptional services to all their customers. The loyalty towards these kinds of companies does not have to be managed by a loyalty program at all. It can simply be built on the high value services they offer as part of their product.

Privileges are one of the most exclusive types of reward when used correctly. Usually privileges will be reserved for the best customers only. As the offered privileges can often not be bought, they represent a form of extra value. Often privileges can act as a good lock-in, once customers have experienced the advantage of the privilege, they will not want to miss it, and are ready to hold or adapt their consumption behaviour to whatever is needed in order to further receive the privilege.

2.5.3   The value of data for relationship management

Data collection

Data to be collected with the loyalty program can be classified into a number of categories. First, there are the basic customer contact details. These must be kept as correctly as possible, incomplete, outdated or duplicate records should be avoided. The second class of data are the transaction oriented recordings of the purchased goods and services, together with a classification of the goods, the price paid and a detailed time and location record. To allow detailed analysis, it is important to hold information on all products, including a classification, marketing information and profit margins.

Based on these records, behavioural data can be extracted for each customer, this allows to assigning each customer to a specific profile. This behavioural information consists of buying patterns, historical transaction dates, amounts and locations.

Data can be gathered from a whole range of sources. It can be collected directly from the customer in interviews or via questionnaires, or it can be collected by observing how the customer interacts with the business or the loyalty programs communication means.

The most common and direct form of data gathering is the completion of an application form when joining the program. It can be used to obtain all basic contact details as name, address, phone number, e-mail and customer preferences. Often application forms are also used to collect data on the customers' demographics, financial situation and lifestyle preferences. It has been shown tough, that customers' become more and more reluctant to disclose personal information to the marketing departments behind loyalty programs (Grönroos 2004, Clark and Clark 2006). One way around this trend, is to offer bonuses or points for the disclosure of detailed data within the program.

Web sites can also be a good source of data, especially when the collected information can be linked to an individual customer. The data collected on web sites is often centred on technical logging of site usage and completed transactions, including return rates, usage duration and purchases.

One of the most important sources of data for loyalty programs consists in the tracking of transactions for each individual customer. This information will allow building an image of each customer's personal buying behaviour. The technical source for this data is the point of sale terminal. The customer therefore must identify himself at the point of sale with a suited loyalty token.

Another interesting source for data that is used to segment customers into profiles or lead personalised dialogues is information from the customer service departments which can be contacted by the customer through a call centre or a web site or at a customer service desk in-store. As well as the repair or replacement centres that can provide data on the customer's experience with products and consumed services.

Data lifecycle, duplication, accuracy, and cleansing

Every collected information has a finite lifetime, a period of time during which the data is useful and can be trusted. The lifetime of each recorded detail in the loyalty database can be different, and is determined by a set of factors defined by the program policies. One of the relevant questions for example is when to remove an inactive customer from the database. It has to be determined whether this customer has left for sure, or whether a potential win-back is possible. Policies on how to decide in these situations must exist in the program and be well defined.

Duplicate entries into the customer database will most likely not disturb the customer as he will use solely one of his identities or use his memberships for different purposes. At the end of the year he will have his total of points collected as with a single membership. The problem of duplicate entries arises when analysis is performed on the data. Each database entry's purchasing behaviour will be calculated separately although they might represent the same customer. Two solutions exist for this problem, the customer's duplicate entries can be merged when identified, and the customer would get a new loyalty token with a new ID. This though would represent a quite rigid process, and might not be appreciated by the customer. Another alternative often applied in loyalty programs, is to merge the records of customers with multiple entries when performing analysis, profiling or clustering (see section 4.7.3.1). In order to reduce duplicate signups with the program, it is important that the customers are continually given an easy option for updating the most current changes of their details.

Benefits of data collection and analysis

The role of data in loyalty

A very important question that needs to be answered when designing a loyalty program is how the collected data will be used by the company that operates the program. Without a clear view on how the collected data will help achieving the goals set out for the program, a loyalty program can not contribute to the success of a business.

When loyalty programs where first introduced, the goal of such programs consisted in targeting offers more accurately towards customers (Clark and Clark 2006). With the advance of technological support for programs, many more uses have evolved. Although, targeting offers to selected customers remains an important function.

Following the advances of customer relationship systems, the knowledge of data analysis and methods such as segmentation or predictive analysis has strongly improved. Customer relationship systems and loyalty programs share a common ground with loyalty programs, namely the improvement of customer relationships through better knowledge of their preferences and behaviours. It has been stated numerously (Grönroos 2004, Bolton et al. 2000, Brumley 2002) that the loyalty program alone does not buy loyalty, what it provides to the operator is information. This information, when turned into knowledge by analysis and aggregation, can help adapting the core business and offerings. This in turn, will be able to raise loyalty among customers. The proposed chain of tasks for the correct use of data within a loyalty program would be: data – analysis – action – loyalty.

Individual customer data analysis

By performing behavioural profiling on the collected data, insight can be gained not only into what customers are buying, but also when exactly and occasionally even why a specific good has been bought. By examining such unrelated factors, individual correlations can be spotted within the customer's behaviour. Brand-switching among goods of the same category in correlation with price changes or promotional offers can be used to determine whether a specific customer is responsive to price offers or promotions.

When targeting promotions to a customer, it can be extremely important to have information on the customer lifecycle and demographic profile of customers. Only through such profiles the suitability of products or certain product categories and related promotions can be evaluated. Premium goods, for example, would rather be promoted among customers who might fall into profiles reflecting wealthier households according to their geographic area or to multiple incomes.

The customer's product preferences and usual repertoire can also offer interesting insights when planning campaigns and selecting appropriate addressees. The preferences are best analysed along categories of products or brands purchased by the customer and help reduce the probability of sending inappropriate promotions to customers. The relationships among product categories and potential cross selling opportunities that can also be identified from the collected data support the design of incentive oriented campaigns, such as couponing promotions.

Pricing strategies are very important to many retail businesses, especially when the competitive landscape is challenging. Long term analysis of customer purchase data can support the development of appropriate pricing strategies. Dynamic and more complex pricing strategies can directly be supported by the loyalty program. Loyalty programs that are based on tiered pricing are becoming popular, these programs offer different prices to members of the program than to other customers therefore the loyalty program acts as a tool for pricing strategy.

One concept well known among e-commerce retailers are shopping suggestions. Based on the previous purchases of the customer, products and goods are recommended that will fit his shopping profile and have a high probability of attracting the customer's attention and interest. When offering a loyalty program, this concept from the e-commerce world can be transferred to the world of traditional retailing.

Segmentation
Based on a complete customer and transaction database, which might contain from all of the following points, segmentation can be performed into a variety of groups based on the many available attributes.

- Demographic information
- Geographic data
- Lifestyle data
- Life stage data
- Customer's interests and hobbies
- Personal preferences
- Transaction history
- Customer service history

The segmentation should represent the requirements of the business and the planned campaign.

A variety of different segmentation strategies exist, which range from the traditional analysis of customer lifetime value (CLV) to the recency, frequency, monetary value (RFM) measure or newer concepts as customer tiering or customer flow analysis.

Detailed information on customer lifetime value for the specific business can only be drawn from long-term database records. It will be difficult to extract the according data from a rather young collection of transaction- and customer histories. In order to offer insight into customer lifetime value, a loyalty program that collects the required data therefore needs to be in place for a fair amount of time. As time passes, the calculated data of course becomes more and more accurate. The knowledge about customer lifetime value will help to put in numbers the effect of losing customers, or from another point of view, it can demonstrate the financial reward of keeping or winning back customers.

Recency, frequency, monetary value has been a well known measure for segmenting customers for a long time. Each of the observed factors: the recency of the last purchase, the general frequency of purchases and the total monetary value spend by the customer is traditionally divided into quintiles. Then a score is calculated for each customer according to his classification in the three categories. The score is usually calculated by simply creating a three digit number consisting of the customer's classification for each of the factors. This leads to a potential of 125 possible groups. This large number of possible segmentation outcomes makes targeted marketing campaigns or the like rather complex. A simplified recency, frequency, monetary value approach has been introduced by dividing the customer base in only two groups per factor, mostly following the 80/20 rule, which leads to only eight possible category outcomes (Woolf 2001).

One segmentation approach that divides customers into spending segments is the customer tiering approach (Woolf 2001). Customers are divided into five groups according to their spending during a fixed period, which could be one week as a minimum and then be aggregated for months, quarters and years. This form of detailed spending threshold analysis can be very useful because it offers an insight into which and how many customers are reducing their spending over the period of analysis, how many are remaining at their level, and how many are increasing their spend (Reichheld 1996). This data can then be used to provide promotions or marketing campaigns that will target customers specifically and follow the intention to move them up through the tiers.

Another metric that builds on segmentation and the collection of data within the loyalty program is the customer flow analysis (Woolf 2001). It is an important measure as it transforms the loyalty program data into business relevant information. This analysis is rather simple, but reported to be potentially very effective (Woolf 2001). Rather than only measuring the sign-up rate of the loyalty program, the outflow of customers which are the ones that turned inactive during the period should also be measured and reported. By looking at both these numbers together, a net customer gain can be calculated which will be a more meaningful performance indicator.

Best customers, defectors, and win-backs

It is often argued that targeting the best customers with special promotions and treats is a very effective and important marketing tool. A case presented by (Clark and Clark 2006) shows how important the top tier customers can be: at a large retail shopping company, the loyal segment spends 175 times as much as the lowest segment on average and the top 7% of customers are responsible for more than 50% of total income. In this case, it can be understandable that keeping these customers loyal, though better services, offers or discounts can be very valuable undertaking.

An important step when trying to keep important customers loyal to the company is to observe the behaviour of customers closely and react upon changes that might lead to a later defection. This kind of early defector detection consists of three different analyses of loyalty data. The first analysis consists in identifying customers how have defected from the company in the past and how are clearly lost from the customer base. These customers can easily be identified from the database by applying a filter to customers with inactive accounts for a reasonably long period. This period, of course, must be a multitude of the average time between customer visits. The second step of analysis is to examine the transaction data of the selected lost customers and to identify patters that might have suggested that these customers were about to defect from the company. It is important when analysing patterns of behaviour, to identify trends in the behaviour of the customers that are relatively unique to the category of defecting customers. The third analysis is then to search customers within the current active customer base that might only shortly have switched into one of the identified patterns that lead to a defection of the customer. Based on this selection of potentially defecting customers, pre-emptive win-back campaigns can be designed that might stop them refraining from the company.

Once customers have ceased from being active with the company, only win back opportunities can offer a last chance in getting back these valuable customers. Based on customer purchasing patterns, win-back promotions can be targeted to the needs of customers and might offer a last chance of re-activating a potentially lost customer.

Generating business intelligence

One form of intelligence that can be gained from data is the personal preference of customers. This data offers potential for differentiation from competitors even in industries where differentiation is usually hard to achieve. The avoidance of wrongly targeted promotions alone can prevent a discontent customer to turn away from the company that is trying hard to persuade him upon a product which he does not need. When on the other side, companies can predict from the data they have the customer's preferred ways of communication, the potential needs, or the triggers for his next purchase, these companies will be able to differentiate themselves from their closest competitor through targeted communication alone.

Once a loyalty program operator has understood what data he really has, they can turn this data and the generated analyses into information that will support them in taking important decisions for the business.

Real-time data analysis offers one approach that moves beyond the evolutionary process of studying historical data towards a proactive and prospective approach. This approach can be interesting when confronted with high churn rates. In this case, a real-time evaluation of which customers are likely to defect in the close future can be very valuable information for marketers. An identification of patterns that help predict the behaviour of customers together with a method to evaluate current customers' potential future behaviour needs to be put in place in order to provide such a proactive system. In the world of Internet and web-analytics, prospective analysis can be used to personalise the user experience in real time and provide content to the user according to his usage of the site.

2.6 Opportunities for interactive media in the marketing mix

The role of the Internet as a purchasing channel is steadily increasing in the business-to-business world as well as in the business-to-consumer and consumer-to-consumer domains. In Austria, 10.8% of total sales by companies are conducted via e-commerce channels. Tourism represents the strongest industry with 15.3% of total sales over the Internet (Statistik Austria 2007a). More than 65% of companies in the EU use a website as a means of communication with their customers (figure 8).

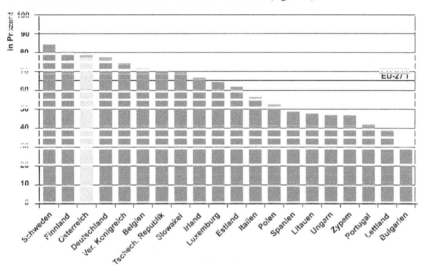

Figure 8: Companies with websites (Statistik Austria 2007b)

Beside the role of the Internet as a transaction channel, its role as an information channel is even more predominant. For many purchases that are conducted offline, research on products, alternatives and prices are conducted online with the help of the Internet (Rösger et al. 2007).

2.6.1 Interactive elements in online retailing

With the first appearance of the World Wide Web and web-browsers as navigation and content representation clients, a more active role of the media-consumer could be observed compared to the predominant TV, newspaper and radio media. The availability of information, its structure, and the way it could be navigated all changes the consumer's behaviour of information consumption (Stähler 2001).

With the advent of new World Wide Web technologies, often referred to under the term of the Web 2.0, the consumer is now directly taking part in the generation of content. This can refer to the creation of media, products, services or new forms of interaction and communication (Rudolph et al. 2007). Participation of users in the creation process of the media is at the heart of most innovative Internet services. The sharing of knowledge, content and resources enables services as Wikipedia, YouTube, Facebook and many others in a rapidly moving domain.

Not many applications that are based on the new trends enabled by customer participation are related to retailing of physical or digital goods. Some applications do not have a business model at all, as for example Wikipedia, and many are based on the generation of advertising revenues by creating large and recurrent user bases. However online retailing is still influenced by the new trends in at least two ways:

- The involvement of the single customer or whole customer base in the product creation process. Referred to as customer-co-creation.
- The use of the Internet as a platform for the customers to share information on products, quality opinions, comparisons and recommendations via forums, blogs and social networks.

The first way, the involvement of customers in the product creation process allows a form of customer orientation for businesses that has not been possible before. The customer's requirements do not have to be anticipated by the company, they are formulated by the customer himself. This approach fits well in the hedonistic schema and experience orientation that is often sought by users on the Internet. Hence, this form of customer-co-creation is especially attractive for products that fit well with these factors and have a high hedonistic nature.

The second influence on online retailing, the use of the Internet as a platform to share and search for product information, enables companies to actively get engaged in these online communities. The active engagement allows for the collection of unfiltered customer feedback at close to no cost when compared to the expensive conduction of customer satisfaction studies. An open dialogue with the customers can further provide an attractive differentiation criterion among community participants from other companies that do not engage with the community.

2.6.2   Interactive media and corporate communication strategies

Customer and user communities

Communities are classified by a "consciousness of kind" among their members, "hared rituals and traditions" and "a sense of moral responsibility" (Muniz and O'Guin 2001). Such communities develop at many positions on the Internet. They emerge around topics of interest, open source software projects or brands. An active creation and management of these communities can help companies to build a loyal customer base with a high level of advocacy.

Experience oriented marketing strategies, which are often employed to escape the flooded world of traditional marketing and advertising gain a new instrument through the introduction of actively managed online-communities. Experience oriented marketing strategies have gained an established position besides traditional marketing strategies and support the notion of consequently orienting all marketing measures along the emotional requirements of the customers and the brand image. The goal of such an experience oriented marketing strategy consists in creating an experience value and an emotional activation of the target group (Kroeber-Riel and Weinberg 2003). The emotional relationship with the community and brand hence leads to a continuing and deep customer loyalty.

This sort of experience oriented marketing strategies, targeting emotional activation of the customers, is often implemented through the build up of brand communities. A platform for social exchange is hence provided to the customers that provides emotional quality and confrontation with the targeted brand and marketing messages of the provider.

For many products, the social value, e.g. the statement transported through the image of a certain clothing brand, is much higher than the functional value of the product. Online brand communities offer a new way to influence the social value of a brand by influencing psycho-social dimensions of the product that can constitute important competitive advantages (Algesheimer et al. 2005). Brand communities can therefore be said to have a positive economic impact on a brand when implemented correctly. Success factors for the economic success of brand communities have been described by Rösger et al. (2007). The authors postulate the mutual-support possibilities among community members, the interaction possibilities between the members and the brand as well as the fulfilment of member requirements, on a functional and an emotional level. Further, brand directories can have a direct economic effect by leading to re-duced transaction and service costs among community members.

Online brand communities often involve a customer-co-creation aspect were the com-munity members openly contribute content to the site. These contributions can be of high value for the community as they enrich the content provided by the online experi-ence. But user generated content, especially in the context of a brand, always requires active management and editing. This form of managing the user generated cont, to-gether with the management of the company's interaction with the community mem-bers, represents a further success factor for interactive online brand communities.

Blogs

Blogs have evolved from being a simple form of a content management system to be-ing a new form of media. Blogging can be defined by the following: "To blog is to continually post one's ideas, opinions, Internet links (including those to other blogs), and so on about things on one's website, which is called a web log" (Smudde 2005).

Blogs also emerge as an attractive means in corporate communication. Corporate communication, in this context, is to be understood as the communication of the com-pany with its environment and therefore represents an important management task (Schmid and Lyczek 2006). Generally it must be differentiated between a bottom-up and a top-down type of corporate blogging strategy.

A bottom-up strategy involves a number of employees that create a real blogging cul-ture within the company. This involves challenges, as the editing and control-mechanisms concerning the information being publicly published on the blogs are re-duced to the decisions taken by the employee himself. This blogging strategy can con-tribute to the company's image when executed correctly, as it is often authentic and gives customers and prospects higher insight into the company's products and proc-esses. It is clearly a means for creating higher transparency towards the company's environment. Guidelines concerning the corporate blogging culture are important for such a bottom-up strategy, as they set the general conditions for either sides, the blog-ging employees and the company itself.

The alternative is a top-down blogging strategy. This approach often follows a targeted information strategy directed to the stakeholders of the company. The source of the information is more centric than in the bottom-up strategy, the content is generated in the marketing or communications department and is edited according to the general corporate guidelines and communication strategies. The blog then serves as a news archive that still supports interesting features for corporate communication: The ability to interactively gain feedback and engage in discussions with readers based on commenting functions of the blog, the ability to distribute the generated content via syndication mechanisms such as RSS (Really Simple Syndication), or the general recency of information associated with blogs and higher frequency of visits than with usual corporate websites.

Generally blogging as a form of presence on the web must be considered when planning a corporate communication strategy. It represents an important factor in the field of current interactive customer communication. Blogging also has relevant impact on mobile strategies as blog content can more easily be distributed to mobile devices through the availability of device and reader-independent syndication mechanisms.

Viral

Personal recommendations have always played an important role in the marketing domain, their role on purchasing behaviour has been analysed and confirmed by empirical research of different sources (Bansal and Voyer 2000). Viral marketing effects are not new to the Internet or the world of new media, word-of-mouth communication has always offered the possibility for the influence of personal purchasing behaviour. The form of recommendation that is the key element in word-of-mouth or viral marketing is based on the theory of interpersonal communication. This theory describes the effect as a process of mutual interpersonal communication of consumers that exchange information on products or services (Cornelsen 2000).

As with many traditional marketing mechanisms, viral marketing must be adapted to the use in the new media context and must further be adapted for the use in the mobile context. The most important aspect of viral marketing is interactivity and communication among customers and potential customers. This interactivity and communication possibilities must therefore be provided be the tools wishing to be used as platforms for online or mobile applications of viral marketing.

Product recommendations are well adapted and appear in large numbers on the Internet. Often the recommendations are part of product reviews that customers provide in which they share their experiences with the product. But these recommendations only partly reflect the idea of word-of-mouth marketing, they lack the personal aspect. Although they provide the information and recommendation, and although they provide a certain asynchronous communication and interactivity between the writer and the reader, they lack the personal factor that makes a recommendation valuable. More effective recommendations must be targeted to the recipient, this is only possible when the writer has the possibility to forward his opinion to the recipients directly and that a personal relationship is existent between them. This is where an important advantage of the mobile channel is existent in terms of being a communication channel for viral marketing.

Targeted use of viral marketing effects on the Internet within the corporate marketing strategy builds on the exponential distribution of information that is possible among users that forward messages containing the information or links to the content. The type of information that is to be distributed through this mechanic requires a medium that supports fast and uncomplicated forwarding from one peer to the next. The goal is to achieve a snowball effect and reach an exponential number of users that have contact with the information for the low cost of initialising the campaign.

Studies have analysed the success factors for viral marketing campaigns on the Internet, most findings can also be applied to the mobile version of the viral marketing effect (Bauer et al. 2007): The key success factors are that campaigns need to provide perceived value to the users, the access to the content must be free, the forwarding of the information must be effortless and the choice of the first transmitters must be made carefully. The value for the user can be created by the positive image of a brand as well as by the experience or entertainment value of the content. The low marginal cost of the forwarding of information on the new media and the easy reproduction of digital content supports the ability of the Internet or the mobile channel to be used for viral marketing.

2.6.3   Interactive instruments in customer relationship management

While the concept of customer relationship management and its instrumentalisation has been discussed in detail in section 2.3, this section provides an analysis of the current state-of-the-art concerning the use of customer relationship elements in online retailing.

The customer relationship instruments that are employed by e-commerce practitioners can best be analysed along the marketing instruments adopted. An adaptation of the traditional marketing mix for online businesses describes following marketing instruments (Wilke et al. 2005): Product line policy, price policy, communication policy and front-end policy. The product line policy comprises all choices regarding the selection of goods that will be offered through the online business, it encompasses the selection of the product line's width and depth. Price policy determines the height of prices as well as discrimination strategies and special offers. The communication policy includes decisions on the content of exchanged messages as well as the selection of channels for communication (Barth et al. 2002) it heavily influences the customer relation by considering personalised and one-to-one communication as well as the communication of the brand image. For online businesses, the front-end policy encompasses the direct interface to the customer. The front-end policy consists of the design and the functionalities of the web presence including features for personalisation and the availability of communication means for users to interact as a community on the site.

A stronger presence of the relationship paradigm together with the current development of the Internet as a channel for customer creation leads to changes among all current online marketing instruments. New applications are created that support new forms of communication between buyers and between the buyer and seller directly.

The product line policy is influenced by the presence of social networks that provide information on the social graph between its users. On social networks, users do not only provide personal profiles of them and administer their relations to other users, but also interact and communicate through these networks. A passive monitoring of the discussion groups and the relations among the users can provide important information for the management of the product line policy. Wikis or similar user driven content generation can also provide added value to the consumers if they get access to a range of information concerning the product they are purchasing. Companies also get the opportunity to learn about the usage patterns of their products on the market and can react by adapting the product line policy efficiently.

Social networks and social shopping platforms can also have an important influence on the price policy of an online business. The monitoring of activities on the social network can provide information on the perception of prices by the customers and can help managing the product pricing. Social shopping platforms represent a federation of users that collectively perform purchasing decisions, an active care of such a community and flexible pricing policies towards their users can offer important sources of revenue.

The interactive nature of the Internet is one of its biggest advantages over other media. Hence corporate communication policies that make use of the Internet can leverage this advantage. Personalised messages, feeds, and newsletters provide interesting opportunities for communication with customers. As discussed above, blogs and viral marketing strategies make heavy use of the interactive nature of the Internet and provide new mechanisms for the corporate communication policy.

Rich media interfaces, customer co-creation and mash-ups constitute the current trends of the front-end policy that influence the customer relationship. Rich media interfaces allow for a richer experience while interacting with the online business, its use also enables for new formats of product presentations and can provide the user with interaction possibilities with the product via simulation or an immersive presentation. Customer co-creation, as discussed above, supports the integration of direct user feedback and communications among users. Mash-ups support the integration of different content sources to provide unique services to the customer, open syndication standards support the creation of such mash-ups and allow for an efficient distribution on the Internet.

3 Mobile infrastructure perspective on the loyalty framework

3.1 Interaction channels supported by mobile devices

3.1.1 Voice communication services

Mobile voice communication is today the most widely used ubiquitous functionality. Its spread has been driven by the sharp drop in prices for connection time, the widely available geographic coverage of networks and the cheap availability of handsets through the co-financing by the network operators.

Looking at the usage of mobile voice communication, it can be noted that there is a high demand for mobile communication, the technical functionality often even gains priority over traditional communication as the mobile device is always kept on by many users and they are ready to accept being interrupted by an incoming phone call during other conversations or tasks (Cooper 2002).

The traditional voice based communication channel in mobile can not only be used in private or business person-to-person communication but can also be used in the context of information systems that provide interfaces via interactive voice response (IVR) systems. This form of person-to-machine communication is an interesting option for integrating mobile communication into information systems and making a remote access possible via a well available voice communication infrastructure. These interfaces can also be used for providing service to customers, they generally reduce costs compared to the operation of a call centre and can, in certain conditions, provide quick and simple solutions that satisfy the customer's requirements. Of course voice based interfaces to information systems underlie a number of limitations: their interactivity is limited to the potential of current voice recognition systems or basic navigation via input on the phone's keypad.

A special form of interactive voice response systems is when the first contact in the communication process is not initiated by a person, but by the machine itself. In this case, the person receives a call automatically conducted by the interactive voice response system and can react upon this call. Voice communication offers great potential to establish an emotional connection and therefore a relationship between a seller and a buyer. This potential is of course reduced when the party on the seller side is replaced by a machine.

Since the success of personal mobile voice communication, research has been oriented towards finding new attractive elements of mobile communication. Video telephony has been one of the advances which are a good example for the motivation to build new services. But until now, none of the proposed services has gained wide acceptance (Yrjänäinen and Neuvo 2002).

3.1.2   Messaging services

Messaging services have brought the biggest and at the same time unexpected success of mobile non-voice services. Especially the short messaging service (SMS) has been a great success for mobile network operators since its launch in 1992. The number of SMS sent daily has surpassed the mark of one billion in 2003 (GSM Association 2005). The functionality provided by SMS consists in sending text messages from and to mobile devices. The text can consist of up to 160 alphanumeric characters. This is due to the actual anticipated use of the functionality of SMS. Originally SMS was implemented solely to serve as a notification service for informing a mobile user of the availability of new messages on his mailbox.

In contrast to voice communication, the communication through SMS is not based on a direct connection of the sender and the receiver of a message. Hence, SMS is an asynchronous communication form, while the transmission time between the sending and the reception can vary between one and two seconds in the most optimal conditions (GSM Association 2005), delays can appear because of different technical reasons. In the case that the recipient is not available through the network at the time of sending, the message is stored by the network's systems and forwarded to the recipient when he comes back online on the network.

The presentation of the message transmitted per SMS can vary, as well as the way it is stored on the recipient's device. A standard SMS will notify the recipient of its arrival, the recipient will then have to navigate through the phone's menu to open the message and show it on the display. In this case, the message is stored on the phone's internal memory and remains there until it is deleted. Another type of SMS messages are FlashSMS messages, these are displayed on the phone's screen directly upon reception and are not stored on the phone after they have been read by the recipient (Yrjänäinen and Neuvo 2002).

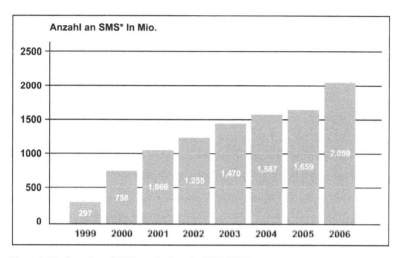

Figure 9: Total number of SMS sent in Austria (RTR 2007)

Simple logos and ringtones can also be transmitted via SMS, as digital attachments to the message itself. The standards for this format vary between handset manufacturers, therefore different formats must be supported by a system that aims for wide adoption.

SMS cannot only be sent and received by mobile phones themselves, but can also be used as a communication interface for an external information system. In the case of SMS messages originating from an information system these messages are referred to as "mobile terminated" messages, in the case of SMS messages which are sent from a user to the information system the messages are referred to as "mobile originated".

With the introduction of the multimedia media messaging system (MMS) messaging possibilities for mobile communication where extended to include multimedia capabilities. From the point of view of the user, the functionality of MMS is very similar to that of SMS. Messages can be sent and received via the mobile device. The sender configures the messages contents and adds a text for the recipient, when the message is delivered to the recipient's device, the user is notified and can choose to download the message's content to his device. Other than SMS messages, MMS messages can also include multimedia content like images, videos, sounds and text or a combination of these formats. The transmission of the multimedia content is achieved through packet switched networking protocols as provided by GPRS networks on top of the GSM stack or via 3rd generation UMTS networks.

One characteristic of MMS messages that might be one cause for the lack of adoption of the service is that MMS messages lead to costs on the recipient's side when downloading the multimedia content of the message. This cost is often not as transparent to the user as the generated data traffic which varies heavily according to the user's contract rate is billed to the user.

The MMS standard is fully compatible with email, this gives the opportunity to integrate mobile communications with standard Internet and email usage. MMS and email share the same asynchronous nature and are therefore well compatible. The multimedia attachments of MMS messages are forwarded as email attachments when handed over by the gateway. But this system integration between mobile messaging and email has not yet yielded a high rate of usage in the European mobile markets.

For the application in the relationship marketing domain, messaging provides a relatively easy to integrate format at manageable costs. Contact can easily be established and intensified with the customer, relevant information can be transmitted in near to real time, and the customer can be kept up to date with information from the company. Messaging is also often used as a response channel for other forms of communication. The biggest limitation is caused by the limited use of characters within SMS messages and the cost involved with sending and receiving MMS messages. The concept of the service must further encompass the threat of being classified as spam by the user. This can be accomplished by providing real value to the customer through the service and letting the customer decide which messages or notifications he wishes to receive.

3.1.3   Mobile internet services

The concept of mobile Internet services consists of providing the ability to access hypertext information via the mobile device. In the first phases of the mobile Internet, this functionality was provided by two different protocols the wireless application protocol (WAP) and the i-mode protocol developed by the Japanese mobile network operator NTT DoCoMo. These protocols where developed for non-data networks that did not support packet switched calls and needed the transmit data over circuit switched networks. Content needed to be developed specifically for the mobile access, integration of traditional existing websites was not possible.

The specification for WAP 1.0 was presented in 1998; it followed the need to establish a standard independent of device manufacturers and network operators. The WAP specification included an own mark-up language that was used to design mobile sites, the wireless mark-up language (WML). WML was not compatible with the hyper text mark-up language (HTML) which was established as the standard language to define web-sites on the Internet.

The new version of the WAP standard, WAP 2.0 also supports protocols well adopted on the Internet as TCP/IP and XHTML. This feature allows for a better integration of the mobile and traditional PC based Internet.

Adoption of mobile Internet services based on WAP and WAP 2.0 are still low. Reasons for this lack of broad adoption can be sought in the promise that was given to users that the mobile Internet experience would be comparable to the one known from the traditional PC based Internet and the high costs associated with the use of data transfer via mobile networks. Further the limitations of mobile devices concerning their screen size that can only present a small portion compared to current PC displays or the lack of input methods that support the input of longer texts. The speed of data transmission over the mobile networks has also been a limitation for the adoption of the mobile Internet, and only slowly, with growing coverage of 3rd generation networks, is the usability of the mobile Internet increasing. And finally it is important to note that the navigation when accessing content and sites on the Internet follows a different logic than the navigation through menus that users are used to on their mobile phones (Helyar 2002).

The second standard of the early mobile Internet was i-mode, launched in 1999 by NTT DoCoMo in Japan and very successful among Japanese mobile users. The service had reached 30 million users by 2001 (NTT DoCoMo 2007). I-mode is an open standard based on HTML as a mark-up language and has a few advantages over WAP. Services can be billed according to the content retrieved rather than the connection time or the data volume alone. This possibility was introduced to the WAP protocol only with the appearance of GPRS supporting networks.

The largest difference between the i-mode network of NTT DoCoMo in Japan and WAP networks in Europe however is not to be sought in the technical specifications. While the offer of WAP content was very poor and prices were kept high in Europe, NTT DoCoMo had involved content providers and developers early in the development phase of i-mode. The service was more open than the restrictive operator portals provided by European mobile network operators. The i-mode success is therefore also due to the adoption of the service on the side of the content providers, more than 2000 mobile i-mode sites existed in 2001 which were officially accepted by NTT DoCoMo and were linked from the provider's mobile Internet portal (Helyar 2002).

The new generation of phones even supports access to standard websites by using the WAP 2.0 protocol as a data transmission layer but also support standard web mark-up languages and optimize their presentation on the mobile device's screen. Some phones of the newest generation even support attractive forms of panning over standard Internet pages that do not fit the phone's screen. This type of access to the rich Internet as it is known from the PC will most probably remain reserved to the more expensive and feature rich smartphones while a trend can be identified that a series of rather cheap "simple phones" will remain on the market covering the demand for easy to operate, simple and cheap devices.

For purposes of managing the customer relation and keeping a customer informed the mobile Internet can provide attractive services that will be used by the consumer when the involved costs are low and transparent and the value generated by the service is perceived by the user. A few technical success factors also exist that the section on the design of the system will further elaborate and propose solutions. While the device can be though as to be belonging to an individual user, there is currently no common way to identify the user when he loads a site via his device. Traditional forms of identification and log-in are complicated given the data entry functionalities of mobile devices. Other challenges next to the identification of users consist in finding the right personalisation technologies to present relevant content to the user as well as strategies to visualise information in a correct format for the reduces screen sizes of mobile displays.

3.1.4   Multimedia support

Integration of multimedia content into the mobile experience counts as an interesting option for mobile non-voice services as the consumption of multimedia content in forms of video or audio are not subject to many of the navigation and usability limitations of the mobile browsing experience.

A range of different technologies exist that support the transport of multimedia content to the mobile device and facilitate its storage and presentation. The content can be downloaded to the mobile device for presentation to the user or streamed to the device via a streaming protocol. With the advance of digital mobile broadcasting standards like Digital Multimedia Broadcasting (DMB) and Digital Video Broadcast for Handhelds (DVB-H) streaming services obtain their own networks, specialised to the distribution of video and audio content to mobile devices.

When making multimedia content available via download, the data has to be transmitted entirely to the mobile device and stared there before the user can access the content. In this case, the device's storage capacities must be large enough to store the content locally, the advantage gained through downloading the content to one's device is the fact that after downloading it once it can be consumed arbitrary times without generating additional data transfer. Another advantage of holding a local copy of the multimedia content is that it can be forwarded to other users via any available channel. Streaming technology on the other hand provides the content as a constant stream of data that is transferred to the mobile device and presented there as it is received. Streaming can either be conducted with live content or with existing content as on-demand streaming. When using a streaming technology to provision content to a mobile device, the player can start presenting the content before it is downloaded completely. Hence, the mobile device only keeps a local copy of a small portion of the content which requires less storage space on the device itself. The disadvantages brought with streaming are that the content cannot be stored and played back at another point of time. When forwarding content that is streamed, the user cannot forward the full content via any available transmission channel, but can only forward the link to the streaming service that provides the content.

Download of multimedia content to the phone is used today mainly for the provisioning of ringtones or videos used as signals for incoming calls. The download of complete songs to the mobile device is the next step in the development of this technology and is supported by the convergence of mobile phones and mobile music players. These devices offer enough storage space for the data downloaded via the network. Streaming services will need the rates for data transmission to be reduced significantly in order to gain wide acceptance. Further the availability of fast networks needs to be guaranteed in order to make the service available to customers independently of their geographic position. Audio streaming requires bandwidth of up to 256 Kbit/s for Audio CD comparable quality and video streaming requires bandwidth of up to 512 Kbit/s for acceptable quality on reduces screen sizes (Zeng and Wen 2002).

Different file formats and transmission standards that are supported by different devices make a full coverage of all mobile devices impossible. When using mobile multimedia content as part of the corporate communication strategy, compatibility with large numbers of existing devices must be ensured.

Mobile multimedia can be used by companies in their customer communication for information services that include product presentations or instruction and support on how to use a product. Multimedia content can also be used to communicate the experience value of a brand and product and support its image. Downloads are useful when wishing to generate a viral effect as the content can be distributed by the user once he has a local copy on his device. The cost for accessing multimedia content via mobile devices is today one of the largest problems of the distribution of such content, but with the decrease of transmission costs for data over mobile networks, and the appearance of flat-rate data packages this barrier will be reduced over time.

3.1.5   Rich applications

Beside the core functionalities of a mobile device that are provided by the operating system of the device, many devices allow for the installation of additional programs on top of the operating system. Such rich applications that run on the device and access its in- and output facilities can run on different platforms that are supported depending on the specification of the device.

Applications based on the Java programming language and running on a Java virtual machine on the mobile device are the most common form of rich applications for mobile phones. Java is supported by many phones in different versions. While the java specification ensures compatibility of the programming language's core functionalities over different platforms, many detail specifications can vary from one device model to another. The Java mobile specification, Java 2 Micro Edition or J2ME, further supports several sub-standards in form of Java specification requests (JSR), only handsets that implement the JSRs required by an application then provide access to the required functionality and only these can act as a host to the application that makes use of these JSR functionalities.

Mobile Java application generally use the mobile interface device profiles API (MIDP) as the user interface technology. MIDP was designed to allow deployment of the same application on devices with varying display and interface specifications. In practice, the implementations of MIDP are not as compatible as the specification suggests and often applications need to be customised to specific devices or device categories.

Besides Java, there are also other types of rich application that can be installed and run on mobile devices. Most alternative however are platform depended or have a coverage that cannot be compared to the coverage of the Java Technology.

Mainly Smartphone platforms like Symbian, Windows Mobile or the Palm Platform come with their own platform dependent programming languages that allow the development of rich applications for the dedicated platform and that provide APIs for the access to phone specific features give the required user authorisation or signing process of the application.

The need to develop an application for each smartphone platform and being confronted with different capabilities of the devices makes developing mobile software that reaches a broad public a very difficult task.

Still, mobile applications that run on the devices of customers can provide interesting opportunities for the company's marketing and customer communication strategy. The notion of desktop ownership has been known in the PC domain for a long time, ownership, in terms of providing core applications to many users, will be similarly interesting on mobile devices as it is now in the PC world. However standardisations of the programming languages as well as common core functionalities need to be provided in order to make the production of such tools feasible in an economical way. The presence of a brand on the mobile phone, eventually through a service program that gives the user access to his services and informs him on currently available offers that fit his profile, can be one of the most attractive forms of how to use the mobile channel to bring the business and related services closer to the customer.

3.2 Mobile devices and services: use and adoption

3.2.1 The adoption of mobile technology

Mobile devices and the related traditional services have seen high adoption rates over the last 10 years. The highest growth rates have been seen in the late 1990s with a breakthrough exponential growth driven by declining prices for both, devices and connection fees offered by the regional service providers. Tough competition on the market for mobile telecommunication has put high pressure on mobile network operators, and has speeded up adoption of the technology.

Mobile technology penetration has reached over 100% in the most highly-developed markets in Western Europe. Even though most statistics only construct a ratio of distributed SIM-cards and total population, which does not represent true usage numbers. SIM-cards today are not only used in personal mobile devices but also in telemetric applications and PC peripheral, although these applications also reflect usage of mobile technology, it cannot be set in relation with population numbers.

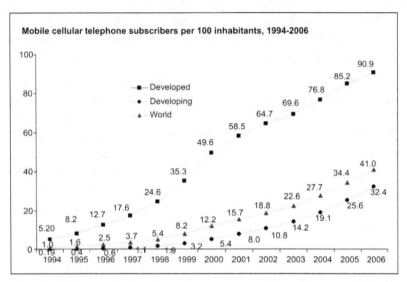

Figure 10: Mobile subscribers per 100 inhabitants (International Telecommunication Union)

While the ratio of the total population to the number of distributed SIM-cards does offer a measure for the relevance of mobile technology in the respective society, it does not give information on the true reach of the technology in terms of people actively using it. It is therefore a rather indicative measure for the personal adoption of mobile technology, as it can be driven equally strong by corporate or industrial adoption of the technology and the individual adoption.

Other available statistics measure the number of contracts as reported by the mobile network providers to the regulating authority. These generally underlie the same problem as counting the number of SIM-card as discussed above, they do not differ between a technology adoption on the personal and on the corporate level or the usage of the SIM-card, voice communication, data communication, telemetric applications or the like. Still these numbers are also often set in relation with the population numbers of the relating area or region.

The possibility to analyse different types of mobile telecommunication contracts however allows for a slightly more detailed insight into the mobile communications market. The figure displaying the development of the Austrian mobile telecommunications market (figure 11) illustrates the important role of prepaid contracts for the spread of mobile technology. Prepaid contracts made mobile telephony accessible to the masses without the threat of long term contracts and the ability to flexibly control costs.

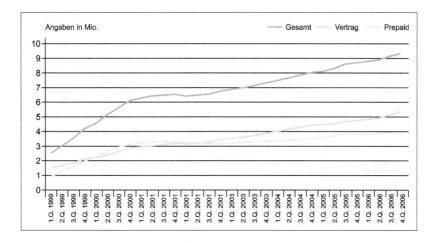

Figure 11: Number of mobile contracts (RTR 2007)

Other strategies in measuring the use of mobile communication, which also fits better into the current situation of a saturated mobile communications market where the distribution of new devices, contracts or SIM-cards does not provide the required sources of growth, are based on the analysis of the real usage of mobile technologies. The Austrian regulating authority collects reports from the mobile network operators on the amount of voice minutes or messages billed to customers in a given period of time (figure 12).

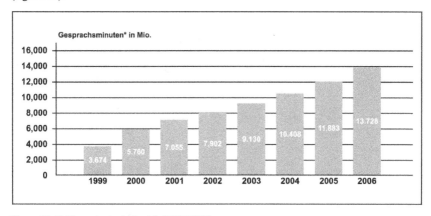

Figure 12: Calling minutes in Austria (RTR 2007)

The number of voice minutes as measured on the network providers' technical systems also demonstrates the ongoing growth of the market, representing an important form of revenue growth and ongoing adoption and use of mobile technology in the situation of a reduction in new participants.

3.2.2   Operating systems and software

Mobile device operating systems and related software have a large influence on how the mobile phone can be used as a communication channel to the customer. The mobile operating system controls the key features of the phone and provides a graphical interface for the user's control of the system. Beyond that, the mobile phone's operating system provides containers and APIs for the installation of additional software on the mobile device. The extent of this layer determines whether rich applications can be provisioned to the respective device, and whether these applications will have access to key features of the phone including mobile data transmission, the initiation of voice calls or access to other applications as the call history or the phonebook.

Generally, more such features are provided by so called smartphones that follow a PC-like software architecture supporting applications that integrate well into the systems themselves. Mobile Java applications, as described in detail in the section on rich mobile applications above, are available on a wide range of phones of both, smartphone and non-smartphone markets, but compatibility and especially the availability of common features is limited.

Figure 13 shows the distribution of smartphone operating systems by different global regions. A significant difference can by identified among the European, Asian and North American markets. While the Symbian operating system dominates the European market, mainly due to the popularity of the Nokia Series 60 devices, Linux only holds dominant market share in Asia while the North American market is the most divers with high shares for Microsoft's Windows Mobile, Palm and Research in Motion.

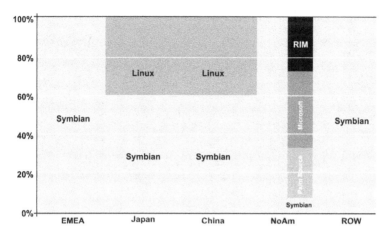

Figure 13: Smartphone operating system market share of sales 2006 (Symbian)

While figure 13 gives an overview of smartphone operating systems, it does not in-clude operating systems attributed to the non-smartphone market which constitute the majority of mobile phones nor does it represent the cross-platform application envi-ronments such as Java Mobile. Still as most rich applications are targeted to smart-phones and require their technical features. However, it must be considered that such applications cannot yield the masses of mobile users as presented by the high mobile penetration rates discussed above.

According to Symbian the Java Mobile installed base is currently about 708 million handsets (Symbian 2007) while the Symbian portion of the graph in figure 13 is 14.4 million devices with an installed base of 40 million devices.

Figure 14 (ARCchart Research 2007) shows a more detailed overview of mobile soft-ware platforms as embedded with most mobile phones that are currently on the market. This figure illustrates that a series of platform providers license their specific software stack to the handset manufacturers independently of the other components offered. For example the Obigo Suit by Teleca AB, a Swedish company with worldwide opera-tions, provides mobile web browsing software to different handset manufacturers for different platforms.

key product metrics

	launched	licensees	models	base
A la Mobile	2H06	0	0	0
Access Linux Platform	1H07	0	0	0
Adobe Flash Lite	2003	13	140	77M
GTK+	1997	3	8	~5M
MiniGUI	1998	1	0	0
Mizi Prizm	2003	1	3	N/A
MontaVista Mobilinux	2003	3	25	25M
Nokia S60	2001	4	39	~60M
Obigo Suite	2001	25	400	300M
Openwave MIDAS	1H06	N/A	0	0
Qualcomm BREW	2001	44	170+	~150M
SavaJe	2004	3	0	0
Symbian OS	1998	12	100+	82M
Trolltech Qtopia	2000	40	11	4M
Windows Mobile	2002	7	22	~5M

Figure 14: Mobile platform and API overview (ARCchart 2007)

Adobe Flash Lite, another notable new player in the mobile industry, is an application platform for mobile device applications. The Flash Lite engine is the mobile equivalent of the Flash player which is a well adopted vector-graphic-based application environment for website development. NTT DoCoMo has strongly supported the development of Flash Lite and has been bundling Flash Lite on every i-mode handset since the 505i series in early 2003, as well as its MOAP-based 3G handsets (ARCchart Research 2007). According to Adobe 13 manufacturers had shipped more than 77 million devices with Flash Lite on over 140 device models by the end of 2006.

With BREW, Qualcomm offers one of the most complete and integrated mobile operating systems solutions. It includes a hardware business that ships over 150 million chipsets a year, the operating system itself and the BREW application execution environment, a UI customisation platform and content delivery platform. The BREW platform is very popular in North America and has an installed base of over 150 million devices.

3.2.3   Mobile networks

The evolution of mobile networks has been an important factor supporting the spread of mobile technology and will continue to play this role as the networks evolve and will enable and support the provisioning of new applications and services to the mobile users on different levels of mobility.

This section will not provide an overview of the evolution of the mobile networks from their introduction in the 1980s until today, it will rather provide an outlook into the current and future developments as far as they are relevant to the design of the mobile customer communication system. The evolution of networks before 2G has been extensively covered in previous research (De Vriendt 2002).

The goal of today's network strategies is to make 3G networks a success as providers for a pervasive wireless world beyond the success of 2G networks. The future of mobile networks will be consisting of a heterogeneous and flexible network architecture that adapts dynamically to the changing environments and utilizes different standards and protocols in different situations (Alcatel 2007).

After many years of success for 2G mobile networks, especially the Global System for Mobile communication (GSM), with double figure growth rates, the shape of wireless networks is now changing. The new forces that will be driving mobile network evolution could turn current threats into opportunities for the mobile network operators. Internet protocol (IP) based communication has long been considered such a threat as it might draw current voice revenues, especially high revenue from international calls, into IP based communication covered by flat rates for data traffic. With new networks, and new business models, these technologies might be the revenue drivers of the future for mobile network providers while allowing customers to access new services at more attractive conditions.

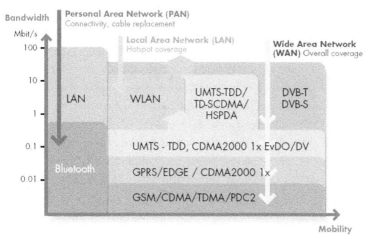

Figure 15: Mobile network evolution (Alcatel 2007)

The target of network providers consists in providing users access to a heterogeneous flexible networking architecture which dynamically adapts to the changing environment, it serves the users need for long range communication as well as short range or personal area communication. Beyond that, the infrastructure can accessed via more different devices and supports flexible switching of devices, generally providing new opportunities for mobile applications (Alcatel 2007).

The next step in the evolution of mobile infrastructure will be the appearance of the IP Multimedia Subsystem (IMS) and all IP strategies by the providers that will be the first enablers for new mobile services.

3.3   Mobile services

The development of digital media, especially the development of the Internet throughout the late 1990s and early 2000s, has shown new ways to create value in terms of products and services. This use of digital media not only as a distribution channel, but also as a transaction medium has made new product and service designs possible. This development leads to the use of the term electronic services, or e-service. An e-service can be defined as "... an interactive, content-centred and Internet-based service, driven by the customer and integrated with related organisational customer support processes and technologies with the goal of strengthening the customer-service provider relationship" (de Ruyter et al. 2000).

"... an interactive, content-centred and Internet-based service, driven by the customer and integrated with related organisational customer support processes and technologies with the goal of strengthening the customer-service provider relationship"
(de Ruyter et al. 2000)

Table 8: Definition of an electronic service

Two general characteristics can be identified for e-services: 1) the service is to be generated via means of information technology 2) the service requires an integration of the consumer via electronic media (Aschmoneit 2003). The definition by De Ruyter given above ads a further dimension to the more general definition of e-services: The strengthening of the relationship among consumer and provider. Electronic services in general can therefore be offered accompanying a core offering, or as independent services.

Mobile services more specifically are a subset of electronic services and follow the property that they are provided via mobile network technologies. The high penetration numbers of mobile technology make mobile services an emerging field with high potential. The evolution of the mobile networks, from circuit switched network to packet switched networks, enabling data transmission as a standard service, has made data-driven services even more accessible on mobile devices. Nevertheless the emergence of applications of this type, that would range beyond voice and messaging services, still is in its infancy and requires new forms of product and service design, as well as new underlying business models that respect the interests of the involved stakeholders.

One important point of differentiation of mobile services from generic electronic services that will mainly be provided via the Internet is the fact that they take into account the characteristics of the mobile channel. A mobile service can therefore be defined as: "... services that make use of some characteristics or context parameters that change with mobility (e.g. information about location)" (Floch et al. 2001). Generally a mobile service is based on an electronic service, its access is provided via mobile networking technology.

"... services that make use of some characteristics or context parameters that change with mobility (e.g. information about location)"
(Floch et al. 2001)

Table 9: Definition of a mobile service

A mobile service is therefore an interactive electronic value proposition provided by a supplier, which is transmitted via mobile networks and consumed by the customer on mobile devices in a ubiquitous way. The strengthening of the supplier-consumer relationship can, as in the definition of electronic services by de Ruyter et al. (2000), provide a further dimension of a mobile service.

3.3.1   Characteristics of mobile services

The development of the Internet, which differentiates itself from traditional media by providing interaction to its users, influences the characteristics of mobile services. In contrast to traditional media, like print, TV or radio, the new media no longer only act as carriers of information, but allow to structure entire information spaces.

Three components are identified by Schmid (2000) that provide the platform for a new media and support the exchange between agents acting on this platform. The carrier system is the first component. In order to support the transport of information among agents, a media requires a system of connections. Such a connection within the carrier system must support the transport of information over time and space. The second component involved in providing a new media platform is the organisation. The organisation includes a range of secondary agents next to those representing senders and consumers of information, these secondary agents provide required infrastructure as transmission services or regulations regarding the provided service. The organisational component therefore acts as a regulating entity for the media by providing and defining all protocols and processes within the new media. The third component is the logical space, defining the syntax and semantics of the information to be exchanged. The logical space also represents meta-information about the media, its carrier system and its organisational components.

In the mobile space, the roles of agents and the components discussed above can be identified clearly and lead to specific characteristics for services provided upon this media, these characteristics will be discussed in the following section.

Location independence

Mobile devices are characterised by the fact that they will accompany their users on the move, independently of their location. Mobile services therefore will be consumed independently of a certain location, while the awareness of the location might be an important factor in providing a valuable service.

Location information can be provided to mobile services via different technologies. Ranging from device-integrated receivers for global positioning system data to network based technologies that allow to identify the user's position by the current network cell or even a multitude of network cells in which the user moves, therefore allowing more precise location information.

The location awareness of a mobile service is therefore one of the characteristics the most specific to mobile services. Information and communication via mobile information systems must be adapted in real time to the location and other context parameters of the user. Only by proving this personalisation, can mobile services make use of one of the most specific features of the mobile media.

The ability of a mobile service to adapt in real time to the context of the user is one of the most important factors in providing a mobile marketing service to a consumer. By optimising the sending of marketing messages and information to contexts where the user is most receptive to them maximizes the impact of these messages and minimises the probability of a negative impact through inappropriate disturbance and the notion of spamming.

Ubiquity

Ubiquity includes the location independence of the device, but goes further from there. It encompasses all factors that make the mobile device an integral part of their user's lives and is defined by the strong integration of the mobile device into everyday tasks.

The device and therefore access to mobile services is available to the user at any time, independently of the user's location or most other contextual influences. This omnipresence of mobile services must also be encompassed in the design of a mobile information system. This can be achieved, as in the case with location information, by constructing mobile services that allow context parameters of the user to influence the behaviour and informational content of the service.

Identification

On a network level, user identification is provided by the means of the transmission and authorisation protocols based on the user's SIM-card (Subscriber Identity Module). The network operator therefore can identify their users in every type of transaction through information gathered on a technical network level.

For service providers outside the infrastructure and information system of the network provider, identification information is more difficult to obtain. Dependent of the service provided and the communication channel in use, identification can be achieved in different ways.

For messaging based services that interact with the network provider via a standardised messaging gateway allowing messages to be sent to the user as mobile terminated messages (MT) as well as to receive messages originating from the user, referred to as mobile originated messaging (MO), identification can be achieved via the users international mobile subscriber identification number (IMSI). This information will mostly be forwarded though the messaging gateway as a parameter and will therefore be available to the service provider for identification of the service user.

For mobile Internet based services, identification of users is mostly more difficult. Especially for services provided outside of the network operators' own portal systems or general infrastructure. Calls to mobile Internet services residing outside the infrastructure of the network operator are mostly passed from the mobile network operator though a gateway to any server on the Internet. Header information for these calls does not include identification information due to privacy and security restrictions as this information would otherwise be available to any service provider without the knowledge of the user. Identification for mobile Internet services is therefore today often implemented by login mechanisms based on usernames and passwords as known from the Internet. These mechanisms however are most often not appropriate for use with mobile devices as the entering of reasonably secure passwords with the limited keypad capacities of many mobile devices results in bad usability of the service and will not find the acceptance of users.

Immediate availability

The availability of mobile services, driven by their ubiquity, allows for immediate action and reaction of all participating agents. This is true for traditional mobile network services as voice calls or the short message service (SMS), but also for the newer data-based mobile services.

These opportunities provided by data services are especially interesting for time critical services that can achieve an increase in value by using the mobile channel. In a customer service environment, customer requests can be handled by mobile information systems to improve feedback time and eliminate delays due to manual processing, therefore increasing the quality of the service and the satisfaction of the customer (Aschmoneit 2003).

3.3.2 Economical characteristics of mobile services

When evaluating mobile services from an economic perspective, it is relevant to consider a system approach. This approach is essential when considering products that produce value within a complex network of components whose interaction is best described by such a system. The value of such products can only be produced by smooth co-action of all components of the system (Katz and Shapiro 1994).

Mobile services provide their value and utility only as a part of a system, the required system components include telecommunication networks, devices, operating systems, software and protocols (Aschmoneit 2003). The design and development of mobile services can therefore not be conducted without considering the other elements and components of the system. The value of the mobile service can therefore not be viewed independently, but always depends on the service's effects within the whole system.

The development of a mobile service consequently requires knowledge, not only about the creation of mobile services, but about all singular system components within the mobile economy and their common interactions.

External effects

External effects are present when a user of a service causes utility or costs to a third party, hence "external" utility or cost. Network effects describe such an external effect in the case of increasing utility with increasing user numbers (the most traditional example being the telephone). Network effects are therefore a positive type of external effects (Katz and Shapiro 1994). Network effects are encountered with many technological innovations that require an investment on the side of the consumer as well as on the side of the provider. Such situations are often referred to as two sided markets.

Products that are subject to network effects require this to be considered when being designed as this effect impacts the product's or service's diffusion. Network effects constrain the adaption of new products, as the small number of users at the beginning provides only a small utility. From a certain number of users, constituting the critical mass, it can be expected that the diffusion process gains in dynamics. Below the critical mass network effects therefore harm the diffusion of a new product or service, above the critical mass, network effects accelerate the adoption.

It is important to consider such network effects when designing and creating mobile services. Two types of services must be differentiated according to the interaction patterns the services wishes to support. One interaction pattern is the communication and interaction among the users of the service. The other interaction pattern is one between a company and its customers on a one-to-one base. In the first case, network effects play an important role, as the possible interactions provide the utility of the service and this utility is increases with the number of participants. Before the critical mass is reached, the service must provide a utility independently of the network effect in order to be able to penetrate a market. After the critical mass is reached, it can be expected that the further diffusion gains a self carrying dynamic. The impact of network effects on diffusion must therefore be considered in the service design by anyone creating a service which is based on the interaction of different users. One solution can consist in targeting closed groups of users that allow a critical mass to be reached more rapidly than within an open system. Another solution can consist in offering the service as a complementary feature to a network that has already been created. In this case an existing pool of users can be reached in a short period of time.

For services that enable communication among a company and its customers, network effects do not play a strong role in the diffusion of the service. It can still be useful to include positive elements of network effects in such services by providing user-to-user interaction, this approach can lead to viral effects in the diffusion of the service.

Negative external effects that accompany network effects must also be considered, these can be caused by limited capacities of the system or high costs of access. The threat lies in having customers willing to use the service that will not have access at all or only under a dire quality of service that will disappoint them. High cost of usage can be another negative effect on diffusion. Hence, negative effects can nullify the positive network effects through shortages of capacity or high entry costs for users. These bottlenecks must be considered when designing the mobile service.

Cost structure

An analysis of the cost structure of mobile services can be conducted by breaking down the costs involved with the provisioning of a service into the cost of the service creation and the cost of running the service and providing transactions within the service.

Compared with any non-electronic-services, electronic services have a generally low proportion of variable cost. Once the service has been developed and can be provisioned, the marginal cost for every further user is relatively low. The provider of a mobile service can therefore expect sinking marginal cost for the provisioning of the service.

These falling marginal costs can also be encountered at the level of the transaction costs of the mobile service. Here, the proportion of fixed cost is relatively low. The main cost factor consists of the variable costs involved with the transmission of data.

The use of standards within the provisioning of electronic services tends to reduce transaction costs. But it has to be noted that standardisation is not yet as advances in the mobile space as in the domain of the stationary Internet (Aschmoneit 2003). Infrastructure and messaging cost currently remain at higher levels in the mobile domain; still falling marginal costs can be expected.

3.4   A classification for mobile marketing applications

With the emergence of more and more applications of mobile marketing in practice, and a relatively young scientific community following and shaping the domain, a range of work has been conducted in order to create a clear classification of the different types of usage of the mobile channel in marketing, advertising and customer communication in general.

A range of early research on the classification of mobile marketing identified several characteristics of such campaigns. Brand building, special offers, timely media teasers, product, service or information requests, competitions and polls were identified as key types of mobile marketing campaigns (Barwise et al. 2002). Kavassalis et al. (2002) proposed three major types of mobile marketing campaigns, including push, pull and dialogue oriented approaches. Further, four general categories of mobile marketing campaigns were identified depending on the type of permission given by customers. One-off push, one-off pull, continued dialogue and fundraising (Jelassi and Enders 2004).

The presented categorisations mainly take into account many of the characteristics of mobile marketing applications, however, they do not give an in depth perspective on the objectives of mobile marketing and their impact on the types of mobile marketing applications. Pousttchi and Wiedemann (2006) present a categorisation of mobile marketing campaigns based on case study research and conduct a morphological analysis also taking into account the marketing objectives that lead to the creation of the mobile marketing campaigns.

This section provides a short overview of the present and existing classifications of mobile marketing applications, and describes which categories the framework for mobile supported loyalty schemes can enable.

3.4.1   Characteristics of mobile marketing applications

A fundamental characteristic of mobile marketing campaigns is the way how content, be it text message, voice or multimedia, gets distributed to the receiver. The two common types of content distribution are the push and the pull strategy (Haig 2002). Campaigns based on the pull strategy for content distribution, require the customer to interact with the marketing system as a trigger and then receive the requested content. Push campaigns send content to a customer without direct action of the customer. Legal requirements either require the customer to register with the service for the reception of mobile content or require the existence of an established business relationship and a close relationship between the existing business relationship and the information sent via the mobile communication channel. Push campaigns and general push mechanisms in direct customer communication always also include the risk of serving unsolicited or unwanted content to the customer leading to negative reaction towards the advertiser and brand (Bauer et al. 2005).

Mobile marketing is said to require a clear value proposition towards the customer (Bauer et al. 2005). In exchange for the access to their personal mobile device, customers expect a clearly visible value from the interaction with mobile marketing campaigns (Kavassalis et al. 2002). Mobile marketing campaigns must therefore provide something of value to the customer. These values can be categorised as information, entertainment, prize games or monetary incentives like coupons (Pousttchi and Wiedemann 2006).

In terms of costs, mobile marketing campaigns characteristically have costs associated with the creation of the campaign, the setup of the technical infrastructure and the direct messaging costs associated with each participant.

The interactive elements of the mobile channel can be used by the mobile marketing campaigns in different levels. From a level of no interactivity at all, like a simple push message, to a reaction that triggers the message, up to the level of a dialogue where a real interactive behaviour is obtained (Rafaeli 1988).

Another characteristic of mobile marketing campaigns is the network the campaign is delivered over and the technology used for communication. These networks can differ by type, protocol and purpose: UMTS, GPRS, W-LAN or PAN networks (Pousttchi and Wiedemann 2006). The available communication channels and appropriate technologies can range from Interactive Voice Response, Short Message Service, Multimedia Messaging Service, mobile Internet applications or rich applications based on mobile runtime environments (see section 3.1).

One possible characteristic of mobile marketing campaigns that is still rather rare in practice, but is being discussed very actively in the academic community (Turowski and Pousttchi 2003, Leppäniemi and Karjaluoto 2005, Dickinger et al. 2004) is the aspect of location based mobile marketing services. Examples would include marketing offers triggered by proximity or services for giving directions to the next relevant store.

Characteristic	Instances						
initiation	push				mail		
medium	print	outdoor advertising	radio	TV	internet	... person	mobile device	other
		information	entertainment		game		identity management	
cost	premium rate		...			none		
opt-in	conventional		electronic		mobile		none	
degree of interactivity	dislodge			reaction		no interactivity		
mobile community technology	WAN			LAN		PAN		
enabling technology	high-level language		WAP		MMS	SMS	IVR	
positioning	mobile network dependent technology		positioning system		...		none	

Figure 16: Morphological box of mobile marketing instances (Pousttchi and Wiedemann 2006)

3.4.2   Objectives of mobile marketing

By analysing 30 mobile marketing campaigns Pousttchi and Wiedemann (2006) provide an overview of marketing objectives linked to the campaigns and group them into six general categories:

- Building brand awareness
- Changing brand image
- Sales Promotion
- Enhancing brand loyalty
- Building a customer database
- Receiving mobile word-of-mouth

The marketing objective of building the brand awareness targets to enhance the recognition and recall of a brand in a purchase situation (Hoyer 1990). It is utterly important for fast moving consumer goods and markets with high competition. In the situation of a product launch, the build up of the brand awareness among the target group is also a key marketing objective. In mobile marketing this objective can be reached by providing information in form of texts or multimedia content like audio podcasts or video trailers with information on the product or brand.

The image that is associated with a product or brand is based on associations to that brand in the customer's memory (Keller 1993). When companies choose to change their brand or product images, they need to change the perception and associations of their customers towards their company or product. Campaigns targeting for a brand image change are often based on events or creating mobile multimedia content that transports the new image.

The typical campaign goal of sales promotion aims for driving sales numbers directly. Case study research shows that this is primarily achieved trough on-pack promotions that promise value-added mobile features linked to the purchase of a certain product (Pousttchi and Wiedemann 2006).

The objective of enhancing the brand loyalty consists of trying to impact customers' repurchase decisions. While the analysis of case studies manly shows newsletter-type applications as marketing oriented approaches to supporting loyalty. The whole set of services that can be provided via the mobile channel to enhance loyalty has been discussed in section 3.1.

A major objective for many marketers conducting mobile marketing campaigns is the collection of customer contact data for customer databases. Together with information on preferences and a purchasing history, this information can then be used to target personalised promotions to the customer with the highest possible relevance to the customer and therefore the highest possible returns. Case study research has shown that the form of mobile marketing used for building customer databases is often the provisioning of a value-added mobile feature linked to the registration or signup with a certain service.

The goal of mobile marketing campaigns that aim for mobile word-of-mouth build upon the idea of viral marketing, the spread of brand related content, that is made available via some mobile technology, through forwarding among peer groups. In this way the marketing message reaches a large number of potential customers through a trusted referral. This method can be a powerful marketing channel as it reduces significantly the cost involved in distributing the marketing message and can build upon the high credibility among peers.

3.4.3   Mobile marketing application types

Based on the characteristics and objectives of mobile marketing campaigns described above, it is possible to deduct major application types of mobile marketing.

With the entertainment based mobile marketing application type the value provided to the user by consuming the message or application provided by the marketer is provided by the entertaining value of the information. Humorous, aesthetic or stylistic elements often serve this type of entertaining value (Wamser 2000).

The monetary value of the provided coupon represents the value added component for the couponing type of mobile marketing campaigns. With the use of the mobile channel for the provisioning of coupons a series of attractive factors can be used beyond the ability of coupons distributed via the traditional media: The coupons can be targeted individually through the delivery via the mobile phone, and the timing of the delivery can be adapted to the consumer's requirements.

The mobile marketing type based on prize games provides added value to the consumer through the perceived value of the potential prize. The mobile channel is often used as the interaction channel in this type of mobile marketing applications, while the campaign itself is advertised via other media.

The last class of mobile marketing applications is the information oriented type of campaigns. The added value provided by the mobile marketing application in this case is an information value that is offered to the consumer. The information is only of value when it is relevant to the user Therefore, intelligent targeting or selection of the information by the user must support this type of applications.

3.5 The integrated product development process for mobile software

The new product development process has been studied extensively in literature throughout the last twenty-five years as an operationalisation of corporate innovation processes. Research roots lie in the analysis of the applied processes in place at companies (Cooper and Kleinschmidt 1986) leading to the identification of most frequently employed activities and their relevance. The advances in research consecutively led to the emergence of a more uniform new product development process based on the application of standardized models and methods (Mahajan and Wind 1992). Beyond the identification of processes in place, strictly following a behavioural research approach, a second research direction evolved seeking insight into the factors influencing project success or failure. Clustering of companies according to their overall innovation success allowed identifying practices tending to positively influence project success. Clear product definition prior to development, multidisciplinary background of involved team members as well as senior management commitment and involvement into the projects were found to be key success factors for new product development projects (Cooper and Kleinschmidt 1995). A meta-analysis of 60 empirical studies identified a range of drivers for new product success: product advantage, market potential, meeting of customer needs, predevelopment proficiency and dedicated resources (Henard and Szymanski 2001). The result of such research has often been a proposed process model describing relevant tasks and associated roles as a guideline to successfully and sustainably conduct innovation management in the pre-project phase of opportunity identification and evaluation as well as in the development and post-project phases.

Traditional analysis of the new product development process and its success criteria focuses strongly on industrial products. While the development of software and software products has also been extensively analyzed, until now there has not been any closer analysis of the process related to mobile software or services. Furthermore, the analysis of the software process has mostly had a very technical and production oriented view, rather than a product view encompassing the market, business models or legal issues.

Based on the broad research coverage on the new product development process, a holistic product development approach for mobile services and applications has been adapted in the course of this research. The resulting process (figure 17) considers a more dynamic competitive environment and the use of common tools for strategic analysis and product development.

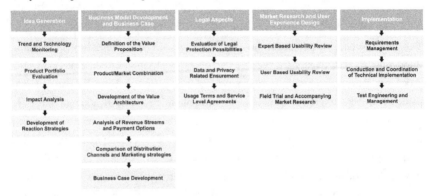

Figure 17: The new product development process for mobile software and services

The core process consists of five phases which are being run through iteratively. The first phase consists of Idea generation, which acts as a constant monitoring task for new opportunities in the pre-project stage. The business model development and business case calculation activities of the second phase act as the economic foundation of the new product. The control and management of legal aspects in the third phase help to ensure the continuity of the project and product. Market research and user experience design are conducted in the fourth phase in order to optimize product acceptance. And finally, implementation and extensive testing constitute the activities of the fifth process phase.

3.5.1   Idea generation and evaluation

Within the innovating entity, idea generation is itself an ongoing repetitive process which ensures technology and trend oriented kick-off of new product development projects. The foundation of a successful idea generation and evaluation process is the close monitoring of relevant trends and technologies mainly within the own industry. Often though, close monitoring of other industries can reveal new opportunities which tend to lead to even more disruptive innovations and a potential convergence of products and services from the different industries.

The model proposes the role of a technology broker in this position. Such entities, which will often reside outside the innovating company, are responsible for linking information on current trends and technological developments from different industries and propose new product projects to the company. This concept has been known for long and has been practiced by some of the most innovative companies for centuries. Thomas Edison's laboratory, responsible for a range of innovations as influential as the modern light bulb or the phonograph, was set in such a network position between different industries, enabling it to bring together innovations from the fields of the electromagnetic, the railway, or the mining industries. Ideo, the famous product design company, today sits in a similar network position, from where it can link experiences from projects in different industries based of different technologies and apply them to new product design projects leading to new and more innovative solutions (Hargadon and Sutton 1997).

The cross-industry trend and technology monitoring must be accompanied by an evaluation of the current product and service portfolio. This assures the alignment of the new product with the core business and allows anticipation of the new product's impact on current offerings, as a complementary product, or as a substitute to existing products within the portfolio.

The impact analysis activity within the idea generation process constitutes the evaluation phase for the newly proposed service including a preliminary economical evaluation, a first feasibility study and a more detailed look at the new product's impact on existing business. The result of this activity is a relevance scoring of the technologies and trends under observation which supports further project related decisions.

Reaction strategies to the elaborated new product opportunities build upon the results of the impact analysis, and include partnering strategies for the new product development, competence acquisition and competence build-up tactics as well as a first project plan of the new product development project including high level time and cost planning.

3.5.2   Business model and business case development

While traditional new product development processes describe a range of functions related to market learning and evaluating success potential for innovations, today's more common approach to evaluating the economic impact and at the same time actively designing value generation and revenue streams for a new product or service consists in the development of an adequate business model.

While a range of definitions exist for the term business model, the definition by Stähler (2002) is followed, proposing a structure of elements which constitute the business model including the definition of the product and the value proposition it provides to customers, the value architecture related to the production and distribution of the product with respect to all involved parties, as well as the associated revenue streams and payment methods (see section 5.2). The specificities of mobile services must be respected when developing a new business model in this field (as described in detail in section 3.3). This includes targeting and branding in the service domain, security and quality of service in the technology domain, network governance in the organisation domain, and revenue sharing in the finance domain (Haaker et al. 2006).

The value proposition defines the utility and therefore the value that the business model provides to the customer and to the value adding partners in the business model (Stähler, 2002). As a result the business model does not only build upon the product itself, but rather upon the generated utility and indirectly on the satisfaction of customers' needs which reflect the value of the product.

Within the definition of the product/ market combination, the product or service and its interfaces are designed and the configuration of the products or bundles of products are determined. The product/ market combination also contains the selection and delimitation of markets for the product. This can be in terms of customer segments, as business or private customers, or geographically. Generally, the product/ market combination defines the product itself and the market it will be offered on and will provide important information needed for the creation of an appropriate business case.

The value architecture as an element of the business model development consists of two separate units of analysis, the internal value architecture and the external value architecture. The internal value architecture consist of the resources needed to provide the product to the market, the definition of the value adding steps conducted within the company and the communication channels and coordination mechanisms with the external value adding partners. The external value architecture defines the interfaces to the customer and to the external partners.

The analysis of revenue streams and payment options pose a major challenge in the development of mobile software and services. In a detailed analysis step, this activity describes how the product will generate revenue, what sources of revenue there are, and together with an analysis of the expected costs, what margins are to be expected from the sale of the product. Different revenue sources can be transaction oriented charges, subscription charges or advertising income, while payment options can be operator based billing, credit card and debit card based payment or integration into web-based payment methods.

The comparison and selection of distribution channels and evaluation of marketing strategies can be seen as an implementation of the results from the previous activities of the process. Based on those findings, precise plans for distribution and marketing of the new product can be defined. Finally, based on the in depth analysis of revenue opportunities and the internal and external costs, a detailed business case as a financial representation of the business model can be developed.

3.5.3 Legal aspects

Three major legal aspects relating to the development of mobile software or services can be identified. The first aspect is the protection from competitors, where the target consist of evaluating potential protection mechanisms ranging from the protection of the product or brand name to a potential patent or protection of the utility model. The second aspect considers characteristics concerning third parties involved in providing or distributing the product or service, this involves the preparation and auditing of contracts and agreements (especially service level agreements) related to offering the service. The third aspect addresses the customer, ensuring the product is in accordance with most current regulations concerning privacy and data protection.

The evaluation of legal protection possibilities comprises the evaluation of registration possibilities for the product or brand name and related symbols or logos on a national or international level depending on the targeted audience for the new product or service. The application possibility of national or international patent rights or utility right protection is mainly dependent on the technical novelty of the product and must be evaluated from case to case.

Third party contracts and service level agreements related to the production, provisioning and distribution of the new product or service must be designed with respect to the specificity of mobile systems and must assure an optimal service to the customer. And audit of related contracts and a mapping to the entities described in the business model can assure coverage of most relevant issues.

Data protection and privacy related ensurement as well as usage terms and end user licence agreements play a major role in any distribution of software, for mobile services these concepts often have to be adapted or re-thought, a first evaluation with relation to the proposed new product should be committed early in the product development process followed by an in-depth analysis later during the ongoing evaluation.

3.5.4   Market research and user experience design

Customer experience is the internal and subjective response customers have to any direct or indirect contact with a company (Meyer and Schwager 2007). The design of the product itself is hence only one part of the overall experience customers make when buying it: Brand, service quality and scope, logistics are all important factors driving customer experience.

Due to low cost and ease of modification, surveys are the overwhelming favourites for measuring past and present patterns of customer experience. But surveys do have limitations, and focus groups, user group forums, blogs, and marketing and observational studies can yield insights that surveys cannot (Meyer and Schwager 2007). This paper concentrates on two phases that have been found to be most relevant to the final user experience in practice: Requirement definition and design. The main challenges posed to usability of mobile services regard the technical limitations of the device, screen size and resolution or keypad, and the properties of the network which is used by the service (AlShaali and Varshney, 2005).

User experience is associated with every product whether it has been intentionally designed or not. In the absence of a user experience professional, the development team creates it by default and thus, the quality of the user experience will often not be very high. This is especially true when developing mobile applications: Developers don't have long-standing experience in designing for smartphones with their reduced screen size, complex interaction possibilities, and APIs that are changing from model to model incredibly fast due to the short product life cycles. Developers thus tend to concentrate on implementing the demanded functionalities so that they are free of software errors, and only a dedicated user experience professional can focus on the user's point of view.

3.5.5   Implementation and testing

The implementation and testing phase combines all tasks directly related to the construction of the software itself. This includes technical specifications as the choice of the platform and programming languages, the task of implementation itself, and the important task of testing which becomes a special challenge when dealing with the diversity of available handsets and the minor differences among devices with the same specification.

The task of requirements specification builds on all results of previous phases of the process, and translates the business and product requirements into technical requirements.

The implementation itself is conducted according to software development standards and requires a specialized team with technical knowledge of the targeted platforms. The proposed software development process is the unified software process as described in (Zuser *et al.* 2001) together with a prototyping oriented approach which enables early evaluation of technical feasibility and early evaluation by usability experts.

Within the implementation phase, testing and debugging are the aspects with the highest specificity for mobile software development. The large number of handsets with different specifications makes detailed testing on the devices themselves a must. A list of targeted and supported handsets relevant for the targeted market should be developed early on in the project. Based on this list, tests should regularly be conducted following standardized test plans and test protocols. When planning the allocation of resources, it must be considered that testing and debugging mobile applications and services demands an exceptionally high effort in terms of organisation and administration. The use of PC based emulators of mobile phone software has not shown to be a means of replacing testing on the devices themselves, the behaviour of the emulator often shows to be different again from the device itself.

4 The reference model for the mobile supported loyalty scheme

4.1 Information systems as enabling technology for mobile relationship marketing

One of the first appearances of information systems in the marketing domain has been with the introduction of database marketing. Database marketing is based on the simple principle of keeping customer records both on a base-record level with key information on the customer himself, as well as on the transaction level by liking every purchase of a customer to his base-record, and therefore enabling detailed analyses on each customer's purchasing history.

There are two possible approaches to the conduction of database marketing: a cognitive analysis approach or a behavioural analysis approach. The cognitive analysis provides insights on the characteristics of customers by analysing their demographic profiles in order to identify the characteristics that customers have in common and use those when marketing the product or service to new groups by targeting potentials with similar characteristics. The behavioural analysis relies on the purchasing history and follows the goal to identify behavioural patterns that allow an effective management of the customer life-cycle.

The large amounts of customers in current retail businesses that employ loyalty schemes make a tracking of individual consumers possible only with the aid of sophisticated marketing database technology. It is the only feasible way on how to capture, analyse and act on the same interpersonal marketing opportunities as applied in earlier and simpler times (Kahan 1998).

4.1.1 Lessons learnt from the Internet as a sales and marketing channel

In the mid-1990's, the Internet was rapidly identified as an important sales and marketing channel. A large number of companies rushed to be present on the Internet without a comprehensive strategy or knowledge about what can be done or cannot be done on the Internet (Brännback 1997).

It was clear that the development and spread of the Internet was leading to a paradigm shift in information technology as well as in the marketing domain. But for many companies, it was unclear how to integrate the new opportunities into their existing marketing strategy. This situation is clearly similar to what is happening today in the mobile domain, where barriers of entry might even be higher than on the Internet as the gate keeping entities, especially the network providers, follow a strategy of actively controlling much of the content available within the domain and have high control over the devices on the market, a strategy that was not followed by Internet service providers during the emergence of the Internet as a mass communication infrastructure.

The appearance of the Internet as an interactive channel has enabled a new marketing approach to spread among companies. A reorientation from the old concept of profits driven by sales with the starting point being production, to a new orientation along the target to meet customer needs. The Internet has therefore lad to a change in the traditional marketing-mix and the dominant logic of marketing (Brännback 1997). An important part of the reorientation was the understanding of the separability of content, context and infrastructure. This led to the ability to distribute goods that had originally been physical goods via the interactive channel. Today's trend of content syndication and aggregation on the web is also based on this approach of separation. As infrastructure (networks, devices) and context (location, state, or user) are two major variables in the provisioning of mobile services, this understanding will gain even more importance in the mobile domain.

It has also been shown that the Internet as a platform for electronic commerce does have influence on companies' information technology structure and their brand portfolios (Treiblmaier and Strebinger 2006). According to the study conducted by Treiblmaier and Strebinger, e-commerce leads to a range of changes concerning information technology structure and brand portfolios among companies on the business to consumer market. Companies where e-commerce has high importance tend to integrate information technology systems beyond department barriers. These same companies also have a higher probability to create an umbrella brand for their prior independent brands.

4.1.2   Computer support in the marketing process

Marketing information systems

Marketing information systems as a subset of management information systems have always been at the forefront of information technology use within companies (see Kotler 1966). The basic framework of such a system is shown in figure 18.

According to the framework by Li et al. a marketing information system relies on three distinctive subsystems to collect the required data. A data processing subsystem that supports the import of data from other sources within the company, the marketing research subsystem for integrating data collected in surveys, and the marketing intelligence subsystem collecting data on the company's economic and regulatory environment. The data processing subsystem is the interface to the company's accounting system, which records every important transaction. The marketing research subsystem therefore integrates data from customer surveys and the analysis of prospects from the target group as well as information from external studies. The marketing intelligence subsystem includes information on the general economic development and the market.

The database of the marketing information system stores the information relevant to the marketing decisions it is aimed at supporting. It consists of information on customers, suppliers, prospects, competitors, governments and the general economic development.

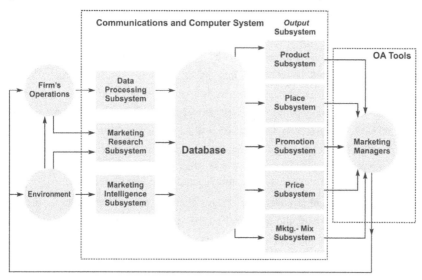

Figure 18: Marketing information system according to Li et al. 2001

The role of the information output subsystems consist in transforming the data stored in the database to information for marketing responsible. Five such subsystems are identified by Li et al. in the marketing information system framework. The first four represent the elements from the traditional marketing mix: product, place, promotion and price. The fifth subsystem represents a strategic perspective on the marketing mix by integrating all the previous outputs.

Computer supported persuasive technologies

Computer programs have implemented motivational strategies such as competition and positive reinforcement since the advent of multimedia capabilities (King and Tester 1999). With the advance of interactive technologies, the idea of the persuasive character of services and applications has spread beyond educational software. King and Tester identify 12 domains with significant potential for persuasive technologies. They describe the four most significant domains as marketing, health, safety and environmental conservation. In the scope of this work, the application of persuasive technologies to marketing is clearly the most interesting. This includes all technologies that promote the buying of products and services or increase the attractiveness of a brand. The strategies used in persuasive technologies are mainly variations of topics that have been used in traditional advertising before. Applications need to leverage the opportunities of the interactive experience of the web or the mobile channel while providing the expected level of trust (Krassnig and Paier 2006).

The influence tactics used by persuasive technologies in order to change the users' attitudes and behaviours are not new, rather they are adaptations of motivational and persuasion strategies that have been used long before the advance of personal computing technology (King and Tester 1999). Information technology still supports the implementation of these old strategies in new ways by providing simulated experiences, surveillance, environments of discovery, virtual groups and personalisation. Simulation and surveillance are the two persuasive strategies that are most directly enabled by information technology as they cannot otherwise be provided efficiently.

4.2 A layered architecture for the mobile supported loyalty scheme

A layered architecture provides a strict separation between the data of an application, referred to as the model, the functional business logic implementation, referred to as the controller, and the presentation elements of a system, generally referred to as the view. This separation makes it possible to develop and modify the implementation of the business logic and the form of the resulting presentation independently of one-another. Based on these three generic layers model, view and controller, the MVC (model-view-controller) paradigm for application architectures has evolved. Its roots lie in the Smalltalk-80 system (Krasner 1985) where the concept was defined as follows: "*Layering divides the functionalities of a software system into separate layers that are stacked vertically, each layer interacts only with the layer directly underneath*".

This design allows for the conduction of changes on any layer with minimal side effects on the other layers, as long as the interfaces to the other layers' remain intact. This property of independence and exchangeability is known as strict layering (Brown et al. 2003).

One major goal of designing systems in layered architectures is to create a reusable domain model that spans the boundaries of a single application. Beyond the three layers of the MVC pattern, the introduction of two additional layers can aid in further decoupling the domain model from the presentation and data source. The five-layer architecture proposed for the development of the mobile customer communication system consists of the presentation layer, the controller layer, the domain layer, the data mapping layer and the data source access layer.

4.2.1   Presentation layer elements

The presentation layer consists of elements for user interaction, to handle user input and present application output. Presentation technologies that are being used within the mobile customer communication system are: Messaging oriented front ends, HTML/JSP, WAP, and rich applications (PC- or mobile-based). The use of a layered technology allows for easy adaptation of the presentation layer, and is therefore ideally suited for the development of mobile systems, as the applications can easily be adapted to new forms of user interaction.

4.2.2   Controller layer elements and business logic

Independent of the presentation technology, requests for domain state and behaviour are performed through a controller object that can be defined for the individual presentation requirements. This controller object implements the mediator design pattern (Gamma et al. 1995). It is important to make sure that domain-specific application logic is not defined in presentation layer, but is rather gained from a mediator-referenced domain object. Presentation layer elements interact with the domain model in generalized ways. Mediator objects decouple application specific functionality from the presentation layer by performing the required domain model requests for the presentation objects. Mediator classes are built to serve a specific application user interface function or use case.

In order to achieve presentation layer independence for the mediator objects, the use of strict layering is required; mediators are not intended to contain direct references to objects of the presentation layer. Mediators are however able to reference domain objects and access their methods and functions. Mediators help capture and control the presentation requirements of the domain model independently of the chosen presentation layer.

4.2.3   Domain layer and entity representations

The domain layer represents the elements of the application domain in form of objects. Based on the paradigm of object orientation, each object represents an element of the real world by defining its properties and available functions.

By implementing all relevant objects of the application domain and their respective functions, the general business logic of the application gets constructed. The elements of this domain layer then constitute the model on which the controller acts when handling requests from the presentation layer. The elements and their functionality as described in the domain model are therefore completely uncoupled from their presentation via any of the possible presentation technologies.

4.2.4   Data mapping layer and data source abstraction

The goal of building a domain layer is that it provides a more abstract view of the domain objects. The domain object itself should not be concerned with implementation specific details. It should rather define its properties and functions. How to store and retrieve elements from a database is therefore not a function that fits well into the notion of a business object. Separating these functions from the business object provides serious benefits, making it possible to change the underlying database or data schema without changing the domain model implementation. Such a design requires a separate layer, referred to as mapping or persistence layer, which enables to store and retract domain objects to and from databases.

4.3 The reference modelling approach

A reference model, or reference architecture, is a conceptual model that, as an abstraction of reality, defines the core concepts that characterise an application domain (Frank 2007). The model solely defines the functional concepts of the targeted application domain, leaving aside the technical part of implementation as a specific information system. According to Frank (2007) a reference model is not only a description of reality, but also includes elements that are prescriptive and contribute new aspects to the domain in the sense of a constructing description. The definition of a standardised vocabulary within the domain of the reference model is another aim of reference models.

4.3.1   Construction of the reference model

In order to follow a rigorous approach in the construction of the reference model for mobile customer communication, a defined process model for the construction of the reference models was identified and applied. The employed model is based on the definition of Schütte (1998), it consists of five phases: Problem definition, construction of the framework for the reference model, construction of the structure of the reference model, model construction and application.

Within the first phase of problem definition, it must be defined which specific problem is to be solved through the application of the reference model and what the major elements of the problem are. The domain for which the reference model is valid is defined in this phase, as well as the future applicants of the model. The next phase consists of the definition of the framework for the reference model. The framework serves the intention to make the model understandable to future applicants and provides an overview of the elements and interfaces of the reference model. In the third phase, construction of the structure of the reference model, the model's level of abstraction is defined, as well as the applied modelling techniques. Further, the elements of the reference model are defined. In the model construction phase, the model is specified in detail by defining the functions of each identified element. And the last phase consists of the application of the created reference model in a specific context of the individual application domain.

4.3.2   Application of reference models

Reference models are applied to a specific situation by constructing an application model based on the reference model. An application model can therefore be considered as an instantiation of the reference model with adaptations according to the defined situation.

Different techniques for the construction of application models from reference models exist, the application technique that should be applied to the reference model must be defined at design time, as the favoured application technique must be compatible to the structure of the reference model.

The construction technique intended for the reference model for mobile customer communication is by means of configuration. The elements of the reference model are therefore designed in a way to support individual configuration of functional elements according to the specific application problem (Brocke and Buddendick 2004).

4.4   Functional requirements for mobile supported loyalty schemes

The framework's functional characteristics will be based on the work conducted on the theoretic foundations of relationship marketing as elaborated in section 2.2. The *social penetration theory* by Altman and Taylor (1973) has been shown to describe the relevant aspects of a buyer-seller relationship most suitably. It provides a model for the representation of the relevant aspects of personalities for describing the evolution and state of the relationship as well as a description of the processes that unfold during the ongoing relationship. In order to construct the reference model for the mobile supported loyalty schemes on the foundation provided by the *social penetration theory*, it is required to formalise the theory's aspects from an information systems perspective and to derive functional requirements for the reference model.

The functional requirements that are derived from the theoretical model are grouped into categories that allow the construction of modules within the reference model. The categories for the functional requirements are: Data collection, analysis, integration, modelling communication and reporting. This list also represents the modules that constitute the reference model for the mobile supported loyalty schemes. Data collection encompasses all relevant features to collect customer and transactional data and link it to the customer entity. The functionalities grouped into the analysis category include all functions related to categorising customers or monitoring customer states. The integration functionalities group all aspects of legacy system integration. The modelling category includes functions that provide the system operators with the possibility to model specific categories, transitions and rules for customer communication. Communication functions provide direct communication to the customer and reporting functions provide relevant management information to the system operators.

4.4.1   *A formal representation of the social penetration theory's personality model*

A formalisation of the personality model must take into account the two major dimensions of the personality model, the personality breadth and depth, as well as their subdimensions. It must also be considered that the personality model is valid for both parties in the relationship. Hence there must be a representation of the customer model for each buyer with which the company keeps a relationship as well as for the company itself. The company's personality model must further support an adoption of certain parameters to fit customer preferences while other characteristics may remain equal among all relationships and constitute the fundamental features of the company.

The social penetration theory's personality model

As discussed in section 2.2, the social penetration process is based on the sharing of information on the relationship parties' personalities. According to the *social penetration theory*, the personalities are structured along two dimensions, the breadth and depth of the personality.

The two dimensions are further divided into sub-dimensions. The breadth of the personality is subdivided into the categories of interaction and the frequencies of interaction. The categories represent the areas that the relationship affects or is related to. The frequency states the number of interactions per category.

The personality depth is sub-divided into layers which reflect the characteristics of one's personality according to the *social penetration theory*. The outer layers of the personality have more elements while these are more superficial. The inner layers are more personal and represent the more central characteristics of one's personality.

The company perspective on the customer

One of the evaluation criteria in the selection of an appropriate underlying theory for the reference model for mobile supported loyalty schemes was the ability to represent both parties of the relationship: The customer and the selling company. The *social penetration theory* accomplishes this requirement by applying the personality model to both entities: The buyer and the seller.

From the company perspective, each customer is represented by his personality model along the dimensions of the personality's breadth and depth. The company can construct an own model of the relationship party's personality and adapt its behaviour towards the customer according to that model. How this approach can be operationalised is one of the major design questions for the reference model describing mobile support for loyalty frameworks.

The customer perspective on the company

As such a personality representation can be conducted for each party of the relationship. Hence, it can also be conducted for the company. As the company is engaged with many customers it must be considered that the company's personality representation in terms of breadth and depth exists in many instances. While some factors of the company's personality remain equal over all instances, some other factors can be personalised towards certain customers according to their preferences.

Adapting the personality model for mobile supported loyalty schemes

In order to support the concept of the personality model in the mobile supported loyalty scheme, the dimensions and sub-dimensions need to be represented in the system's data model: The personality breadth with its sub-dimensions frequency and
category as well as the personality depth with its sub-dimensions layer and characteristics.

The personality breadth dimension

The personality breadth can be represented through the details of the customer's interaction with the system: Each customer interaction must therefore be recorded by the
system with a reference to the customer record itself and the product category the interaction refers to. In order to be able to provide these records, the system must support identification of the customer for any interaction conducted. The system must further be aware of the available product categories as well as a mapping for the interaction type to the affected product category. Figure 19 represents such a basic data model
that holds customer information together with the information on customer interactions and affected product categories.

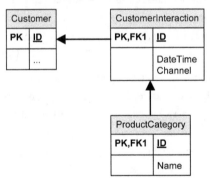

Figure 19: Data model for the representation of the personality breadth

In order to then deduct the frequency per category for each customer, an aggregation
of all customer interactions per category can be conducted. A relational data model
facilitates such an aggregation. Table 10 illustrates this type of aggregation for three
customers A, B and C, three available product categories I, II, III and a number of
typical communication channels.

By conducting this aggregation, customers can be grouped into segments representing
the current state of the personality breadth perspective on the relationship. According
to the *social penetration theory*, these fields of topics with prior experience form the

foundation of the customer relationship. These categories represent those topics that the customer is familiar with and associated with the company. A personalised experience can be provided to the customer by offering him content that matches his interests and previously touched categories. The channel preference can also be derived from this analysis on a customer and product category level. The selection of communication channels for future communication can therefore be adapted to the collected preferences of the customer.

Customer/ Category	Channel:			
	In store	Mobile Internet	Mobile messaging	Stationary Internet
A	1	2	3	1
I			2	
II		2	1	
III	1			1
B	5	3	2	2
I	1	1	1	
II	1	2	1	1
III	3			1
C	2	1	3	1
I		1	2	
II	1		1	
III	1			1
Total	8	6	8	4

Table 10: Aggregated view on customer interactions by product category and channel

The personality depth dimension

The personality depth, represented in the social penetrations theory via the personality's characteristics arranged in layers, can be represented within the reference model for mobile supported loyalty schemes as the known preferences of the customer within the preferred product categories. These preferences can include preference for certain brands within product categories, or specific customer requirements with respect to product categories.

These personal preferences that get exchanged during the evolution of the relationship need to be recorded by the system in order to monitor the customer preferences that get exposed to the company during the relationship and can be used in order to provide the customer with a shopping experience unmatched by competitors that cannot leverage this level of customer insight. The given example of the preferred communication channel per product category represented in figure 19 and table 10 represent one such knowledge item that allows further personalisation of the customer relationship.

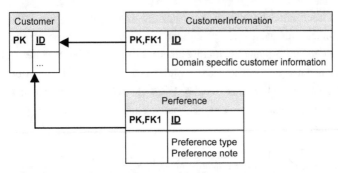

Figure 20: Data model for the representation of the personality depth

Figure 20 represents a reference data model for the representation of the personality depth. It consists of two relations that are attached to the customer entity. The customer information relation must be defined per application domain according to the personalisation data that is relevant to the domain. While a bank would need to record financial information on their customers and spending habits or savings preferences, a retail clothing store may require information on customer's sizes and style or colour preferences.

The preference relation defines standard preference types that need to be recorded for each customer as the relationship evolves and the customer is willing to disclose preferences towards the seller. For each preference type, a note on the according preference is taken. Based on data analysis, preferences can be extracted for customer behaviour that can be monitored as the customer's interaction with interactive communication channels and the customer's purchasing history. A detailed analysis of the extraction of potential customer preferences from interaction and purchasing history and strategies to test these extracted preferences for validity will be discussed in the course of this section.

Major functional requirements derived from the social penetration theory's personality model

Following functional requirements can be derived through the formalisation of the personality model as discussed above. The identified functional requirements will further be elaborated as part of the construction of the reference model from the implementation perspective.

The elements are classified along the functional categories as defined in the introductory section to this chapter. The assigned identifier will support short references to the functional requirement during the construction of the reference model.

Identifier	Functional description	Functional category
customer identification	Channel-independent identification of the customer within the system in order to support the recording of customer interactions.	Communication
interaction recording	Recording every product category related customer inter- action.	Data collection
interaction category assignment	Assignment of every interaction to the selected product category.	Analysis
preference construction	Aggregation of customer preferences by product category and communication channel.	Analysis
preference recording	Recording of customer preferences that are disclosed over the course of the relationship.	Data collection
customer information collection	Recording of customer information that is being used in the service process.	Data collection
preference extraction	Extraction of potential preferences through analysis of interaction and purchasing histories.	Analysis
multichannel output	Channel independent output of customer information ac- cording to the customers' preferences.	Communication

Table 11: Requirements derived from the personality model

4.4.2 Supporting the social penetration process

The process model of the *social penetration theory* as described by Altman and Taylor (1973) describes the dynamics of a relationship and can be applied to inter-personal as well as to buyer-seller relationships. The process model describes changes along eight specific dimensions as the relationship evolves. The information that drives the development of the process is gained through the exchange of information among the relationship parties on their individual personality model as described above.

Dimensions of the process model

The information that is available in order to control the evolution of the social penetration process as a formal representation is captured in the model elaborated above for the representation of the relationship parties' personality model. Hence, the data models representing personality breadth and depth must be incorporated into the process model and control its advance.

The process model consists of eight specific dimensions that affect the communication within the relationship: Interaction diversity, which represents a broadening of personality breadth over the course of the contact as well as adding new communication channels to the relationship over time. Interaction uniqueness which is driven by retained customer information and the knowledge on customer's preferences. Replaceability and equivalence describes a dimension that allows for different ways of communicating a message that will be understood based on the knowledge of one-another. Openness is based on the trust that emerges within a lasting relationship and describes the appearance of new topics within the relationship. The understanding of roles as a dimension of the process model of social penetration describes an inter-personal effect that is less appropriate for the dynamic aspects of a buyer-seller relationship as the roles are clearly defined among the relationship parties. The increasing informality is another dimension that does not directly apply to buyer-seller relationships as they are supported by the developed reference model and will therefore not be included in the formal process model. The possibility and acceptance of criticism is an important element that supports the deepening and development of a customer relationship, the importance and validity of feedback increases with the evolving relationship. The increasing exchange efficiency is the last dimension of the process model and describes the economic advantages gained by the close relationship these should be made measurable through the formalisation of the process in order to be able to measure the return on the efforts invested into the relationship. Of course, these advantages evolve dynamically with the development of the relationship.

A Formal representation of the social penetration process model

Interaction diversity

Interaction diversity represents the broadening of personality breadth over the course of the relationship. For formalisation as an element of the mobile supported loyalty reference model this dimension of the process model can be understood as the extension of the buyer-seller relationship to new product categories over time, the interaction therefore gains in diversity. It can be of value to have insight on the typical evolvement of the dynamic dimension in order to predict a customer's future purchasing behaviour and transition patterns. With the evolution of the relationship, an evolution can also occur concerning the favoured communication channels, a quick adoption to the customer's new preferences can support a positive service experience.

The evolving breath of the relationship is represented and monitored through the data model for the personality breadth, communication preferences are represented and monitored through the data model of the personality depth. The requirement to capture the dynamic aspects and development over time of these characteristics introduces a new analytical layer to the system that tracks changes and transitions in customer personality records in real time in order to support an adoption of the personalised customer communication to the new demand.

Derived requirements:

- Understanding of typical customer behaviour patterns and the domain specific development of the breadth and depth of customer relationships over time.

- Identifying transitions in behavioural patterns near to real time.

- Acting upon these to be expected transitions by being aware, controlling and accelerating them.

Interaction uniqueness

The process model's dimension of interaction uniqueness, which is driven by acquired customer information and the knowledge on customer's preferences, supports the notion of personalisation within the mobile loyalty reference model. As with the monitoring of the interaction diversity discussed above, the data source for managing the dynamic aspect of interaction uniqueness is provided by the data models of the relationship's breadth and depth.

In order to provide a personalised and consequently unique communication experience to the customer that is tailored to his needs the according customer information needs to be matched with available communication and information items. These Items must be configured by the company and annotated with the categories and situations that they are appropriate for. Such Information Items might be marketing messages containing product or pricing information or special offers that are personalised to the customers' requirements.

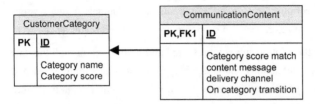

Figure 21: Data model for the representation of content categories and customer category matching

In order to enable this matching of customer requirements and communication content, a finite number of customer categories must be defined along with rules based on the personality breadth and depth data how customers are assigned into these categories.

Derived requirements:

- Possibility to define customer categories and create rules for the classification of the customers into the categories.

- Automated execution of classification rules when specific customer related events occur.

- Possibility to define communication content for different channels and assign it to a customer category.

- Automatic triggering of communication content according to rules concerning category state or category transition.

Replaceability and equivalence

Replaceability and equivalence describes a dimension of the social penetration process that allows for different ways of communicating a message that has equivalent sense to both relationship parties and therefore will be understood based on the knowledge of one-another.

With the deepening off a relationship, this concept states, that messages can be simplified and formalisms might be left out as the relationship parties have had the ability to get to know the formal aspects of the communication. And therefore have constructed appropriate associations with the relationship partner's behaviour in terms of formality and communication style. The possibility to simplify messages and abbreviate communication can lead to higher efficiency within the relationship.

For the mobile loyalty framework, the main application of the replaceability and equivalence dimension is the selection of the communication channel. Based on the adaption of messaged and their simplification based on prior experience and knowledge, the best suited communication channel can be selected. This flexible selection of a communication channel can support a better customer experience and at the same time reduce communication costs on the side of the seller as simpler and cheaper communication channels can be used for customer communication with deepening familiarisation of the customer with the company.

Within the larger scope of customer relationship management a simplification of processes is a common scenario of this process model dimension. Hence, a customer that is known to the company might not require the same complex registration and evaluation process that a new customer requires. But this deeply affects the company's core processes and lies outside the scope of the mobile loyalty framework.

Derived requirements:

- Flexible selection of communication channel based on customer preferences and the customers' familiarity with the company derived from interaction and purchasing histories.

Openness

Openness is based on the trust that emerges within a lasting relationship and describes the appearance of new topics within the relationship. In the context of customer relationships, this can be understood as the introduction of new product categories to the customer based on the customer's trust that was gained via an existing relationship.

The dimension of openness allows for the control of the extension of the relationship to new areas of personality breadth, hence new product categories. This process dimensions must support the coordination and timing of marketing messages related to product categories in which the customer has not yet established a relationship with the company.

In order to represent the process dimension of openness in the reference model, it is required to be able to determine the relationship quality in order to derive the level of openness towards other products and services per customer and product category. It is also required to define the relationships among product categories as these can stand in no particular relation to each other or represent supplementary or complementary goods.

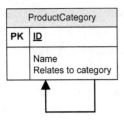

Figure 22: Relations among product categories

This relation as represented in the data model as shown in figure 22 allows determining which category can be recommended to a customer that is already involved with the company in another product category. Specific communication content can then be targeted to customers who match the rule pattern that represents openness and where it is possible to derive a recommendation from the category relationships.

Derived requirements:

- Measure relationship quality per category to determine openness to new relationship areas.

- Allow for modelling relationships among categories.

- Enable personalised marketing messages for new product categories based on customer information per category and relationships among categories.

The possibility and acceptance of criticism

The possibility and acceptance of criticism is an important element that supports the deepening and development of a customer relationship, the importance and validity of feedback increases with the evolving relationship. In the context of the reference model for the mobile supported loyalty scheme, the possibility, management and reaction to feedback plays an important role in the management of the customer relationship (Bruhn 2003).

The company's service channels are the hubs that collect feedback by customers on products and services, these service channels and their quality play an important role in the customer experience and the quality of service as perceived by the customer. The reference model for the more communication oriented mobile elements of a loyalty framework supporting mobile interaction can add to this service quality by providing interactive communication channels that enable customer feedback and help providing service quality to the customer by providing an ability to interact rapidly and interactively to customer requests or inquiries.

In order to be able to integrate mobile communication with the service organisation and its tools, it is required to define adapters to the legacy systems and manage the integration of the incoming and outgoing messages along all available communication channels. Incoming and outgoing communication must be multichannel enabled and the service quality must be provided independently of the communication channel.

Derived requirements:

- Provide adapters to the customer service channels for mobile customer communication.
- Support multichannel integration for customer feedback and reaction.

The increasing exchange efficiency

The increasing exchange efficiency as a dimension of the process model and describes the economic advantages gained by the established relationship between buyer and seller. These economic results should be made measurable through the formalisation of the process in order to be able to measure the return on the efforts invested into the relationship. Only when the returns on the investments into the customer relationships can be made explicitly visible will it be possible to maintain a high standard in customer satisfaction and retention over the long term.

The economic value of a relationship has two major components. The value of the additional business that can be conducted through the existence and active management of the relationship, and the value of the savings that can be achieved through the servicing of a customer based on the knowledge previously acquired on his preferences.

The bottom line success of relationship marketing efforts is always measurable via the mid and long term economic returns on the efforts and investments. It is therefore required to actively measure the economic return in order to determine the success of the activities put in place. The reference model incorporates the measuring of the economic success through the tracking of a customer's life time value and a prediction based on previous customers' lifetime value developments. In order to achieve this it is required to conduct data analysis on all customer master data, interaction records and purchasing records as well as category transitions and other available behavioural information to be able to predict economic return on the relationship investments.

Derived requirements:

- Calculation of real present customer value based on purchasing history, turnover and margins.

-   Predictive analysis of customer lifetime value based on the total customer base.

Major functional requirements derived from the social penetration theory's process model

Following functional requirements can be derived through the formalisation of the process model as discussed above. The identified functional requirements will further be elaborated as part of the construction of the reference model from the implementation perspective.

The elements are classified along the functional categories as defined in the introductory section to this chapter. The assigned identifier will support short references to the functional requirement during the construction of the reference model.

Process model dimension		
Identifier	**Functional description**	**Functional category**
Interaction diversity		
behaviour patterns	Understanding of typical customer behaviour patterns and the domain specific development of the breadth and depth of customer relationships over time.	Integration/ Analysis
pattern transitions	Identifying transitions in behavioural patterns near to real time.	Analysis
transition management	Acting upon these to be expected transitions by being aware, controlling and accelerating them.	Modelling/ Communication
Interaction uniqueness		
class definition	Possibility to define customer categories and create rules for the classification of the customers into the categories.	Modelling
automated classification	Automated execution of classification rules when specific customer related events occur.	Analysis
message definition	Possibility to define communication content for different channels and assign it to a customer category.	Modelling
communication triggering	Automatic triggering of communication content according to rules concerning category state or category transition.	Communication

Replaceability and equivalence		
automated multichannel output	Flexible selection of communication channel based on customer preferences and the customers' familiarity with the company derived from interaction and purchasing histories.	Analysis/ Communication
Openness		
relationship monitoring	Measure relationship quality per category to determine openness to new relationship areas.	Analysis
category relations	Allow for modelling relationships among categories.	Modelling
cross category messaging	Enable personalised marketing messages for new product categories based on customer information per category and relationships among categories.	Communication
The possibility and acceptance of criticism		
service system integration	Provide adapters to the customer service channels for mobile customer communication.	Integration
multichannel input	Support multichannel integration for customer feedback and reaction.	Integration/ Communication
The increasing exchange efficiency		
present customer value	Calculation of real present customer value based on purchasing history, turnover and margins.	Analysis/ Reporting
customer lifetime value analysis	Predictive analysis of customer lifetime value based on the total customer base.	Analysis/ Reporting

Table 12: Requirements derived from the process model

4.4.3 Monitoring and management of the interaction of relationship entities

The analysis of the personality model and the process model of the *social penetration theory* delivers a whole range of requirements for the reference model to encompass. Further requirements can be gained from an analysis of the process model of follow-on interaction that was presented in section 0 and that is also an element of the *social penetration theory*. Finally, an analysis of the relationship marketing instruments, as presented in section 2.3, provides the last set of theory derived functionalities for the reference model representation of the mobile supported loyalty framework.

Incorporating the process model of follow-on interaction into the reference model

A further element of the *social penetration theory* is the process model of follow-on interactions. This process model allows the analysis of subsequent transactions and explains why they occur. In order to accomplish this analysis, as discussed earlier, the social penetrations theory draws back on the *social exchange theory* and adapts its notion of comparison levels. Based on past interactions and exchanges, the customer predicts future outcomes of exchanges and decides on whether to continue interacting or terminate the relationship.

In the context of relationship marketing, the follow-on interactions can be understood as repeated purchasing events. Hence, the customer is keeping the buyer-seller relationship upright. According to the theory, the repeated purchase is conducted by the customer when the evaluation of the previous interaction, be it a purchase or purely informational, is evaluated as a positive experience from the point of view of the customer. This evaluation is conducted by the customer by comparing eventual alternatives and is therefore always relative to the customer's alternative options.

In order to represent the model of follow-on interactions within the reference model it is required to draw upon the data collection functions as they have been defined above. In order to employ the model as to track and predict the evaluation-action cycles that take place on the customer side it is required to have access to each single customer's identified purchasing history. Based on this purchasing history the customer side evaluation can be reconstructed. In the case of a repeated purchase it can be concluded that the evaluation phase has been positive on the client side. In the case of a reduction in purchasing frequency or a total stop in demand from the customer, it must be concluded that either the demand pattern of the customer has changed naturally, which can be an attribute of the product itself, or that the evaluation phase of the follow-on-interaction has led to a negative result. This case needs to be identified by the system, the negative influence and the related event needs to be identified and according communication towards the customer needs to be initiated. The support of this requirement builds on accurate repeat purchase and purchasing behaviour monitoring and the ability to react thereon.

The exploitation of this model will only be applicable to businesses that are confronted with regular repurchase cycles, if the interaction mechanisms are of higher complexity the model of follow-on-interactions might not be able to describe and explain the drivers for ongoing or discontinued relationships.

Major functional requirements derived from the process model of follow-on interaction

Following functional requirements can be derived through the formalisation of the process model of follow-on interaction as discussed above. The elements are classified along the functional categories as defined in the introductory section to this chapter. The assigned identifier will support short references to the functional requirement during the construction of the reference model.

Identifier	Functional description	Functional category
customer event monitoring	Accurate monitoring of interaction and purchasing history per customer on an individual basis.	Data Collection
repurchase cycle analysis	Analysis of repurchase cycles and identifications of pattern transitions.	Analysis
repurchase pattern transition reaction	Reaction to repurchase pattern transitions based on defined interaction rules.	Modelling/ Communication

Table 13: Requirements derived from the model of follow-on interactions

Linking the transactional and relationship views

The analysis of customer related information on past transactions and the prediction of further outcomes constitute the link of the transaction sphere to the relationship sphere according to the *social penetration theory*. It embeds the transactional nature of businesses with a time spanning perspective on the entire relationship. Within the reference model this is achieved by keeping record of interactions and transactions and conducting various analyses that enable an identification of the current state of the relationship and allow taking the appropriate measures in order to offer the customer a personalised and need-covering experience.

The foundation of the business thus remains the transactional processing of customer requests. Marketing however adopts the relationship approach when communicating to the customer. While changes at the foundation of the business, like product design or business models, might be implemented to fit the transactional approach, the instruments provided by the reference model enable the construction of a relationship layer on top of any transactional business with only few requirements of adoption by the core business.

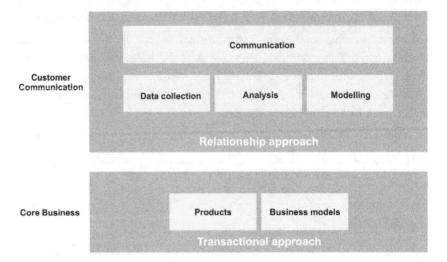

Figure 23: Linking the transactional and relationship views

The focus of the reference framework is therefore put on customer interaction and related touch points as to offer an ideal and personalised service experience to the customer. The elaborated functional requirements of the communication category represent this focus and are driven by the businesses rule sets defined through the modelling functions as well as the analysis functions that aggregate collected data in order to derive decisions to control the communication flow between the relationship parties as illustrated in figure 23.

Customer relationship instruments in the reference model

Instruments of customer relationship managements have been introduced and discussed from the marketing point of view in section 2.3, this section presents the results of the analysis on how the instruments and their mechanisms can be implemented within the reference model for mobile supported loyalty schemes. The instruments as discussed in section 2.3 will briefly be introduced in the context of a technical implementation and mobile communication and the derived functional requirements will be presented and discussed.

Overview of customer relationship instruments

For the customer acquisition phase, a series of relationship marketing instruments have been identified: Product promotion in terms of push- or pull-based customer information, sales promotion, extension of the use of the whole product line and re-purchase promotions as well as the support for a rapid and seamless acclimatisation of the customer to the products and the company are the major instruments of the first phase of the customer lifecycle.

The customer persuasion must be achieved through the demonstration of the ability to satisfy customer needs by the company. Customers expectations can actively be managed by the use of pull and push promotions. Push promotion refers to the traditional advertising oriented promotion where the company provides information to the customer via the advertising channel. Pull promotion provides information to the customer if and when it is requested. In the next step, an instrument must be put in place to stimulate the use of the product and service. Short-term stimulation can be achieved by sales promotions at the point-of-sale. Strategies for long-term stimulation are more efficient for building real customer relationships. This can be achieved by actively stimulating the repeated purchase by a customer or stimulating the use of multiple products of that company by offering bundles. Acclimatisation directly through the product can be achieved by providing customer with training for the product, a special platform for customer service or very particular product characteristics

Relationship instruments for retention management find application during the growth and saturation phases of the customer lifecycle. Within the growth phase, customisation of products according to the requirements and wishes of the customer can provide an important instrument to gain advantage over competitors lacking the personal customer information needed for the personalisation of the goods. The offering of value-added services can be another instrument of managing the customer relation within the growth phase. An important instrument for supporting growth is cross selling, the intentional management of sales activity to raise the customer's sales level by either selling related products to the customer or raising the purchasing frequency. Switching barriers and developing efficiency improvements can act as relationship management instruments in the saturation phase of the relationship. Switching barriers can consist of contractual-, economic- or functional switching barriers (Shapiro and Varian 1999). Efficiency improvements can be achieved through cost reduction by standardisation, unit cost reduction and taking full advantage of the customer's willingness to pay.

After the termination of the relationship with the customer, instruments for recovery management can be put into action. Frequently, the triggers for the imperilment phase are errors and failures in the products, services or interactions of the company with the customer. Possible instruments to respond to this status are the rectification of eventual errors and restitution of possible mistakes. Promotion and pricing policies can be tools to provide rectification and restitution. The termination of the relationship follows a non-averted imperilment. There is only room for a reactivation of the customer relationship with instruments similar to those of the initiation phase: customer persuasion and customer stimulation. The instruments can be adapted to the type of defection that is encountered. Different types of defections must be considered: company induced defection, competitor induced defection, or customer induced defection.

Derived functional requirements from relationship marketing instruments

The analysis of the relationship marketing instruments reveals that they can be grouped into two distinctive categories. The category of product and business model related instruments and the category of promotion related instruments. While the product and business model related instruments cannot be represented within the communication layer as the encompassing layer for the reference model, the promotional instruments do call for functional support through the reference model.

Therefore potential functional requirements are raised through the instruments that call for product promotion in terms of push- or pull-based customer information, sales promotion, cross selling as well as promotion and pricing policies as tools to provide rectification and the resulting termination of the relationship following a non-averted imperilment. Some of these functionalities have been addressed in earlier analysis of the theory based functional requirements.

Servicing customers on interactions and reacting to their personal preferences has been addressed in the analysis of the process model. It is encompassed in the functional requirement of communication triggering. Cross selling strategies have been defined as a functional requirement based on the dimension of openness of the social penetration process it is defined as the cross category messaging requirement. General defection prevention has been addressed in the analysis of the process model of follow-on interactions, the derived functional requirements are repurchase cycle analysis and repurchase pattern transition reaction.

Dynamic pricing can be raised as a new functional requirement derived from the relationship marketing instrument of the recovery management phase. It has not yet been derived from any of the theoretical foundations. It can be implemented on top of the purchasing histories of individual customers and an aggregated purchasing history describing demand patterns and price sensitivity. In order to be employed as an instrument to prohibit defections, it can be used in close conjunction with the functional requirements of repurchase cycle analysis and repurchase pattern transition reaction.

Identifier	Functional description	Functional category
Dynamic pricing	Adapt prices within defined ranges and target personalised pricing promotions towards customers in order to prohibit price based customer defections.	Analysis/ Communication

Table 14: Requirements derived from relationship marketing instruments

4.4.4 Functional features for the reference model

Requirement ID	Identifier	Functional description	Functional category
D1	customer event monitoring	Accurate monitoring of interaction and purchasing history per customer on an individual basis.	Data Collection
D2	interaction recording	Recording every customer interaction independently of the channel.	Data collection/ Integration
D3	preference recording	Recording of customer preferences that are disclosed over the course of the relationship.	Data collection
D4	customer information collection	Recording of customer information that is being used in the service process.	Data collection
M1	class definition	Possibility to define customer categories and create rules for the classification of the customers into the categories.	Modelling
M2	message definition	Possibility to define communication content for different channels and assign it to a customer category.	Modelling
M3	category relations	Allow for modelling relationships among categories.	Modelling
MC1	repurchase pattern transition reaction	Reaction to repurchase pattern transitions based on defined interaction rules.	Modelling/ Communication
MC2	transition management	Acting upon these to be expected transitions by being aware, controlling and accelerating them.	Modelling/ Communication
A1	repurchase cycle analysis	Analysis of repurchase cycles and identifications of pattern transitions.	Analysis

A.2	pattern transitions	Identifying transitions in behavioural patterns near to real time.	Analysis
A.3	automated classification	Automated execution of classification rules when specific customer related events occur.	Analysis
A.4	relationship monitoring	Measure relationship quality per category to determine openness to new relationship areas.	Analysis
A.5	interaction category assignment	Assignment of every interaction to the selected product category.	Analysis
A.6	preference construction	Aggregation of customer preferences by product category and communication channel.	Analysis
A.7	preference extraction	Extraction of potential preferences through analysis of interaction and purchasing histories.	Analysis
AC1	dynamic pricing	Adapt prices within defined ranges and target personalised pricing promotions towards customers in order to prohibit price based customer defections.	Analysis/ Communication
AC2	automated multichannel output	Flexible selection of communication channel based on customer preferences and the customers' familiarity with the company derived from interaction and purchasing histories.	Analysis/ Communication
AR1	present customer value	Calculation of real present customer value based on purchasing history, turnover and margins.	Analysis/ Reporting

AR2	customer lifetime value analysis	Predictive analysis of customer lifetime value based on the total customer base.	Analysis/ Reporting
I1	service system integration	Provide adapters to the customer service channels for mobile customer communication.	Integration
IA1	behaviour patterns	Understanding of typical customer behaviour patterns and the domain specific development of the breadth and depth of customer relationships over time.	Integration/ Analysis
IC1	multichannel input	Support multichannel integration for customer feedback and reaction.	Integration/ Communication
C1	communication triggering	Automatic triggering of communication content according to rules concerning category state or category transition.	Communication
C2	cross category messaging	Enable personalised marketing messages for new product categories based on customer information per category and relationships among categories.	Communication
C3	customer identification	Channel-independent identification of the customer within the system in order to support the recording of customer interactions.	Communication
C4	multichannel output communication	Channel independent output of customer information according to the customers' preferences.	Communication

Table 15: List of major functional requirements and identifiers

4.5 Modules of the framework for mobile supported loyalty schemes

The development of the data model for the mobile loyalty scheme framework is conducted as a domain model in UML (unified modelling language) notation representing the data items that correspond to the information generated and consumed by the functionalities of the system as defined in section 4.4. Based on the domain model, relevant information items can be identified for each instantiation of the reference model and a relational data model can easily be derived according to the specific project requirements.

4.5.1 The underlying data model for relationship status representation

The functional requirements defined in the previous section provide the groundwork for the development of a generic data model that represents the data elements that are necessary in order to be able to provide those functions within the framework. An overview of the derived data model is presented as a domain model in UML notation in figure 24. The data model represents all information items that are required as inputs to the analysis-, reporting- and communication-supporting functions. The analysis functions perform different examinations of the collected customer data and output, either new customer related data like categorisations or state of the relationship, or triggers for communication events. The reporting functionalities extract and aggregate relevant data in order to provide feedback to the operators on different key metrics of the scheme. The communication-supporting functions provide the messaging capability towards the customer within the system and are based on analysis results, state transitions or current states of the relationship and its defining items.

The customer object represents each identified buyer as defined by the role model of the *social penetration theory*. The object represents all available and required base data on the customer including contact details and basic personalisation information. The customer object is the key identifier for all other data items that relate to the buyer and therefore allows analysis functions to select and aggregate data on and individual customer level. Analysis of data on category or general level can still be conducted by selecting and aggregating data without filtering via the customer object.

The customer information object represents application specific information that is recurrently required within the production or service process. By recording this information systematically, the information is available when needed and must not be collected from the customer and the information can be used within analyses to provide deeper insights into customer preferences, needs and segments. The customer preference object represents a specific type of customer information and inherits all attributes of the customer information object. Customer preferences describe specific preferences that have been stated by the customer or extracted from previous interactions. These preferences apply to the features of the mobile loyalty scheme and define preferred communication channels, the specific customer's repurchase patterns, and the like.

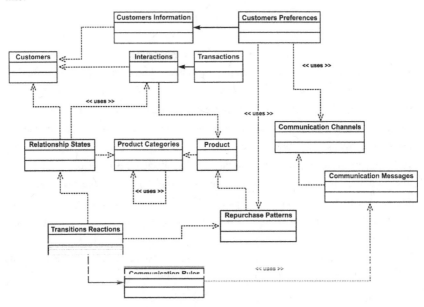

Figure 24: Representation of the reference model's data model

The interaction object, and the more specific transaction object that extends it, refer to the customer's inquiries and the customer's conducted purchasing transactions. As stated in functional requirement C3, it is required to identify the customer at the points of inquiry and the points of purchase which does cause limitations to the application as will be shown when analysing specific applications of the framework. Interactions are related to products and hence product categories and can be grouped and aggregated via these for analysis purposes.

Product category and product objects represent the company's products and services together with all relevant attributes that are required in order to conduct the defined analyses and trigger the defined transitions. This includes information on product prices and margins as well as relations among product categories in order to support the recommendation of new product categories that fit the customers present and past purchasing behaviour. Based on the information on prices and margins, calculations on the present customer value as well as predictions on the lifetime customer value can be made. For the support of personalised dynamic pricing, the range of price variance that the system can offer must be defined on product or product category level. Products that follow certain specific repurchase patters are extended with the information on typical intervals and amounts in order to be able to monitor a customer's repurchasing behaviour with the product's repurchasing characteristics.

The communication messages that are available to the system are represented by the accordant object and must be configurable by the program operators. The event that triggers the sending of the message as well as the content of the message must be stored by the object. The content must be able to hold personalised fields that get filled at execution time from information within the event context of the event that triggers the sending of the message. Depending on the message type, it can be useful to define different delivery channels and hence different formats of the message depending on the channel it should be delivered over. The available communication channels are represented via the communication channel object that holds specific information on each available channel ranging from channel characteristics like synchronous or asynchronous to the definition of ranges for delivery time that might be more flexible for channels like email or print output then for mobile messaging or voice communication where a real time reachability of the receiver is to be expected. Preferences for communication channels can be represented by linking customer preference objects with the respective communication channel objects.

Communication rule objects and the derived transition reaction objects are part of the data that represents the modelled interaction schemes of the system. Communication rule objects link specific events to communication message objects and define the handling process for the message including characteristics like delivery delay, grouping of messages, message thresholds and the like. Transition reaction objects represent the model that defines what reaction are taken when a transition, between categories or within repurchasing patterns, is encountered, these reactions constitute of process definitions that can include messaging, agent notification or other activities.

The object representing the relationship state holds information on the product categories that the customer is currently active in and the level of activity that the customer currently demonstrates. By aggregating information on interactions and determining interaction frequency as well as monitoring repurchasing patters the relationship state object identifies and triggers transition in purchasing behaviour that lead to the activation of the according communication process.

Data sources and integration

When implementing the reference model for the mobile supported loyalty framework inside an existing marketing and information systems architecture, there is to be expected that various data sources exist that need to be integrated into the system in order to provide it with the required data as defined above. Figure 25 shows the data model for the reference model and highlights the data objects that are typically to be expected to be stored, updated and maintained within external data sources that are present prior the introduction of the mobile support for the loyalty system and thus used by other processes within the company. It will typically not be possible to restructure total data holding because of the presence of other existing applications making use of these data sources and a total reengineering of all applications provides a non-acceptable hurdle to the implementation of mobile features. It is therefore required to extract the data and transform it appropriately to be able to load it into the data model for the mobile loyalty schemes.

The data representing the customer object will typically be present in the form of a customer database that will have either its own interfaces for data manipulation or be a part of a customer relationship system that provides the interfaces and holds further data sources with detailed information on interactions and transactions. The required attributes per customer include names, salutations, contact data and a unique ID that allows for referencing the customer object to other customer related data items.

The data for the customer information object will typically either reside in the customer relationship system, or in an enterprise resource planning system that controls the production process. Another potential source of data for customer information objects are records on service interaction or service cases were customer details have been collected. Again, this information must be extracted from its current data sources, transformed into the required format and loaded into the system's data model. Potential extraction possibilities and different sources of data will be discussed later in this section.

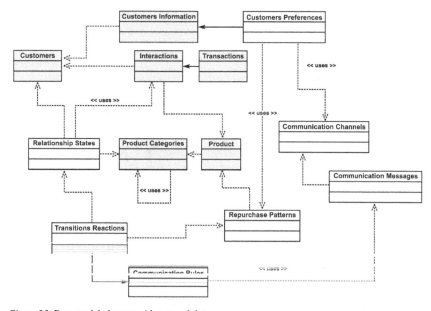

Figure 25: Data model element with external data sources

Data on interactions and transactions will be present either in the existing customer relationship system or as transactional records in the financial information system. Service interactions might be present in help desk or similar applications. The possibility to relate transactions and interactions to single individual customers is essential as it is required to evaluate single customers' behaviour towards the company. When loading external interaction and transaction data into the system's data model, it is possible to aggregate available data in terms of a data warehousing application. When analysis and reaction processes are wanted to be close to real time, which may be an important factor for some defined functions, the loading of data from the original source needs to be conducted in close intervals or directly at update of the original data source.

Data on products and product categories can be available through the databases of inventory control systems or enterprise resource management systems. This data typically does not move that rapidly and can therefore be updated in longer cycles. The data might require some extensions that are not available through the existent data. The relationships amongst product categories for cross-category recommendations or data on dynamic pricing thresholds might have to be added in the system's data model. Interfaces for this type of manipulation are to be provided.

Real time data handling

An important aspect concerning the integration of external data sources into the framework is the question on how well the data within the framework can be held in synchronisation with the master data sources. The loading of production data into systems that conduct analysis or archive data is a well established process within corporate information systems management (Bauer and Günzel 2004). However, these processes often do not have the requirement of getting access to data in close to real time as the applications that make use of the data generate their outputs, reports on data aggregations, periodically and the loading of the data updates can be conducted in coordination with the periodic timing of the analysis processes. When wanting to fulfil the requirements of some of the defined requirements, a close to real time processing of the data is, however, necessary.

The advantage of the mobile communication channel in the context of customer communication lies in the ability to reach the customer without experiencing the delay caused by other communication channels. This advantage can only be leveraged appropriately when the available data can be processes in real time in such a way that enables rapid reaction to changes in the data representing customer behaviour. It is therefore required to integrate external data sources in a way that enables an update frequency that is adapted to the functionalities that have been selected when assembling the system instance by adapting the reference model to the specific requirements of the application domain.

It is a major task to identify the truly required update frequency for the system's internal data model. Over performing and keeping the data synchronised to a level that is not being leveraged by the system's functionalities might lead to high costs in the implementation and operation of the system, while achieving a lower than necessary rate of updates might lead to incorrect functioning and inappropriate customer communication due to delays in the handling of the data and triggering of customer communication. The actually required update frequency can be determined by analysing the defined functionalities and identification of the data sources that drive the according event and communication. Based on the identified data source, an analysis must be conducted at what intervals and with what frequency the data can change and how these possible changes might affect the triggering of the event in the mobile communication system. This enquiry can then support the definition of the most appropriate synchronisation intervals.

Technically, two different approaches can be selected in order to achieve tight data integration between external sources and the mobile customer communication system. The external data sources can be queried directly and on-the-fly by the system or, alternatively, the external data sources can regularly be mirrored into the system through an extraction, transformation, loading (ETL) process. Both options come with advantages and disadvantages. While the possibility to query the external data source directly, with read only operations, offers access to the most recent data, it might lead to interferences with other running systems that need access to the database and the database might not be suited for the types of operations required by the system. Still, if possible, direct access to the data allows for access to the most current versions of the data. Read only mode ensures that no inappropriate write operations are executed on the data, and it is not required to hold duplicate copies of the data for different purposes and synchronise these data inventories. If the mobile communication system needs extensions to certain data attributes that are not available within the original data source but must be calculated at the typical transformation step, these calculations can eventually be conducted at real time by defining views that include the respective operations.

The second solution, that consists in implementing a high frequency ETL process, with the frequency depending on the requirements elaborated as described above, ensures that the target data structures and database are appropriately designed for the target system and that the data is available as expected by the system by the means of the transformation process that ensures data quality. On the negative side, this option demands to keep two copies of mostly equal data which is a solution that does not scale beyond certain limits. The replication process is also not optimal, as, in its simplest form, it consists of copying the whole data from the original source to the target. A solution to this problem can consist in only running updates of the data that has changed since the last synchronisation instead of complete replications at each synchronisation event.

4.5.2 Data analysis and sources of business intelligence

Adapting the customer communication to the individual requirements of every customer is vital to the effective use of the mobile channel. Up to a certain scale, personalised communication is provided by the close interpersonal relationships that exist between the buyer and the seller. Beyond that scale, in today's common mass markets, where a company serves large numbers of customers over global locations and without a personal attachment between the customer and a company representative, the targeting and personalisation of communication messages must be supported by information systems. Specifically, information systems support the implementation of data analysis methods that evaluate each and every customer's interactions with the company and derive a personalised communication process.

Functional modules for data analysis

The modules that provide the analysis functions within the reference model, in order to support the personalisation of communication, have been derived from the theoretic foundations in section 4.4 and are illustrated in Figure 26 as a hierarchical representation that explains the interrelation of the analysis functions. Multi channel output, supporting the dynamic selection of communication channels, stands at the top of the hierarchy as it is the core functionality that is supported by all other analysis functionalities. Monitoring of the relationship evaluates the current state of the relationship and is based on the recorded customer activities and resulting categorisations. Transitions from one category to another or changes in repurchasing cycles lead to changes in the customer profile and, hence, in the status of the relationship that is represented via the relationship monitoring module. The analysis of present customer value and customer lifetime value provide the economic perspective on the management of the customer relations and evaluate customer transaction data as part of the analysis. The construction and extraction of customer preferences serves as a foundation for the selection of communication content one the one side, and the parameterisation of the communication on the other side. The parameterisation includes the definition of communication channels that the customer favours, as well as the intensity and timing preferences for the communication. The data sources on which the extraction of preferences is based are the previous customer reactions to communication events.

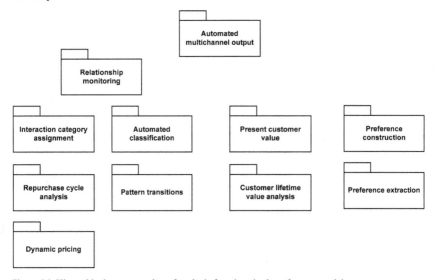

Figure 26: Hierarchical representation of analysis functions in the reference model

The analysis modules can further be categorised based on the methods that are applied within them. While some analysis models are purely rule based and execute a finite set of preconfigured rules on the provided input data, other modules are dependent on more sophisticated methods of data analysis from the domain of machine learning that support the extraction and identification of significant attributes from large sets of data. These attribute then support the adaptation of the communication strategy to the personal requirements of the customer.

4.5.3 Workflow management and rule-based communication

A core functionality of the framework for mobile supported loyalty schemes is the ability to process defined workflows based on customer data and analysis results. This feature supports the automation of processes and enables a company to provide a personalised experience to every participating customer event at large scale.

The customer dialogues are controlled based on the customer segments and the defined business rules and processes. The customer segments are defined by attributes and characteristics of the customer master data and the interaction and transaction data collected for each customer. The segmentation process that assigns customers to their respective categories is executed regularly by a scheduler. The business rules define activity chains that are executed when triggered by specific events, for instance when a customer is reassigned from one category to another. Such an activity chain can consist of a customer dialogue that is started based on the specific event.

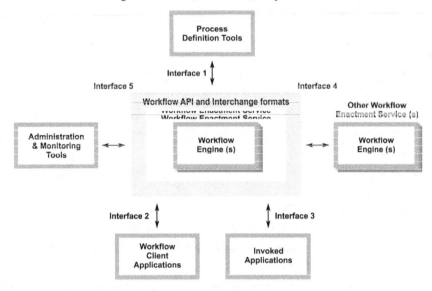

Figure 27: Workflow components and interfaces (Hollingsworth 1995)

According to Hollingsworth (1995) a workflow management system consists of the core enactment service that hosts instances of the workflow engine that execute defined processes (Figure 27). During execution time, the workflows can use standardised interfaces to call upon external applications through interface 3 and proceed with their execution based on external results. Workflows can also interact with other workflows that are being executed in remote enactment services via interface 4. Workflow client applications trigger the execution of the workflows and receive status notifications and execution triggered events. This communication is provided through interface 2. Runtime monitoring of the processes is provided through interface 5 and supports interactive tracking of process states and statistics. The process definitions are created with external tools that support the modelling of the processes the final definitions are provided to the enactment system via interface 1.

Modelling interactions

The modelling of potential interaction patterns within the system has two distinctive characteristics. It is represented by the modelling of the processes that are executed as workflows and defines the human-computer interaction that must be in accordance with the cognition involved in human-computer interaction (Olson and Olson 1990). As the communication is executed and processed through an information system, potential human reactions to the interaction must be anticipated and considered in the interaction model.

The modelling of interactions is related to two major functionality categories, modelling and communication. Modelling functions provide the ability to configure system elements and processes in order to constantly adapt the system to customer requirements without the need to reengineer program code. The communication functionalities provide all customer facing interfaces for inbound and outbound communication with the mobile communication technologies as the main innovative interaction driver.

The communication functionalities must be flexible in order to adapt to individual communication behaviour of the customer and reflect the customer interaction patterns. This includes the selection of the favoured communication channel or preferred daytime for message delivery.

The most central interaction model in the reference framework is the triggering of a communication message based on an event raised by one of the analysis modules. Based on the calling event, the interaction model defines a specific message or a set of messages to be sent to the regarding customer. In the most basic case a single event triggers the transmission of one single message. In more elaborate cases, the model selects messages from an available set based on the parameters of the calling event, selects the communication channel according to the customer's preferences and schedules the message for a particular time as derived from customer preferences.

Dialogue management

Dialogues represent more advanced forms of interactions. Multiple inbound and outbound communication events, or interactions, are grouped into one dialogue. The dialogue management consists of the execution of defined rules and process models for determining the system's reaction to inbound messages and returning information to the customer.

Dialogues therefore represent all communication interaction between the company and the customer from a specific triggered event, a category specific campaign, a change in purchasing behaviour or the like, up to the defined goal, a closed sale per instance.

Dialogues can be defined as workflows equivalently to interactions. The basic principle of interactions as defined above needs to be extended for the processing of incoming messages and the ability to react based on their content. The processing of incoming messages must be enabled for all possible inbound channels that support automated processing. Extraction of content and reaction on the inbound message is possible through the application of machine learning algorithms or the use of predefined reply messages and forms that can be processed automatically or semi-automatically. Such predefined reply forms or well defined reply formats for email and sms communication make the handling of dialogues much simpler than the processing of free text from which the customer's intent must be extracted with the help of statistical methods.

Supporting multichannel workflows

The need to support multichannel outbound and inbound communication has been stated at multiple stages of the development process for the reference model for mobile supported customer communication, it is driven by the requirement to adapt the communication process to the customer's preferences while enabling the use of the advantages of each channel for specific communication purposes.

The channels that should be supported in a specific implementation of the reference model must be defined independently per case. The reference model cannot provide an exhaustive list of potential communication channels to be supported as these may vary from implementation domain to implementation domain. The technical definition of the communication modules includes generic inbound and outbound communication adapters that can be implemented for any arbitrary communication technology. The reference model includes specified adapters for mobile messaging, the mobile Internet, email, fixed line Internet and paper mail processing. For each of these communication channels, adapters for inbound and outbound communication are specified (see section 4.6).

The selection of the communication channel for outbound messaging can be defined at multiple levels. It can be an attribute of the message itself, it can be derived from customer preferences or as a process rule that evaluates any other parameters that are produced in the course of the process. In this way, the process can adapt to the customer's current communication preferences and dynamically return information to the customer via the channel the request was received.

4.5.4 Mobile interaction elements for the framework

While the framework encompasses multichannel communication the emphasis is on the use of mobile communication and the leveraging of the advantages that the mobile communication channel provides to customer communication. Thus, this section will focus on the customer touch points that newly arise when first employing the mobile channel in a domain. The functional broadness of the reference model will most certainly lead to the creation of new touch points within every domain that have not yet been served with mobile customer communication functions.

Customer touch points

A fundamental aspect of employing mobile communication in marketing is the need to understand the newly arising customer touch points that have no previous equivalent and hence require the development of a new understanding for how the represented topic in each domain is accepted by the customer via the mobile channel.

The customer touch points are defined through the elements defined in the functional category of communication. These include the reactions to the customers' interactions with the company and changes within the interaction patterns, information on product categories that might be of interest to the customer or other information that is adapted to the collected preferences of the customer as far as available to the system.

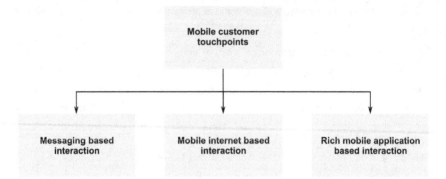

Figure 28: Mobile customer touch points

As these customer touch points take place via the mobile phone, they can be transported via the different available technologies as elaborated in section 2.5.1. An overview of the touch points and their specific characteristics is given in the following section and helps in further defining the derived requirements of section 4.4.

Mobile web

For purposes of supporting the buyer-seller relation and keeping customers informed on new products and special offers, the mobile Internet can be used as a channel to provide attractive services to the customer. The technical success factors include the identification of a user and the personalisation of the content based on this identification. While the mobile device is a heavily personal device that can be associated with a single user in most cases, most mobile network operators do not allow the user information out beyond the Internet gateway that connects the mobile network to the Internet and enables the mobile user to access content hosted on the Internet. This leads to the situation where a mobile website that gets accessed through a mobile device cannot retrieve information about the user that is typically associated with the device. Traditional forms of identification and log-in are complicated given the data entry functionalities of mobile devices.

When looking at the elaborated functionalities of the reference model as defined in section 4.4, a number of communication oriented functionalities can be identified as especially suited for the exchange of information via mobile Internet sites or portals. The functionality supporting transition management (functionality MC2) might well use a messaging oriented form of communication for notification of the customer, but core information on incentives for the customer can be transported via the mobile Internet. Dynamic pricing (AC1) provides personalised prices within certain defined ranges to customers in order to raise sales levels or prohibit defections. While the mobile Internet channel, again, must rely on other channels for the active notification of the customer, the follow up information on the notification can be provided via mobile websites. As mentioned above, the mobile Internet channel lacks a standardised identification feature as required for the fulfilment of the customer identification functionality (C3). Through the close integration of a service provider for the hosting of mobile sites with the mobile network providers, a technical solution for the passing of the user's MSISDN through the gateway can be achieved.

The mobile Internet generally can support the provisioning of deeper follow up information to notification that can actively be pushed to the customer via messaging channels. With the technical ability to display rich information content and text of unlimited length, the mobile Internet provides the ability for a richer interaction experience than pure messaging. Questionnaires and forms further support the effect of feedback and interaction without being restricted by the need for exact use of keywords and other formats.

Mobile messaging

For the support of specific communication functionalities within the reference model, messaging provides a relatively easy to integrate communication format at manageable costs. Contact can easily be established and intensified with the customer, relevant information can be transmitted in near to real time, and the customer can be kept up to date with information that is relevant to him as it matches his personalised profile. Messaging is also often used as a response channel for other forms of communication. The biggest limitation is caused by the limited use of characters within SMS messages and the cost involved with sending and receiving MMS messages.

The concept of any service based on mobile messaging must further encompass the risk of being classified as spam by the customer. This risk can be eliminated by providing relevant information and real value to the customer through the service and letting the customer decide which messages or notifications he wishes to receive.

An analysis of the functionalities from the communication category reveals that many of these functionalities can be provided based on mobile messaging. The functionality defined as repurchase pattern transition reaction (functionality MC1) can seriously be enhanced through making use of the benefits of the mobile communication channel as it can gain from the benefit of a direct and closely timed company initiated interaction with the customer. The active management of transitions (MC2) supports the provisioning of incentives to the customer in order to actively control and accelerate positive relationship transitions through positive effects that are provided towards the customer. The delivery of these incentives via traditional communication channels is often expensive and the caused delays can lead to unwanted effects. Dynamic pricing is another functionality that can profit from messaging based communication. Dynamic pricing (AC1) is highly relevant in the saturation phase of the relationship were the threat of defection is high. When a high probability for defection is identified for an individual customer, a rapid contact is required in order to provide the customer with a valuable service experience and a real time incentive to maintain the relationship. Functionality C1, communication triggering, concerns all company initiated customer communication that is triggered through analysis results, relationship state transitions or specific customer driven events. Many of these communication items rely on a fast delivery to the customer in order to support the notion of fast reaction to customer behaviour as expected by many customers today. Notifications for specific information can be sent to the customer via mobile messaging while follow up information consisting on details is delivered via other channels that are referenced in the mobile message. Customer identification (C3) is supported by the mobile messaging channel as the source of any mobile message can by identified via the senders unique MSISDN and can therefore be referenced to the respective customer master data record that also holds the MSISDN as an identification attribute.

The analysis shows that messaging based communication supports company-initiated customer activation. This is especially valuable when it is wanted to activate the customer at a specific point in time that relates to an action conducted by the customer himself. When designed with the notion of the customer's cognitive processes in mind as described in the introductory section on customer interaction processes, powerful service experiences can be provided to the customer through mobile messaging based applications.

The lack of possibilities to deliver rich content or even longer text content via mobile messages makes the messaging channel a good channel for the initialisation of dialogues, while more information on the topic can be provided through other channels, for instance via mobile Internet services or interactive voice response systems.

Rich mobile application

Mobile applications that are installed directly on the devices of customers can provide interesting opportunities for a company's marketing and customer communication strategy. The presence of a brand on the mobile phone, possibly through programs that give the user access to the company's services and inform him on currently available offers that fit his profile, can be one forms of how to use the mobile channel to bring the business and related services closer to the customer.

The strategic application possibilities for rich mobile application in the context of the defined requirements based on the selected theoretic approach to customer relationship management are limited. The advantages of rich mobile application clients are rather brand building- and service-oriented than customer communication driven. While many of the features that where described to be possible via the mobile Internet, would be possible through dedicated applications, the required effort in the production of these applications for the large amounts of different handset would make acceptable coverage very costly.

The approach of the *social penetration theory*, when applied to relationship marketing, as in the development of the reference model, offers insights on the communication layer and the interactions among a relationship parties. The service and product layer that could be served through specific applications is hardly addressed as was already noted in Figure 23. This fact certainly represents one of the current drawbacks of the model and theoretic approach. While service integration and rapid access to services are important features for successful customer relations, they reside on the layer not represented in the current model.

4.6   Communication infrastructure

4.6.1   Supporting multichannel communication

The core driver for multichannel communication in the management of customer relations is the empowerment of customers with the choice in how and when they wish to interact with the company. The target is the maintaining of a high level of customer satisfaction by fulfilling the customer's expectations. Independently of the channel the customer selects when initiating the interaction, the company needs to reply consistently through any supported communication channel in order to meet the customer's service level expectations. In order to provide this service efficiently, tasks that can be automated in the processing of these messages must be supported by the system in order to free operator time for the processing of the requests.

Automation of inbound communication processing

Automation of the processing and routing of incoming messages is a key factor for providing efficient multichannel customer communication. The automated processing can add value to two independent targets of the customer communication strategy. The ability to provide high quality and fast responses to customer enquiries, and the capability to reduce labour intensive manual classification of messages, support cost effectiveness and quality of service for the customer.

Based on natural language processing, it is possible to conduct a content analysis on the incoming message or request and classify the message. Classification can support indentifying the customer that sent the message based on data from the customer database, understanding the messages priority and the according service levels required, as well as more information about the contents of the message, as the product or service of concern, or the type of request. Once the classification has been conducted, the system can auto respond to the message in an accurate manner, providing a better customer experience than automatically replying to every message with a generic automated response message confirming the reception of the enquiry. Based on the classification and extraction results, the system can further perform any internal action or forward the message to the most appropriate operators to handle the request.

4.6.2 Customer facing functions and outbound communication modules

A company's customer communication strategy must satisfy the needs and expectations of the company's customers to a full extent. Many companies are confronted not only with one specific category of customers but must serve a whole range of different segments. These segments often will favour much different communication channels for conducting business with the company. Customers heavily integrate communication channels. Studies show that 50% of shoppers consult the Internet before they shop at a physical store (CMO Counsil 2005). These shoppers research products and alternatives online.

A variety of interaction possibilities exist between the buyer and the seller. These range from the traditional communication channels via the interactive communication on the Internet towards mobile services as described in section 2.6.3. The mobile communication applications and a mapping to the defined functionalities of the reference model have been elaborated above. An analysis of the most common communication channels beyond the mobile channels and how these can be integrated into the reference model constitutes the next section and provides a perspective on the integration of other communication channels with the mobile loyalty framework.

Email

The marketing literature often refers to email solely as a push marketing medium (Jupiter Research 2005), while its relevance as an interactive communication channel that customers actively use in order to get in touch with a company to receive information on products and prices or to file any other types of enquiries. The power of email lays in its asynchronous nature and its speed. Email messages are delivered around the world within a few moments, but do not require the recipient to be present or to react instantly.

At the same time, the email communication channel suffers heavily under the load of spam that is transmitted and the lack of security provided by the underlying protocols. As has been discussed in section 0, email as a marketing channel is suffering seriously under the problem of ever growing amounts of spam messages that make users restrain from accepting this channel as an essential source of information. As a means of direct communication and dialogue email can still be a powerful customer communication channel.

In order to support email communication in a multichannel environment in a cost efficient way, automation of email processing, or at least automated support in the processing of email enquiries, is a key factor in providing a high standard in customer experience.

Email classification is the first step to the automation of incoming email processing. Content based classification algorithms have been adapted early for the classification of emails, and basic implementations can yield good results in classification based on trained categories (Segaran 2007). Besides the assignment of an incoming message to the appropriate category, a process for the handling of messages within each category needs to be put in place. This process must define the appropriate operators to handle the messages of each category within the company, as well as the service level required within each category. Some processes might include further steps that can be conducted automatically based on content extraction from the incoming messages. An incoming email message with a service request could hence be automatically processed in order to identify the product affected by the request, the customer that sent the request and be filed in the ticketing system from where the enquiry can be followed up and resolved. The manual steps that would be required to identify that the email contains a service request, the product affected and the transfer of data from the email into the company's tracking system would require time and lead to delays in the resolving of the customer's issue.

Automated processing of incoming email is therefore an important aspect of a solid multichannel customer communication strategy. Depending on the numbers of customers to serve and the frequency of email interactions, the level of automation in the processing must be defined while leaving potential to update the system when levels increase.

Fax and mail

Incoming fax and paper mail documents still constitute an important amount of customer communication in most companies. This development is partly due to the fact that a number of processes require formal paper documents to be signed by the customer and sent to the company. Depending on the industry of the company the intensity of these requirements may vary, but telecommunication companies or banks are heavily dependent on these processes.

Mail or fax documents that can generally be referred to as paper documents can be classified into different document type classes according to their level of structuring. When developing a strategy to automatically process mail or fax documents, it must be differed among structured, semi structured or unstructured documents. Structured documents refer to forms that have been designed by the company and are sent to the customer for ease of returning feedback or conducting orders. Semi structured document refer to documents that have not been standardised to the level of forms, but that always obey specific characteristics. The standard example for semi structured documents include invoices, these are standardised by certain legal requirements and have common content but are still designed individually by each company. Unstructured documents are documents that cannot be classified by their structure; these include all types of standard business letters.

Different automation processes are needed according to the level of structuring of the incoming information. While handling and processing of structured documents can easily be automated with appropriate software, semi structured documents require higher complexity in processing and more sophisticated software tools that support machine learning algorithms in order to train a classifier based on previously classified documents. Structured documents must be identified at reception. This is often supported by including fields with document identifiers at fixed positions on the document that can be read with the help of optical character recognition (OCR) software. These identifiers then allow the identification of the form, based on the knowledge on the form's fields. These can be extracted from the document with the help of OCR and processed electronically based on the rules defined upon reception of this type of document. Semi structured documents must be classified by either processing the image data and retrieving information on the document class by analysing patterns of pixels on the image or by performing OCR on the document or specific parts of the document in order to retrieve text information that can support the classification of the document. Unstructured documents can be classified according to their content only as the structure does not reveal any information on the document class. Full page OCR must be conducted and based on the retrieved text information, content based classification, similar to the processing of email, can be conducted on the documents.

As with the automated processing of email messages, after the classification of the document and extraction of relevant data a process must be defined for the further processing of the incoming documents. This process must be supported by tools when aiming for high rates of efficiency in the customer service domain.

4.7 System integration, data collection and analysis

The foundation of the reference model as a communication driven systems lies in the data that provides the information to personalise the communication content to individual needs. The information is extracted from the data through the application of analysis functions as defined in the reference model. The integration of data that is managed by external systems must be integrated into a central data repository to allow analysis features access to all relevant data. Strategies for data integration and methods of data analysis are presented in the following section.

4.7.1   Integrating legacy systems

The operation of the defined features of the reference model requires a tight integration into existing systems to be able to draw on available information when executing the mobile customer communication processes. The external data elements have been identified in the course of the development of the reference model. These include data on products, prices, margins and product categories as well as data on customers if these are already available as stored by customer relationship management systems.

Applications that store this data are present in most companies prior to the implementation of the reference model. Therefore, strategies need to be developed in order to integrate data from these systems into the data model that drives the features of the mobile communication reference model. The proposed strategy for the integration of available application is based on the concept that most data stored by external applications, like existing customer relationship systems and enterprise resource planning systems, is stored in relational databases that can be accessed by third party applications through direct connections to the database management system that hosts the database.

By defining an extraction and transformation module that has access to all relevant data sources and knowledge of the data sources' data models, an integration strategy based on the data warehousing concept can be implemented. The extraction and transformation module is configured as to extract the required data from the available external data sources, and transform them into a standardised data model that represents the view required by the reference model in order to operate the selected features.

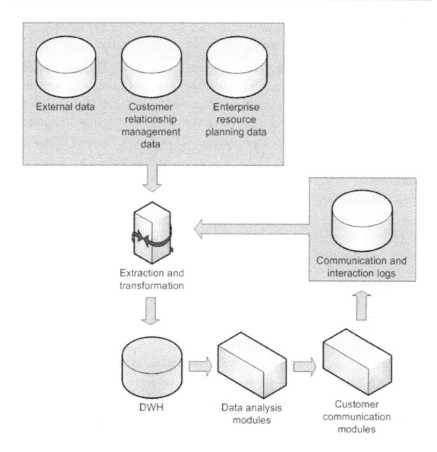

Figure 29: Data integration strategy for the reference model

Based on the external data sources, an extraction and transformation process is defined and implemented with an according software tool. The aim of this tool is the construction of a database for analytical purposes. The selection of primary data sources for the construction of this data warehouse depends on multiple criteria: The aim of the data warehouse, the quality of available primary data, and the general availability of the data, legally and technically. The aim of the data warehouse can differ depending on the selected features of the reference model that wish to be implemented. Quality and availability of primary data are influenced by the quality of the information infrastructure in place at the implementing company. A clean and strategy-aligned information infrastructure is a definitive requirement for the implementation of any loyalty scheme or analytical data-driven application.

Unlike the primary data sources, data warehouses usually do not implement relational data models. The representation of data in data warehouses is optimised for analytical purposes and therefore implements a multidimensional data model. Multidimensional data models define facts and dimensions as well as the classification relationships among them (Sapia et al. 1998). Facts and their values represent the core entities that will be analysed, classification dimensions represent attributes that define the facts and values and allow grouping and aggregation of facts by dimension. By this representation, analytical tools can access data in the data warehouse by defining the facts and values to be selected and the dimensions to be set as filters and aggregators for the fact's values.

4.7.2   Aggregating information from external data sources

The system integration strategy of the reference model follows a data warehousing approach by integrating data from various available data sources into one standardised analysis format which allows for the construction of analytical queries consumed by the functions of the reference model's analytical layer. The creation of the central data source, that represents a data warehouse, is conducted through a standardised process according to Bauer and Günzel (2004). The process consists of five distinctive phases that describe the monitoring of external data sources in order to identify changes, the extraction of the data from the different data sources, the transformation of data in order to standardise formats and representation of records that might differ among data sources, the loading of integrated data into the central data store, as well as the analysis based on the newly created multidimensional view on the data.

Monitoring of external data sources

The monitoring process serves as a means to observe the primary data sources in order to discover changes that are relevant to the central data warehouse. The monitoring function is therefore a key element in providing the mobile customer communication system with information in near to real time for the data sources where this is appropriate and required. The monitor controls the whole process of data aggregation, as it triggers the extraction, transformation and loading elements, as defined in its rules.

Different technical options exist for the implementation of monitoring within a data warehousing process. Monitoring is an integral part of the data warehouse system, as it controls the complete data aggregation process, technically, however, monitoring must be seen as a component of the primary data source, as it needs to integrates deeply with the database management system that hosts the primary data source in order to discover the relevant changes to the data that require a new execution of the complete data aggregation process. Depending on the features of the database management system in use for hosting the primary data source, monitoring can be conducted based on internal mechanisms of the database management system or must be conducted externally via a specialised tool that can integrate with the system. The selection of the monitoring technology will mostly depend on whether the available database system offers a possibility for monitoring or whether it will have to be provided through an external tool that might conduct comparison operations on periodical extracts of the primary data source (Bauer and Günzel 2004).

Active monitoring mechanisms are offered by some database management systems as an integral feature and allow defining triggers based on state changes within the database (Widom and Ceri 1996). These systems implement the concept of ECA-Rules consisting of the triples event, condition and action that represent the rule to be executed at every occurrence of the specified event. These ECA-Rules can be used in order to identify operations on relevant data within the primary data source and trigger the data aggregation process so that the central data warehouse is updated with the new data from the primary data source.

Replication based monitoring mechanisms represent an alternative to active monitoring systems that can be used with database management systems that do not implement the concept of ECA-Rules. Replication is a concept that is provided by many database management systems and allows duplication of all data manipulation operations to a secondary image of the data base. Based on the replication mechanism that propagates the changes made to a database to an external system, a monitoring strategy can be implemented.

Protocol based monitoring mechanisms can be implemented for almost any data storage infrastructure that is able to create a log on the data manipulation. When the protocol contains enough of the relevant information that is required for an external tool that analyses the protocol to identify changes to relevant data and execute rules defined for specific events, a protocol based monitoring strategy can be implemented. Typically the protocol is copied to a defined location periodically, where the analysis tool can access the log and identify changes that are relevant to the central data warehouse.

Extraction of data from legacy systems

The process of data extraction is heavily dependent on the primary data sources and the monitoring mechanisms in place. The underlying design decision is which data needs to be extracted from the primary data source into the data warehouse. The relevance of the data for the analytical operations to be conducted on the data warehouse is the main factor influencing this decision. In the extraction phase, the data identified by the monitoring process is read from the primary data source and copied into a working-area in which it can be manipulated in the transformation phase.

Extraction from the primary data source can be triggered periodically, at request, by event or by immediate replication (Kimball et al. 1998). With periodical extraction, data is drawn from the primary data source at defined regular intervals. These intervals are defined depending on the characteristics of the source data like the frequency of changes of records and depending on the requirement to keep the data in the data warehouse up to date. Extraction at request is implemented when there is no requirement for automated extraction, e.g. when all analytic queries are executed manually. In this case, the preparation step of extraction can also be executed manually in advance. Event driven extraction can support certain monitoring strategies that trigger the extraction process based on defined monitoring rules that are executed upon data manipulation operations on the primary data source. Immediate extraction fulfils the requirement of having access to real time data in the data warehouse, while it can be complex to integrate data sources in real time that require high levels of transformation in order to be inserted into the data warehouse, this strategy can support many of the requirements for the ability to react to customer actions in real time as demanded by certain functions of the reference model.

Transformation and standardisation of data records

Because the data warehouse integrates data from various systems and data sources, data fields and types as well as unique identifiers will not be available in identical form over the different primary data sources. A data transformation process according to defined mapping structures therefore needs to be conducted before data can be integrated into the data warehouse.

Unique identifiers and keys that represent the same entity might vary among different primary data sources. In this case, a mapping strategy for the different keys needs to be developed and defined as a process step in the data transformation process. In order to support system wide unique identifiers for data that needs to be integrated, a strategy can be followed to create the system wide unique identifiers for every data record on the level of the primary data sources. These keys are referred to as surrogates as defined by Wieringa and Jonge (1991).

Different data types in the primary data sources also need to be identified in the design phase, conversion rules need to be defined in order to be executed upon the records of the primary data source before loading the data into the data warehouse. These rules define the treatment of different date or number formats, unify codification of attributes and conduct data cleansing by removing incomplete records or duplicates. The goal of the transformation process is to achieve a high quality of the data in the data warehouse.

4.7.3   *Customer insight and knowledge through data mining methods*

In order to provide personalised communication and recommendations to large numbers of customers, methods must be applied that extract relevant knowledge from the available data on these individual customers. The analysis functions of the reference model rely on two major categories of data examination. Firstly, the classification of customers, products or product categories into defined groups that share certain characteristics or configurations of characteristics. And secondly, the identification of items, communication content or products, that might fit the customer's preferences based on data from previous interactions with the customer and data from other customers.

Data analysis methods

Two methodologies for data analysis, that are required in order to provide the functions as defined in the reference model, will be presented in this section. The first method can be applied for the classification of items based on their characteristics. The second method can be applied for creating recommendations based on different customers' data on products or other items.

Methodologies for data classification and recommendation

Classification as used in this context can be defined as the process of clustering data into groups that share specific characteristics which describe them as being closely related to each other. Customers with similar purchasing patterns, for example, can be identified by such algorithms based on the data on their previous purchasing behaviour. Classifications based on information on customer's real behaviour are much more powerful than the often encountered of grouping of customers by demographic characteristics like age, income or location.

Different approaches to classification exist. The two major approaches are supervised and unsupervised classification methods. Supervised clustering methods require the manual classification of data sets into groups in order to be able to "train" the classifier. The rules created from this approach are based on the characteristics that are found to be distinctive among the available groups. After the training phase, the constructed classifier can be applied to data sets that are not pre-classified and can attribute them to the defined group that best fits its characteristics. Unsupervised classification algorithms do not require to be trained with pre-classified data. Their aim is to discover the natural groups within a data set. In order to identify groups of customers with similar preferences, such clustering methods can be employed.

In order to be able to apply a clustering algorithm to specific data sets, a description of the characteristics that describe the underlying data must be defined. In the case of the mobile customer communication framework, the relevant characteristics that describe the customer are his purchasing history in terms of products and product categories. The frequencies of purchases of products can be used as the characteristic for the classification of customers.

Based on these characteristics, clustering algorithms can be used to discover groups of customers that have similar purchasing behaviour or groups of products that are often purchased together. One specific clustering algorithm is *hierarchical clustering*. This algorithm calculates similarity among items based on their characteristics and joins them into groups and treating newly aggregated groups as single items in the next iteration (Jain et al. 1999). The similarity among items is calculated using a distance metric like the *Pearson correlation score* that defines the similarity of items based on the values of their characteristics, in this case the number of purchases of specific products.

Based on the identified product groups that represent products that are often purchased together by customers, analysis functions from the reference model can determine products to use for cross-selling strategies and recommend products that fit the customer's purchasing behaviour but that have not yet been purchased.

Besides creating recommendations based on classifications, product recommendations can also be constructed based on direct comparison of the characteristics of individual customers or products. These characteristics again can be representations of the products purchased by customers or ratings of the products by customers. The term collaborative filtering was introduced by Goldberg et al. (1992) as to describe the method of extracting recommendations from large data sets based on the similarity of user preferences.

An important design question when implementing collaborative filtering is whether to construct recommendations based on users, in this case, customers, or items. User-based collaborative filtering incorporates all data from all customers in order to determine recommendations, for very large data sets, this method gets slow as a customer needs to be compared to all other customers and the products they have bought or rated (Segaran 2007). Item-based collaborative filtering follows another approach by comparing items based on the group of customers that have bought or rated the item (Sarwar et al. 2001). As the relationships and similarities between items do not change as dynamically as the data behind customers, the item similarities can be computed in advance and used upon request in order to identify items that are similar to those recently purchased by the customer.

As discussed above, similarity among users can be measured by calculating correlation scores of users based on their characteristics. The *Euclidean distance score* is a simple measure for correlation among users, it calculates the sum of squares of the differences among the characteristics of customers and returns a value between 0 and 1 that corresponds to the similarity of the users. The *Pearson correlation score* introduced above is slightly more complex in terms of calculation, but compensates for some typical data imperfections (Segaran 2007).

Based on the similarity scores calculated among each pair of items or users, depending on the type of filtering selected, recommendations can be derived by searching users or items that have high similarity scores to the current user or item for which according recommendations are sought.

5 Analysis of business models for the mobile supported loyalty scheme

The foundation for a business model for the provisioning of the elements defined in the reference model for the mobile supported loyalty schemes can only be the economic return that can be achieved through the successful implementation of such a scheme. The economic return on the application is therefore based on the results of higher rates of customer retention and better customer service supported via the program. The first chapter of this section provides an overview on the economic impact of loyalty and the management of customer relations. Based on these findings, an appropriate business model for the provisioning of services around the framework can be constructed.

In the second section of this chapter, business model design fundamentals are discussed and a definition of the term for use in the present context is given. The elements that need to be described in order to define a specific business model are presented and will be used throughout the construction of different business models to be applied in the context of the reference model. Based on the common business models in mobile and the common business models in the loyalty domain business models for the application of the reference model will be developed.

5.1 The business case for mobile supported loyalty

For the design of a business model behind a technological innovation that is constructed as to support reaching goals of customer loyalty management, it is utterly important to understand the economic impact of customer loyalty and an increase therein on the company's financial results. An increasingly important measure that companies make use of when evaluating new technology investments is the measure of return on investment (Rai et al. 1997). Return on Investment (ROI) gives information, beside others, on the time span that is required in order to refinance the investment through the gains leveraged by the investment. In order to achieve this, it is required to understand the gains from higher levels of customer loyalty in terms of financial value. This section introduces the concepts on which a valuation of customer relationships can be based. The following sections draw on these concepts in order to develop a business model for the technical implementation of the reference model for the mobile supported loyalty schemes that provides value through rapid ROI to potential users of the system.

In today's standard financial representation of a company's assets as evaluated by accounting standards, there is no means as to express the value of customers or to differentiate between customers depending on relationship state. Accounting standards do not differentiate between revenue generated by new customers or existing customers and investments in customer acquisition is often treated as a current expense in accounting rather than being assigned to the specific customer account and amortised over the lifetime of the customer relationship with the revenues and margins generated by that respective customer (Reichheld 1996).

A clear increase of customer present value can be identified among a whole range of industries when the company achieves to increase the customer retention rate. Figure 30 illustrates the findings from a cross industry study that examines the impact of a five present rise in customer retention on the net present customer value. It shows that an auto service company can increase the profits from an average customer by 81 percent if the company can manage to retain another 5 percent of its customers from the previous year. Two specific elements drive this respectable increase in customer value. The first effect is the pure growth of the company that follows the lower defection rates. The second effect is due to the higher margins that customers that remain with the company generate over time.

The first effect, growth through fewer defections, is very intuitive. If a company can reduce customer defection while adding new customers, its total customer base will grow faster than that of a comparable company that adds new customers at the same rate but looses more customers each period. The second effect, higher margins over time, is a more complex component of customer relationship gains. It is based on the assumption that profits gained from customers that are acquainted to the company are higher than the profits gained from new customers. Figure 30 shows an analysis of a customer's profits over a lifetime period of five years in different industries.

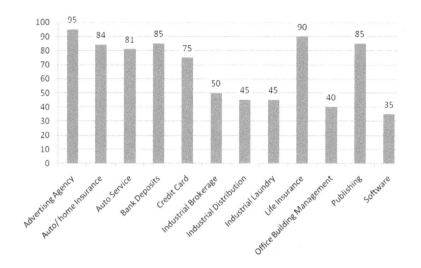

Figure 30: Customer net present value change in percent for a five percent increase in customer retention (Reichheld 1996)

The figures show that the loss of long term customers can not be compensated by a
one-on-one replacement with new customers. In some industries money is even lost in
early relationship phases due to high customer acquisition costs, these investments can
only be made up by an enduring customer relationship beyond the point of break even
for each respective customer or at least a majority of customers. Even in those industries that have positive margins on their customers in early phases, margins increase
with the ongoing relationship and retained customer contribute higher profits than
newly acquired ones.

The increase in profits of the development of the relationship can be attributed to a
range of effects that have been identified to have positive influence on profits over
time. A comparison shows that these effects align well with the theoretic foundation of
the reference model for mobile supported loyalty schemes. A more detailed analysis is
presented below. The core effects are the base profit of each customer, revenue growth
with lasting relationships, cost savings of serving an acquainted customer, referrals by
satisfied customers and a price premium that can be gained within lasting relationships. The next section will analyse these effects in more detail and present how these
contribute to higher margins over the course of a customer relationship.

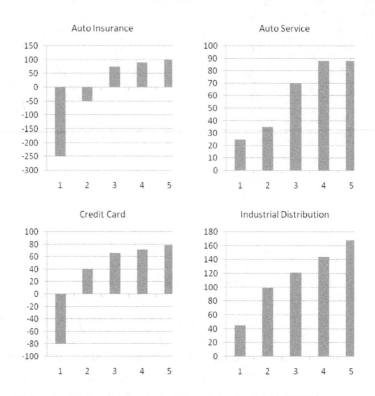

Figure 31: Customer lifetime profit pattern in different industries (Reichheld 1996)

5.1.1 Elements of loyalty return

An important step in understanding the returns on customer loyalty efforts for a specific business is to create the ability to quantify the profits for a typical customer over the typical customer lifetime. At the foundation of this analysis is the knowledge of how new customers differ from acquainted ones in terms of the cash flow that they produce and how this difference evolves over time. The general single elements driving this difference can be categorised into the effects introduced above that will be elaborated in more depth within this section:

- Base profits
- Revenue growth
- Cost savings

- Referrals

- Price premium

The base profit is the revenue and profit stream that comes from a customer based on the simple purchase of any product or service. Any revenue should naturally contribute a margin to the business and hence be able to contribute to the business' profit. It is assumed that this base profit is not affected by time, loyalty or increasing efficiency. With this simple and static profit stream, the impact of retaining a customer can easily be analysed. With every period that the customer can be retained the margin from the base revenue can contribute to the recovery of the acquisition cost involved with winning the customer.

Revenue growth in lasting relationships

A growth of revenue and hence a growth of profits over time within an ongoing customer relationship can be driven by different sources. With an increasing number of interactions, the customer might get more familiar with the company's full product line. This factor has been encompassed in the framework for mobile supported loyalty schemes as the requirement to support cross category messaging as a tool to provide a customer with access to products or service that he has not yet had contact with, but that fit the customer's profile.

It can be seen as typical customer behaviour to extend the range of products purchased at a supplier that offers high value to the customer and achieves good levels of customer satisfaction with most businesses that allow for extension of the product categories where these patterns apply (Reichheld 1997).

Another set of requirements defined for the reference model supports the notion of growing revenues with lasting customer relationships. The requirements defined in the analysis category support the active management of cross- and up-selling in accordance with the customer profile and therefore provide a means to actively influence the growth in revenue from additional purchases over time. In order to provide incentives for purchases in new product categories, offers can be targeted individually to customers that fit the pattern and the transition can be accelerated. Personalised offers, rewards and dynamic pricing can be important variable in this process.

Cost savings of serving acquainted customers

Over time, within an ongoing customer relation, customers get to know the company and learn to be increasingly efficient in the interaction with the business. At the same time, the company gets to know the customer and his preferences and can react to interaction with fewer needs for clarification than with a new customer.

Customers gain insights on the company's products and services and require less direct support from the company's employees when purchasing or operating the products. In some industries the savings on servicing returning customers can be related directly to the interpersonal relationship that emerges among the customer and an employee of the company. These advantages and gains as described here have one important drawback, they cannot easily be quantified and hence do not contribute to the goal of making the returns on loyalty investments measurable in terms of financial results.

In order to provide quantifiable results, the costs involved with serving the customer must be made transparent on an individual customer level or at least on a customer-segment level that allows a differentiation among customers in different phases of the customer lifecycle. Allocation of servicing costs can then be attributed to the customer segment in which they occur and allocated on the customer accounts in this segment. This measure of course can only be taken where the costs can be identified on a level of enough detail.

Industries with large advantages from serving customers repeatedly over multiple periods are retailing and distribution. These industries profit from the ability to predict demand very well based on the customers' previous purchasing behaviours. A constant set of customers can hence support the streamlining of inventory management and logistics.

Referrals by satisfied customers

The importance of referrals varies widely from industry to industry. While it is a vital marketing channel is some industries, especially in the business-to-consumer domain, it can be of far less importance in other industries. As the framework for mobile loyalty primarily targets business-to-consumer markets, referrals are an important aspect of the framework. Elements of viral marketing that support the process of recommending the services, offers or products of the business to peers and incentivises, are a core element in one of the evaluation case studies. Tracking of the according customer behaviour is a key element for enabling better active management of this viral marketing channel and rewarding the customers that lead to many referrals (Reichheld 1997).

Another important aspect about referrals is that studies show that customers who are directed to the company through referrals tend to be more profitable over the course of their customer lifecycle. Customers won through advertising campaigns or price promotions are seen to be less profitable over time. According to Reichheld (1997), this might be due to the fact that the existing customers who recommend the company to their peers have deep insight on the products or services of the company, as well as good knowledge of the requirements of the peers to which they recommend the company.

Price premiums within lasting relationships

Prices paid by persistent customers are seen to be effectively higher than those of newly acquired customers. This is due to an important part to the fact that new customers are regularly offered trial discounts as an incentive to purchase a product or service for the first time. Generally it can be stated that customers that remain with the business for longer periods are less price sensitive. They get accustomed to the values that are traded in the regular exchange, and are less exposed to price driven incentives.

In order to quantify the profitability gains from price premiums within lasting customer relationships, it is required to measure each customer's transactions with the individual price paid. Often this is not the case as prices and margins are recorded at product level and averaged before customer profitability is calculated based on the average prices and margins (Reichheld 1997). This procedure hides the effect that different customers pay different prices and contribute different margins when purchasing the same product. Transactions must therefore be aggregated on the customer level, only then it is possible to measure a customer's individual contribution to the margin based on his transactions.

5.2 Business model design fundamentals

As the aim of this section is the development of a business model for the provisioning of services or products derived from the reference model for mobile supported loyalty schemes, it is required to first define the term business model and how it is understood in this context.

5.2.1 Definition of the term business model

Traditionally, strategic analysis of a business includes perspectives on business units, the market and the company (Aaker 2001). But these units of analysis have shown to be of less relevance when applied to new business concept or fast moving markets. The representatives of the market-based view as illustrated by Caves and Porter (1977) argue that the structure of the industry that a company is active in determines the strategic options and success factors for that company. However, innovative new products are often confronted with the fact that the market for the product must be created or will be changed critically through the introduction of the new product or service. Hence, a market based analysis as a means to determine a strategic position for the new service or product cannot be conducted. The representatives of the resource-based view on corporate strategy provide a more internal view on the strategic success factors of a company, by attributing major importance to the internal resources of a company (Foss 1998).

Based on the shortcomings of both perspectives on corporate strategy, especially when confronted with fast moving markets or highly innovative products, the notion of the business model as a unit of analysis has evolved and gained prevalence in management literature (Stähler 2001). A range of definitions have been given for the term business model. Stähler (2001) defines the business model as a concept for a business that consists of three units that need to be defined: the value proposition, the architecture of the value chain and the revenue model. Timmers (1998) defines a business model as *"An architecture for the product, service and information flows, including a description of the potential benefits for the various business actors, and a description of the sources of revenues."*

Wirtz (2001) applies Timmers' business model definition to a single business and hence defines it as the representation of the company's production and value adding system. It consists of the required inout resources as well as the definition of the transformation process that leads to the addition of value. Petrovic et al. (2001) extend the model by Wirtz and define seven sub-modules that define the logic by which a company creates value. These sub-models include the definition of the value model, the resource model, the production model, the customer relations model, the revenue model, the capital model and the market model.

The process for the development of business models as presented by Stähler (2001) represents a theory derived path of development that can be followed when practically developing a business model. This approach offers the applicable perspective to business models and will therefore be adapted to define the business model for the mobile loyalty framework. The business model accordingly consists of the definition of the value proposition, the architecture of the value chain and the revenue model. The architecture of the value chain is further subdivided into the product/ market perspective and the level of stability of the architecture.

5.2.2 Elements of the business model

The value proposition as the first element in business model design defines the utility and consequently the value that the business model provides to the customers and to the value adding partners in the business model (Stähler 2001). As a result the business model does not only build upon the product or service itself, but rather upon the created value and indirectly on the satisfaction of customers' needs which reflect the value of the product or service.

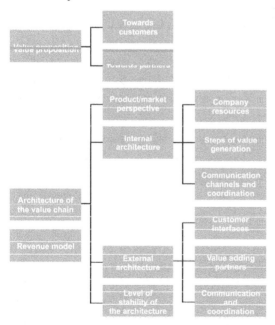

Figure 32: Elements of the business model (adapted from Stähler 2001)

The product/ market perspective defines how the product or service and its interfaces are designed. The configuration of the products or bundles of products and services are described. The product/ market perspective also comprises the selection and delimitation of markets for the product. This delimitation can take place in terms of customer segments, like business or private customers, or geographically. Generally, the product/ market perspective defines the product itself and the market it will be offered on. It therefore provides important information needed for the creation of an appropriate business case that will act as the quantitative representation of the business model.

The architecture of the value chain as an element of the business model definition consists of two separate units of analysis, the definition of the internal value chain elements and the definition of the external value chain elements. The internal value chain elements consist of the resources needed to provide the product to the market, the definition of the value adding steps conducted within the company and the communication channels and coordination mechanisms with the external value adding partners. The external value chain elements define the interfaces to the customer and to the external partners.

The definition of the architecture of the value chain further includes the definition of the level of stability of the architecture. The definition on how stable or how dynamic the architecture of the value chain is specified has a major impact on the flexibility of the business. A loosely configured partner network allows for rapid adaptation and change while more tightly and long-term oriented partnerships might allow deeper process integration and efficiency.

The analysis of revenue streams and payment options pose a major challenge in the development of business models. As a detailed plan of revenue sources, this element must describe how the product will generate revenue and what sources of revenue there are. Together with the analysis of the expected costs, the achievable margins that are to be expected from the sale of the product a financial analysis of the business model can be conducted. The different revenue sources can be transaction oriented charges, subscription charges or advertising income, while payment options can be operator based billing, credit card and debit card based payment or integration into web-based payment methods (Stähler 2001).

The comparison and selection of distribution channels and evaluation of marketing strategies can be seen as an implementation of the results from the previous activities of the process. Based on those findings, precise plans for distribution and marketing of the new product can be defined. Finally, based on the in depth analysis of revenue opportunities and the internal and external costs, a detailed business case as a financial representation of the business model can be developed.

5.3 Business models in mobile business

Within the mobile domain, specific business models have evolved that constitute different parts of the value architecture in order to provide voice and data transmission as well as services based on the transmission channels to customers. While a certain level of saturation is reached on the market for basic voice and data transmission, value added services on top of the communication infrastructure provide growth potential for the mobile domain (Simonitsch 2003).

5.3.1 The value architecture for mobile business

Third party service providers that act as an extension to the mobile network operators business, provide value added services on top of the mobile infrastructure as provided by the mobile network operator. In a traditional understanding, the value architecture for the provisioning of mobile services is configured as illustrated in figure 33. The flow of revenues originates from the end customer, billing is provided by the mobile network operator, and revenues are distributed to other parties in the value architecture. The cooperation among mobile network operators, third party service providers, content providers and hardware and handset manufacturers allows for a concentration on to core competencies for each role of the value architecture. This concentration on core competencies leading to specialisation among the parties of the value network allows for a limitation of risk in a dynamic market by offering higher flexibility and access to large numbers of resources through the network of cooperation partners (Neudorfer 2004).

Experts predict a transformation of mobile business models driven by the extension of mobile services from essential voice and data transmission to services that run on top of the basic communication infrastructure. Figure 33 illustrates the rising importance of the role of wireless application service providers in the architecture of the mobile value chain. It is expected that the number and relevance of wireless application service providers will rise in future (Steinbock 2003). While network operators were providing most of the services to their customers directly based on infrastructure acquired from manufacturers, the newly appearing parties add features and services to the networks. This modular value architecture allows for a more flexible adaptation to the fast moving and dynamic market environment. The major concern of the mobile network operator remains the increase in traffic and transactions that take place over the respective network.

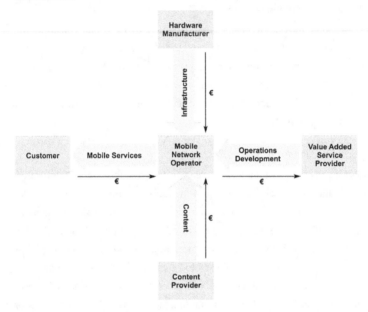

Figure 33: Traditional role of the value added service provider (Neudorfer 2003)

5.3.2 Mobile third party service providers

The mobile third party service provider, as presented in figure 33 and described in literature (e.g. Neudorfer 2004), are to provide customisable applications as value added service to the mobile network operator's customers. According to the prevalent definitions as cited above, the mobile third party service providers take a position as intermediates between the mobile network operator and the customer to provide the development and operation of mobile applications that fulfil the customer's requirements.

Two major factors are seldom discussed in literature but highly relevant for the operation of successful mobile applications. Firstly the integration of multiple or all mobile network operators on a market in order to be able to provide services to users independently of their provider and reach a broader public with the application. And secondly the considerations of a second group of customers besides the end customers of mobile network operator, namely those companies that which to reach their users or customers via the mobile channel. The design of the business model for the mobile loyalty framework will encompass both these factors and propose solutions as elaborated in the case studies.

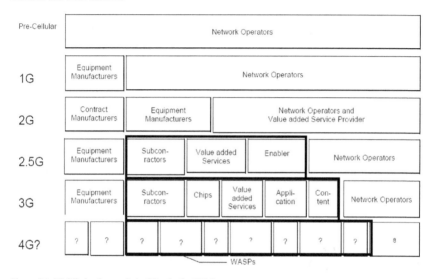

Figure 34: Mobile business chain (Neudorfer 2004)

The cooperation of network operators and service providers in the provisioning of mobile services to consumers and other companies as a means to communicate with their customers is supported by a range of specific effects. The distribution of tasks and functions among value adding partners allows for a concentration on core competencies for each of the involved tiers. The requirement for fast time-to-market is only attainable through tight cooperation among partners and a sharing of competences in the context of development projects. Finally, the cooperation allows reducing risk, for the network and infrastructure provider, as well as for the end customer.

Beyond the cooperation with mobile network operators in order to provide value added services and applications to the network operator's customers, service providers become a new distribution channel for value added products on top of the network provider's communication infrastructure. The service provider creates value added services for third parties outside the mobile domain by bundling services of the network provider with custom applications to enable the third party company the provisioning of a mobile communication channel towards their customers.

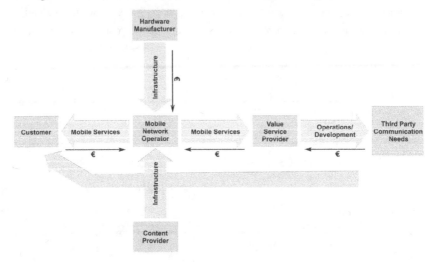

Figure 35: Role of the third party service provider

5.4   Loyalty systems business models

Loyalty systems generally have two specific points of integration within a company. They are to be seen as part of the information technology infrastructure and must be operated and maintained as an information system including the coverage of topics like data security, system uptime and other operational aspects of information systems. The second point of integration is the incorporation of the system into the corporate marketing strategy. The loyalty system, while consisting of information technology components in order to provide the defined services, must serve the strategic goals and orientation as defined by the marketing strategy.

The implementation of systems is therefore driven by two perspectives, the information systems perspective, and the corporate marketing perspective. The business models behind the provisioning of loyalty systems equally target both approaches. While information technology driven business models aim for the distribution of underlying infrastructure in terms of hard- and software, the marketing driven business models build on consulting for the setup phase and external operation of the required infrastructure in the execution phase of the system's lifecycle.

5.4.1 Technology provider business models

Infrastructure providers

The business model of the infrastructure providers consists in the distribution of hardware and software components that serve as the infrastructure layer for the operation of loyalty systems. These components include databases, transaction software, analysis software, application development environments and middleware and integration components.

In the context of loyalty systems, the value proposition offered by infrastructure providers consists of the provisioning of software tools that enable the creation of systems that cover the requirements for the loyalty system as defined by the marketing strategy. This is the value proposition as offered to the customers of the infrastructure providers. Traditionally infrastructure providers offer strong value propositions towards partners. These partners distribute the infrastructure provider's products, and accompany the implementation phase by bundling the infrastructure products with services and consulting.

The architecture of the value chain for infrastructure providers consists of value adding steps by providing higher levels of abstraction on top of basic software components. Higher levels of abstraction on the technology layer usually lead to faster and simpler implementation cycles as core elements that can be reused among applications are made available by the infrastructure provider's tools. The value adding steps in the internal architecture of the value chain for infrastructure providers are provided by software engineering processes. The required company resources consist of skilled personnel and technical infrastructure.

The external architecture often consists of a strong partner network that distributes the provider's products to customers and bundles the products with value added extensions or services that fit the requirements of the customer. The level of stability of the architecture is highly dynamic and can rapidly be reconfigured according to customer requirements. Revenue models in this domain are often based on licensing fees that need to be paid periodically based on the components that are being used by the system.

System providers

System providers enable a company to license an existing loyalty or customer relationship solution as a bundled product. This approach still requires extensive resources at the implementing company. Even when implementing a licensed customer relationship solution, companies need to create the information technology infrastructure and integrate the new system with the existing infrastructure. The offered applications are often organised in modules which can therefore be sold and implemented independently of one another. In this way the system can be adapted to the defined marketing requirements.

The value proposition offered by system providers towards their customers is the availability of readily developed modules for elements required for the implementation of loyalty systems. These systems often have a proven record of success and there are existing application examples that prove that the system has worked for other customers. System providers also often provide a strong value proposition towards their partners. As the infrastructure providers, the system providers rely on partners for the distribution and implementation of their products. The partners are compensated by receiving revenue shares based on the sold products and the ability to charge the customer for services involved with the implementation of the system.

The architecture of the value chain for system providers is similar to that of the infrastructure providers, generally it can be said that the system providers offer a further level of abstraction form the technology layer and specialise on specific applications while the infrastructure providers often deliver domain independent software products. The internal architecture of value creation is based on software development processes and the company resources consist of skilled personnel, technological infrastructure and access to underlying software products.

The external architecture of the value creation process is strongly dependent on distribution and implementation partners that integrate the systems into the customer's infrastructure and provide according consulting and support services. These value added partners also provide strong customer interfaces and allow wide presence through a strong partner network. The revenue model for system providers consists of licensing fees payable periodically as well as project based consulting and maintenance that can be billed to the customer independently.

5.4.2 Service provider business model

The service provider business model is based on the trend of outsourcing non-core company processes to external, specialised, companies. While the distribution and marketing strategies must be considered as core tasks of nearly every company, the operation of complex information systems might be outside of the company's core competencies scope. In a service provider model, the service provider manages the required hardware, software and provides the required resources to maintain and operate the system. The implementation of this model usually takes less time as the applications are already build and the operating infrastructure is already in place.

This model comes with a few advantages for the company wishing to implement a loyalty system. The setup costs are lower than in the previously presented approaches as the companies do not need to pay upfront for software licenses or hardware costs. There is no requirement to develop internal information technology and operation skills to manage the new application. The pricing models of service providers are often flexible and can adapt to various requirements and company sizes. On the down side, the service provider solutions cannot be adapted to the individual requirements as flexibly as the other presented models. If adaptations are possible these need to be implemented by the service provider which might involve high cost and time delays even for minor adaptations.

The value proposition offered by service providers consists not only of the provisioning of a software solution that needs to be incorporated into the company's infrastructure. It extends this proposition by taking over the operation and maintenance of the system as an external service to its customer. The value proposition towards the customer thus consists of a full solution for all loyalty system needs including software, hardware and the operation of the infrastructure. The selected marketing strategy and derived requirements for an information system can therefore be supported with the tools provided by the service provider. Partners play a less important role in the value architecture of service providers as the applications are distributed to customers directly and the implementation and adaptation requirements are low for each additional customer once the system is in place.

Service providers add a further value adding step to the architecture of the value chain of systems and infrastructure providers by operating and maintaining the systems for their customers. The internal architecture hence gets more complex as the business does not consist in the development and distribution of software, but also in the operation of the systems for a number of different customers. In terms of resources, service providers require an operational infrastructure and the personnel to maintain the system. Due to the investments required in the build up of such infrastructures, the level of stability of the architecture must be more stable in order to guaranty mid-term return on investment. The revenue model for service providers is based on periodical charges for the provisioning of the full service to the customers.

5.5   A business model for the provisioning of mobile supported loyalty schemes

While the reference model as presented in the course of this thesis can be adapted and implemented by any provider of a loyalty scheme, the complexity of integrating mobile communications technology and access to mobile interfaces with the information systems supporting the marketing and communication strategies can lead to high risk and costs of implementation. Therefore the research question, as elaborated in the introductory section, encompasses the aspect of how the service can be made available to providers of loyalty schemes, either as a complete customer communication solution, or as an extension to existing environments in order to provide and extend them with mobile communication features.

5.5.1 The role as a mobile third party service provider

The reference model for the mobile customer communication framework relies on specific mobile services in order to provide the communication features as derived from relationship marketing theory.

As discussed above, two major factors are relevant for the operation of the broad provisioning of mobile applications. The integration of all mobile network operators on the market, in order to be able to provide the service to all users independently of their mobile network operator, and the considerations of a second group of customers besides the end customers of mobile network operator, namely those companies that wish to reach their users or customers via the mobile channel.

The business model for the mobile loyalty framework must thus encompass both these factors and propose solutions in order to provide a valuable service to the operator of the scheme as well as to the consumers that use the provided mobile services. The provider for the mobile loyalty schemes must therefore take a position as a value added service provider in the mobile domain and bundle mobile telecommunication capabilities with the value added services that enable direct customer communication via the mobile channel. In this way the provider can offer the application based on the reference model together with the capabilities to provide mobile communication to his customers. The positioning within the mobile domain as a value added service provider enables the scheme operator to provide services that go beyond to what service providers can offer. A tight integration with the mobile network providers and their infrastructure enables the service provider close access to the consumer's mobile devices allowing more exact feedback on usage behaviours and a better understanding of how the services are used. A close technical integration can further be used to provide services at lower cost and to create new schemes for billing mobile services to the consumers, eventually making them available for free when they are backed by a company that wishes to use this communication channel towards their customers.

Within its role as a mobile third party service provider, the provider of the mobile loyalty scheme hence establishes the technical communication infrastructure to provide the communication channel towards the customers. Through a close integration with the mobile network providers, aspects of mobile communication can be integrated into the communication processes that would not be available when offering the service through other more generic third party service providers. These aspects might include the identification of users when accessing mobile Internet sites, the retrieval of location information or deeper information on the users' mobile behavioural patterns.

5.5.2 The role as a loyalty system provider

As a loyalty systems provider for applications based on the mobile customer communications reference model, two possible options exist. The provider can act in the role of a systems provider and enable a company to license the existing loyalty or customer relationship solution as a bundled product. As elaborated above, this approach requires the availability of resources for implementation and operation of the solution as the companies need to create the information technology infrastructure and integrate the new system with the existing infrastructure.

The second option consists of offering the applications based on the reference model as a value added service provider, in this way, the applications can be bundled with the value added mobile communication services as described above and offered to the customer as a bundle. Technological uncertainties and implementation risks can hence be minimised through the provisioning of the system through a service provider model.

The operation of mobile information systems can be considered outside of most companies' core competencies, hence a service provider model can minimise the required resources and associated risks with the setup of new technology. In the service provider model, the service provider manages the required hardware and software and by bundling the application with tight integration into the mobile infrastructure of the network operators, a position of a one-stop-shop for mobile customer communication can be achieved. The advantages for the company wishing to implement a loyalty system are the low setup costs when compared to the development of an own solution and build up of an own infrastructure, and the potential availability of pricing models that can adapt to various requirements and company sizes.

5.5.3 Business model components

According to the scope of analysis as defined for business model development in section 5.2, the value proposition, the architecture of the value chain consisting of the internal and external perspective on the value creation as well as the revenue model for the mobile supported loyalty schemes will be discussed. Finally an analysis of the target group from the perspective of a mobile customer communication service provider will be presented.

Value proposition

The service provider's customers are the companies wishing to implement mobile customer communication systems as a means to enhance customer relationship and leverage the benefits of customer relationship managements as discussed in section 5.1.1. The returns from successful customer relationship management that lead to higher retention rates and an effective leveraging of profitable long term customer relations represent an increase in bottom line profits for the company that implements a successful strategy. Hence, the value delivered to the customer is a means to enhance the return on the conducted business. As the technical solution for supporting mobile customer communication is only one aspect of a much wider customer relationship strategy, not all gains from enhanced customer relationship management can be attributed to the value proposition of the service provider. But the service provider is an enabler for the last step in customer relationship management and therefore facilitates a beneficial communication channel towards the customer.

A range of partners are involved in order to enable the business model for the provisioning of the service for mobile customer communication. The service provider integrates products from various software vendors, hardware manufacturers and builds the service on top of an existing mobile and wired network infrastructure. The value proposition towards the software vendors and hardware manufacturers results from the simple purchasing and licensing of their products in order to be able to operate the system on top of them. A more complex form of value exchange is required in the cooperation with the mobile network providers that need to integrate the new service provider into their systems and fulfil the advanced requirements that are required in order to provide the deep level of integration required for the support of the customer communication features. The value created for the network operator results from increased traffic and transactions and the creation of a new revenue stream coming from companies that are willing to finance their customer's mobile transactions when interacting with them.

Architecture of the value chain

The product/ market perspective is the first element within the definition of the business model's value architecture. It defines how the product or service and its interfaces are designed and comprises the selection of markets for the product. For the mobile loyalty scheme, the product can be defined as the infrastructure that supports mobile customer communication as an element of customer relationship management process through implementation of the functions as defined in the reference model for the mobile customer communication framework. The market for the services is constituted by the companies wishing to implement customer communication functionalities via the mobile channel. A closer analysis of the target market and the prerequisites for the implementation of the reference model is provided later in this section.

The internal architecture of the value chain consist of the resources needed to provide the product to the market, the definition of the value adding steps conducted within the company and the communication channels and coordination mechanisms with the external value adding partners. In the case of the business model for the mobile supported loyalty schemes, the internal architecture must provide the development of the applications, their operation and the integration of the applications with the mobile communication infrastructure as well as the data sources from the customer's existing infrastructure.

As defined above, the external value chain elements define the interfaces to the customers and to the external partners. The most important partner in the business model is the provider of the mobile communication infrastructure. The systems of the mobile network operator must be interconnected with the applications of the service provider in order to support the requirements as defined by the reference model. The technical connections of the systems represent the interfaces between the service provider and the mobile network provider. The interfaces to the customers are also provided through the applications and the data access and transmission channels that must be put in place when setting up the cooperation. Through these interfaces, the data required for the mobile communication infrastructure can be exchanged and customised messages can be transmitted to the consumers.

The level of stability of the architecture is heavily influenced by the closeness of the partners within the value architecture. In this case, the integration with mobile network operators is a base requirement in order to provide the service. If the cooperation with one of the mobile network operators fails, the service cannot be provided to the whole consumer market and the value for the direct customers is drastically reduced. A high degree of stability is therefore required in the value creating architecture.

Revenue model

The business model, as elaborated above, is based on a service provider approach. The analysis of revenue streams and payment options must therefore be conducted based on this type of markets' common revenue models.

The plan of revenue sources must describe how the product will generate revenue and what sources of revenue there are. Potential revenue models in this sector that can be applied individually or that can be combined with each other are (Hohmann 2003):

- Charging a periodical fee for the access to the application,
- Charging per transaction or other measurable unit,
- Charging for services related to the provisioning of the application,
- Charging a percentage of the revenue received or of the costs saved from the operation of the application.

By charging a periodical fee for the access to the application, the operator of the system can cover bottom line costs and generate regular, predictable, revenue. Due to the cost structure involved in operating the service, which is heavily driven by the fixed costs of running the infrastructure for the service, charging for access to the system periodically does fit well with the overall financial plan of the business model. The sources of revenue, when charging periodically for the access to the application, are the service provider's customers in terms of companies that use the service as their communication channel towards their own customers, mostly consumers. This revenue model can be combined with any one of the other revenue models. In a configuration with other revenue streams, this element would represent the constant income communicated to the customers as a base fee for gaining access to the service.

The revenue model of charging per transaction or any other measurable unit is common to mobile business models as the transactions over the mobile networks can be measured exactly and the value to the customer is closely related to the transactions committed over the course of the billing period, although this revenue model does not fit the cost structure for the mobile network operator industry, that is also strongly driven by fixed costs. Within the revenue model of the service provider for mobile customer communication, charging per transactions for the communication between the companies and their customers is an important aspect of covering the cost of messaging and data transfer that needs to be bought from the network operators and redistributed to the customers through the role of a third party service provider in the mobile industry. The source of this revenue stream, again, are the companies employing the system for their customer communication. The amount for each company is related to the intensity of usage of the system. The income generated is therefore less predictable. As the transaction based revenue stream can be calculated as a cost plus model, by charging the cost of each transaction plus a defined margin, the revenue cover costs and contribute to profit directly.

By charging for services related to the provisioning of the application, the service provider can enhance revenue flow on top of regular base fee income and transaction oriented charges. Services can include consulting for the implementation of relationship management instruments from business and technical perspectives, support in the operation of the system or technical adaptations and customisation of the application. Service revenues are often attractive to software companies as the margins are high and the fixed costs of providing service to customers is low (Hohmann 2003). A service revenue stream can be considered as independent from the other streams of revenue and not related to any other costs in the provisioning of the application. The source for service revenues can be different from those mentioned above for the other revenue models, besides the service provider's customers, services can be delivered to mobile network operators and other players in the mobile domain as well as players in the loyalty domain wishing to integrate mobile features with their systems. The high requirements in knowhow and resources for the provisioning of service to customers are a drawback in the setup of this revenue channel in early phases of the service provider's lifecycle.

Generating revenue by charging a percentage of the revenue received or of the costs saved from the operation of the application is an innovative approach to service that limits a customer's risk significantly (Zeidler 2004). Of course the risk is transferred to the service provider whose revenue will be dependent on the success of the application with respect to the customer's benefits solely. The second major drawback with this revenue model is the measurability of the bottom line results for the end customer. In the context of the proposed framework, a model has been discussed to measure the profitability of customer retention and loyalty, but besides mobile communication a range of other factors also can drive loyalty success or failure. A clear definition on which gains are achieved through the provided application can therefore be hard to determine. In specific cases, where the target measures for the success of the program can be defined clearly among the service provider and the customer, this model can offer an attractive alternative to the base revenue model as discussed above. The complexity of setup and the requirement of negotiation and the definition of the appropriate measure, involving the risk of choosing an unsuitable measure, make the model difficult to implement in the first place.

Target group for the mobile loyalty service provider

In order to define the potential market for the provisioning of services and applications based on an implementation of the proposed reference model, a framework has been developed that encompasses the major criteria as to be capable of integrating the application into the corporate information systems. The framework consists of nine criteria that describe the ability of a company to implement a system based on the requirements derived in the course of the development of the reference model.

The first criterion is derived from the fact that an association of each transaction to the respective customer should be present in order to conduct the analyses on which the communication and personalisation functions are based. Companies that have a mapping of transactions to individual customers based on the nature of the business or transaction type are in a big advantage when implementing personalised communication and relationship management strategies. The availability of customer-level transaction data is therefore a key criterion when implementing the reference model.

The level of retention benefits, as discussed in section 5.1.1, describes how strong the financial impact is that results from higher levels of customer loyalty. This figure differs among industries and companies. While a broad assessment can be conducted based on the industry, detailed company based numbers will usually not be available and need to be calculated from the specific company's transactional and financial data. The higher the benefits of enhanced customer retention rates, the more a multichannel approach including mobile functions will be able to contribute to bottom line results.

The number and types of current customer interactions are another factor for determining the applicability of the reference model for a specific company. Companies with decreasing customer contact have larger benefits from a personalised interactive communication channel than companies with regular personal customer contact. The type and frequency of customer contacts is mostly defined on the industry level. Industries can therefore by assigned scores with respect to these criteria and each company can be evaluated according to the respective industry.

While the adoption of mobile technology is broadly spread across all demographic groups, certain groups can be identified to be more receptive to communication with companies through the mobile communication channel. The question on how much the company's core target group fits into the demographic spectrum of interactive mobile communication will be another factor for determining the applicability of the reference model for a specific company.

The type of business, in terms of having a transactional business model or a more relationship based business model will have influence on the applicability of the reference model. A business based on mostly independent transactions with the customer's ability to switch sellers without difficulty requires strong instruments to enable a relationship on top of the transactional approach. Businesses that are based on relationships between the seller and the buyer often have strong instruments in place that can be extended through mobile communications. Hence, the approach to the two groups from the perspective of the reference model is different and must be taken into account when defining the market segments.

The market environment, in general terms of competitiveness, can have strong influence on the need to put relationship marketing instruments in place. In monopolistic markets, the requirements for relationship marketing tend to be low, as the customers have no other option than to fulfil their requirements through the monopolistic supplier. In more competitive markets, relationship marketing plays an increasing role and can be understood as a competitive advantage (Aaker 2001). In order to leverage the advantage from relationship marketing, according instruments need to be put in place and operated. The service provider for mobile loyalty services can offer applications that support this effort.

The way how companies currently differentiate themselves from their competition is another factor influencing the adoption of mobile customer relationship instruments. Companies that have focussed differentiation strategies, for example through a positioning as price discounters, a relationship approach will be less appropriate. For companies in the middle and high price segments without a specific positioning through their brand, relationship instruments with features delivered over the mobile channel can be of high value in order to strengthen the competitive position.

Because of the need to integrate tightly with the current loyalty and relationship marketing strategy and existing systems, the current infrastructure and strategy of a company has a strong influence on its suitability as a customer for the mobile loyalty service provider. Companies with existing strategies and systems in place, have the advantage of having customer databases, transaction mapping to customer records and communication strategies in place. When setting up the mobile extension, the existing infrastructure serves as a solid foundation for the future system. Companies that do not have a loyalty or relationship marketing strategy or infrastructure in place represent another segment for the service provider. These companies require intensive consulting for the definition of the program and its objectives as well as a baseline technical analysis on how to gather the required customer and transactional information and the implementation of the according technical means along the company's core processes.

The information technology integration abilities of the customer company represent the last factor determining the ability to serve as a customer for a potential service provider of applications based on the developed reference model. IT integration is required in order to link the service provider's systems to the customer's internal systems. This integration is required in order to fulfil the requirements defined as parts of the integration strategy and data exchange in the reference model. Companies that operate state-of-the-art information technology systems will be able to integrate new standard compliant elements into their system easier than those who do not have an appropriate IT infrastructure or operate legacy systems that are not compliant with today's interface and data exchange standards.

Influencing Factor	Description
Availability of data	Association of each transaction to the respective customer in order to conduct the analyses for controlling the communication and personalisation functions.
Level of retention benefits	Strength of the financial impact from higher levels of customer loyalty.
Number and types of customer contacts	Companies with decreasing customer contact have larger benefits from a personalised interactive communication channel than companies with regular personal customer contact.
Customers present in mobile target group	Certain customer groups can be identified to be more receptive to communication with companies through the mobile communication channel.
Type of business	Businesses based on independent transactions require strong instruments to enable a relationship on top of the transactional approach. Businesses that are based on relationships between the seller and the buyer have strong instruments in place that can be extended through mobile communications.

Market environment	Competitiveness has strong influence on the need to put relationship marketing instruments in place.
Differentiation strategies	The role of mobile customer communication is influenced by the chosen differentiation strategy.
Existing loyalty efforts	The current infrastructure and strategy of a company has a strong influence on its suitability as a customer for the mobile loyalty service provider.
IT integration abilities	Integration is required in order to fulfil the requirements defined as parts the reference model. Companies that operate state-of-the-art information technology systems will be able to integrate new standard compliant elements into their system.

Table 16: Factors influencing the adaption of mobile loyalty services

6 Reference model evaluation

6.1 Evaluation through case study research

In the course of the conduction of the presented research, the elements of the reference model for mobile customer communication as a means to support relationship marketing have been applied and redefined iteratively in different contexts. The gained insights from the application of the elements in the corporate environment have been used to refine the reference model itself and extend it in order to serve the requirements as encountered in valid and authentic application environments.

The case studies have been conducted at different levels of depth. While the *retail industry case study*, and the *multi partner program operator case study* led to a concept on how the mobile features of the reference model could be implemented within the existing program and infrastructure based on interviews and research of the current strategies and programs, the *banking industry case study* led to an implementation of a mobile customer communication system in two phases as a real operative application based on the concepts as elaborated during the design phase.

In order to follow a rigorous approach to the case studies and the evaluation of the results from the application of the reference model, the case studies have been designed according to the methodological approach recommended for case study research (Eisenhardt 1989, Flyvbjerg 2006, Stake 1995, Yin 2002). The process that was pursued in the course of the research consists of following steps for each case study:

- Determination and definition of the detailed research question
- Selection of the case
- Collection of data on current systems and applications
- Collaborative design of mobile elements based on the reference model
- Analysis of implementation specificities for the reference model elements
- Refinement of the reference model based on learnings from the case study.

This process has been run through for each of the three case studies and the research question has been adapted for testing specific elements of the reference model in different industry contexts. The gained insights have been incorporated into a new version of the reference model which has therefore been adapted iteratively based on the gained knowledge of its application in the context of the case studies.

For reasons of nondisclosure, the case studies have been made anonymous and specific details of marketing strategies and operational systems have had to be removed from the presentation. All factors relevant to the evaluation of the reference model and the traceability of the development and refinement process have been kept and are presented individually for each of the conducted case studies in the following sections.

6.2   Banking industry case study

The *banking industry case study* was conducted in cooperation with an Austrian group of banks. The banking industry has very specific requirements toward the communication with customers. The industry is very sensitive to the notion of unwanted or misleading communication content. At the same time, a lot of information related to the banking business that can be of value to the customer can be transferred to the customer in real time through the mobile channel.

The case study has been conducted in two phases. In the first phase, a mobile marketing program was implemented and tested in a selected number of branches. The marketing program was independent of the banking systems data, no customer data was retrieved in order to personalise the messages. The system kept its own data on the users' interactions with the system, and was operated independently of the core banking processes. The target group for this mobile marketing system was defined as students from local schools, colleges and universities. The target of the campaign was to increase customer frequency in the branches within the target group and leverage the increase in frequency for product sales. In the second phase, the mobile customer communication system was designed as to provide personalised communication to customers based on the banks customer data records. Integration into the banks data systems was thus required. Through the extension of the mobile system with bank oriented customer communication, the target group for the system was extended to all customers with an affinity towards mobile communications.

6.2.1 Applied elements of the reference model

In the first phase of implementation of the mobile customer communication framework, the application was oriented to support brand positioning by using the notion of being able to provide an innovative mobile service to customers. While the reference model, as being strongly based on relationship marketing foundations, does not include elements targeting the strengthening of a brand, the application was still based on elements of the reference model. Specifically, *interaction recording* (D2) in order to be able to attribute every interaction with the system to a specific user, *preference recording* (D3) as to determine the customers preferences over time that are disclosed through the interactions with the system, *customer information collection* (D4) to serve the customer based on information gathered throughout the communication process like the type of handset in use, *relationship monitoring* (A4) in order to measure the customer's involvement with specific categories offered through the service, *multichannel input* (IC1) to support multiple option of interaction with the system for multiple roles and actors, and *customer identification* (C3) in order to support personalised communication and interaction with the system.

Based on these functions, a mobile couponing system was developed that served registered user with coupons in a defined regular interval which they could retrieve through a device in each participating branch. The technology used in order to identify participating users and print the according coupon was a data matrix code that can be transmitted to the mobile device, displayed on the screen by the user, and read by the device that would validate the current coupon and print a paper coupon for redemption at the advertising partner's site.

In the second phase of the case study, the system was extended to provide new functions and integrate with the data of the core banking system's customer master records. By adding integration with the banking systems' data sources, higher level of personalisation and features based on business related transaction could be supported by the system.

The elements of the reference system on which the functional extensions of phase two are based were *message definition* (M2) allowing definition of communication content for different events that can be raised within the system based on the customer master data integration, *service system integration* (I1) to provide the data adaptors to the banking system, and *cross category messaging* (C2) to allow participating banks to select customers based on current product configuration and trigger mobile dialogues based on the selection.

The case study consequently encompassed a total of nine elements from the reference model that were developed and refined based on the experiences made within the design, implementation and operation phases. The insight gained within the application has been encompassed into the reference model as assures validity applicability of the presented concepts in accordance with the selected process for the construction of the reference model.

6.2.2 Identification and design of the mobile customer touch points

In the first phase of the implementation of a mobile customer communication system, a mobile-based couponing application was developed and rolled out to selected branches with a close relation to the defined target group. Customers were attracted to the service through traditional advertising. Flyers were distributed on nearby campuses and an attractive presentation of the stand with the scanner device inside the banks was ensured. Users would register for the service through their mobile phone by sending a message including a defined keyword to a number referring to the sms gateway of the system as communicated through the marketing channels. After signing up, the users would receive a welcome message and their data matrix code that allows them to redeem coupons as they are distributed to the customers. For each distributed coupon, the system would the simply send a notification per SMS to the user who would then be able to come to the bank and redeem the coupon with his unique data matrix code that was issued at registration. In case of a loss of the code, the code could be reissued by simply sending a message to the systems SMS gateway number.

In this first mobile customer communication application the element of *interaction recording* (D2) from the reference model was implemented based on the fact that only two types of operations where possible for the user of the system in the role of the bank's customer. For each of these interaction types, a method to support *customer identification* (C3) was implemented. The first type of interaction is the messaging based communication of the user with the system through its SMS gateway, the second type of interaction is the redemption of coupons by scanning the data matrix code at the bank. In this setup, the scanner was connected to the backend system via an over-the-air GPRS (General Packet Radio Service) data connection. The data matrix codes that encode a unique ID for each user were decoded by the scanner, sent to the backend system via the GPRS connection and validated against the database by checking which coupon was currently assigned to the user. The backend system would then return a command to the scanner to print a coupon or display a message on the scanner's interface. The identification of users when exchanging messages was conducted via the handset's MSISDN (Mobile Subscriber Integrated Services Digital Network Number), the unique identifier simply representing the user's mobile phone number. These two mechanisms, MSISDN when interacting through messaging, and the data matrix encoded ID when using the scanner, allowed for a recording of every interaction of the user with the system on an individual user perspective.

In order to support the reference model requirement of *preference recording* (D3), an analysis was conducted on how specific customer preferences can be discovered through the use of the system. The analysis revealed that the best indicator for customer preferences in this type of system was to be based on a categorisation of the coupons sent to the customers. Each coupon was therefore attributed to a specific category and the redemption of coupons by the users was tracked. Preferences for certain types of coupons hence could be derived from the transaction logs of scanner based redemptions.

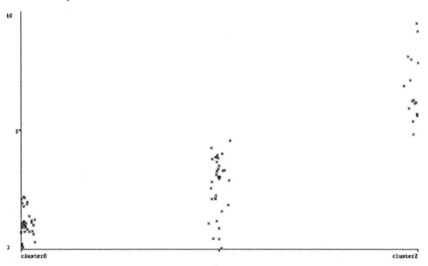

Figure 36: Results from clustering of users based on transaction data (y-axis = number of transactions)

Based on the elements of *interaction recording* (D2) and *preference recording* (D3), a further functional requirement from the reference model could be tested within the case study, *customer information collection* (D4). Specific groups of customer where identified based on their previous interactions with the system and the common information on these groups could be used to target new messages more directly to the members. Figure 36 illustrates a result from clustering transaction data and displaying the clusters with the amounts of conducted transactions on the y-axis. A clear correlation between the cluster membership and the number of redemptions can be recognized.

Based on these clustering results from the application of decision tree classifiers and the data collected through the functions discussed above, the element of *relationship monitoring* (A4) could be implemented into the system. For each of the available couponing categories, the personal preferences could be evaluated through simple queries on the transaction logs. Based on the result from these queries, the intensity of contact in each category could be evaluated for every user. This information was then used to control the system and determine the potential performance of coupons before they were sent out based on the number of users interested in the respective category.

Multichannel input (IC1) was supported in the system through the provisioning of a web interface for the system operators in each bank. In this way, users could be registered directly by the bank during a personal conversation. The web interface also provided access to reports and statistical data on the performance of the system for each bank.

In phase two of the case study, the couponing solution was extended by multiple features that required an exchange of data between the mobile communication system and the bank's customer records. Based on this integration of the mobile customer communication system with the bank's data on its customer more valuable service could be provided to the users of the system.

For the more complex communication processes that emerged from the integration of detailed customer data from the bank's information systems, the reference model's function of *message definition* (M2) needed to be implemented. For each communication process available in the system, messages were defined including the definition of dynamic fields that would be filled at runtime with specific customer information. The predefined communication content would be retrieved based on process rules defined for specific events that the underlying system would raise. All of the message definitions and respective processes are administrable through a web interface and can be adapted to requirements as they evolve.

Service system integration (I1) is provided based on the tight integration on the data level. The information on participation in the mobile communications program is available through the standard customer relationship management interface that is available to the bank's staff. The communication via the mobile channel can be controlled from the customer relationship system's interfaces in the known environment without the need for new tools to be set up.

The element of *cross category messaging* (C2) from the reference model can also be controlled via the customer relationship management system through the integrated functionalities and interfaces. Bank staff can select customers based on their product preferences from the customer relationship management system and trigger messages and communication dialogues with these customers based on the selected data. All messages can be personalised according to the rules and messaging content details as defined in the implementation of the *message definition* (M2) functionality.

6.2.3 System integration

For the implementation of the first phase, no specific IT integration into the banking systems was required. The mobile couponing system was operated independently of the bank's customer data records. The registered users were therefore not identified as specific customers of the bank and no information beyond their mobile phone numbers and information on their interactions with the system were known. Based on this system, the acceptance of the mobile communication channel could be measured, but the application was not integrated with the bank's knowledge of its customers and could not be made to react upon customer transactions and interactions concerning the core business.

A tighter integration with the bank's information systems was designed and implemented in the second phase of the case study project. The newly added features to the mobile communication channel were then driven by the customer data provided by the bank and integrated into the mobile communication system. Due to the security limitations that go in hand with the management of bank customer records, a secure and restrictive data exchange mechanism needed to be designed for the transfer of data between the bank's core infrastructure and the mobile marketing system that was operated within the bank's own computing centre.

A classic extraction and loading process was defined for the data that needed to be transferred between the systems. Periodical updates were scheduled on a daily basis in order to keep the mobile information system up to date with data changes of the customer master records as kept by the bank's systems. Within the bank's data model, a field was defined to store relevant information for the customers' opt-ins into the participation in the mobile communication offering. This field served as a selection operator in order to extract the relevant information for the data transmission to the mobile information system. The regularly transmitted data was then loaded into the mobile communication system and all changes were recorded in the system as updates of the existing entries. Based on these updated entries, the system could then trigger the appropriate communication as defined in the rule set.

6.2.4 Results from program operation

The results from this particular case study can certainly be expressed at best detail, as the system was put in operation in a real application context and was used by customers of the participating bank. The operation of the system allowed measuring its impact in two ways. Firstly, the specific transaction and user data could be analysed and the number of registered users or total transactions were used as performance measures for the system. Secondly, the users of the systems could be interviewed on their perception of the communication system and its advantages and disadvantages.

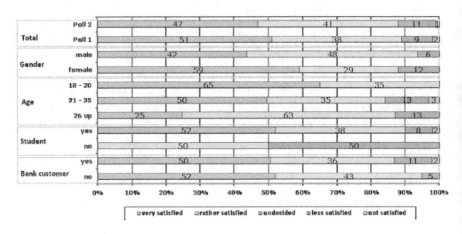

Figure 37: Satisfaction of participants with the mobile service (evolaris)

Participation numbers exceeded all expectations. Over 1.700 users registered to the system during the first phase and user response to the offered coupons by far exceeded the expectations. Customer frequency in the participating branches was increased significantly and direct sales could be attributed to the program.

Surveys were conducted among users of the mobile service. Figure 37 shows the results from one such study conducted during the case study. The figure illustrates that 88% of the participants were very or rather satisfied with the service. While the top satisfaction mark loses with the increased age of users, general satisfaction with the service remains high among all age groups.

The learnings from the design and implementation of the mobile customer communication system for the bank contributed to the refinement of the reference model by exposing the concepts and elements to real world conditions. The gained insight on industry requirements towards the system that were generated and processed during the case study have been incorporated in the final version of the reference model. Major contribution include the definition of strategies for customer identification and customer interaction recording as well as the implementation of a dynamic system to support message definition and process oriented sending of personalised messages.

6.3 Retail industry case study

The *retail industry case study* was conducted in cooperation with an Austrian retail chain that operates multiple department stores and specialised stores in Austria and neighbouring countries. The retail industry is one of the industries that historically have invested heavily into programs to increase their customer relationships. The largest loyalty programs are operated by companies from the retail industry and the gained knowledge on customer and their purchasing behaviour often constitutes important sources of information for the strategic decisions of these companies.

The retail industry typically has one very specific disadvantage to the situation previously presented for the banking industry. The customer's transactions are not naturally related to the customer by a specified means of identification. Therefore the retail industry has come up with the notion of loyalty cards that have reached high rates of distribution among households. The functional aim of the loyalty card, which must be shown at each purchase, is to gain the ability to relate the purchasing transaction to a specific customer or at least household. As an incentive to disclose their shopping behaviour through the presentation of the card at each transaction, the customers are offered special rebates or other types of incentive that correlate with the number and value of the conducted transactions.

The notion of providing valuable content to retail customers can be perceived as difficult as the communication content will mostly be advertising oriented and less of personal relevance to the customer. But through cooperation with content providers or through the creation of own content, attractive information for customers can be created and combined with targeted product offers.

In the course of the *retail industry case study* a detailed analysis of the existing loyalty system was conducted. Based on this analysis, a concept was developed for the integration of mobile communication features into the existing system in order to enhance its functionality. Unlike the *banking industry case study* the system has not been implemented in the course of the research, but the insights gained from the design phase for a mobile extension of the current system have contributed strongly to the definition of the elements of the reference model as presented in section 4.4.

6.3.1 Applied elements of the reference model

The developed concept for the mobile loyalty program extension in the *retail industry case study* is based on a range of functionalities defined in the reference model for the mobile customer communication framework. The focus in the development of the concept was put on functionalities from the data collection and analysis groups as well as functionalities from the communication and interaction modelling group.

A function supporting *customer event monitoring* (D1) was already in place within the existing system but was extended in the concept with mobile features in order to enhance the accurate monitoring of interactions and purchasing history for each customer. The element of *interaction recording* (D2) is supported trough the integration of existing identification measure and new mobile identification measures. *Preference recording* (D3) supports the recording of the customers' preferences as they are disclosed over the course of the relationship through the regular purchasing decisions and undertaken interactions. The feature of *class definition* (M1) supports the definition of customer segments as classes and the creation of rules for the classification of customers into the segments in order to address communication with respect to the customer's general preferences. The feature of *Category relations* (M3) allows for the modelling of relationships among categories to support *cross category messaging* (C2) that triggers marketing messages related to product lines that are defined as compatible with the customer's current purchasing behaviour. The concept for mobile customer communication from the *retail industry case study* includes the reference model's aspect on repurchasing cycle analysis and communication based on this analysis.

The function of *repurchase cycle analysis* (A1) constitutes the foundation for the analysis of repurchase cycles by identifying purchasing patterns from the transactional data. The *pattern transition* (A2) elements support the identification of changes in the customers purchasing behaviour. *Repurchase pattern transition reaction* (MC1) features manage the sending of messages in reaction to transitions in repurchasing cycles. *Transition management* (MC2) manages the processes and dialogues that are designed to support welcome transitions and prevent unwanted transitions in purchasing behaviour.

6.3.2 Identification and design of the mobile customer touch points

The concept developed within the *retail industry case study* was based on the goal to extend a successful existing retail loyalty program with mobile features according to the elements specified in the reference model. The existing loyalty program was based on the use of a typical loyalty card as a means of identification at the point of sale. Customer transactions were then recorded by individual customer and total revenue per customer was calculated as the key measure for all other loyalty efforts. The incentive offered to the customers for participation in the program and regular presentation of their loyalty card when purchasing goods, was the redemption of a percentage of total sales in form of a cash coupon at the end of the year. Other soft benefits were related to the use of the card, including free parking at the department store when purchasing goods over a certain amount, or participation in special offers or sales campaigns. A special version of the card further encompassed a payment function that was handled by the store itself through a direct debit system. Customers were offered delays in payment when opting for this card and no bank card or cash was required for shopping.

The program was successful in terms of numbers of participating customers and in terms of usage rates among participating customers, hence, a large number of customers who once joined the program would recurrently use their cards when purchasing goods. The drivers for usage were mostly the soft incentives that offered customers a real time benefit from the usage of the card. The program lacked a clear strategy for the use of the collected data. The only analysis conducted was based on the customers total spending and customers were grouped into three segments according to this measure. Since no detailed customer segmentation was conducted based on the collected data, the communication strategy towards customers was not personalised to customer's preferences nor was it targeted sensibly to the most valuable customers.

The elements selected for the concept describing the integration of the mobile customer communications framework into the exiting program were chosen in order to enhance the existing program where the strongest shortcomings had been identified. Therefore, elements from the functional categories of data analysis and communication form the core of the concept for the integration of mobile customer communication.

The function of *customer event monitoring* (D1) supporting the accurate monitoring of interactions and purchasing history per customer is provided in the existing system through the identification of the customer with his loyalty card. This function can be extended by identification features supported by the mobile phone. Potential technologies are data matrix based codes to be displayed and scanned with specialised hardware from the mobile phone, of near field communication (NFC) or radio frequency identification (RFID) based applications provided via the mobile phone.

Element of the Program	Mobile Function	Gain from Mobile
Collecting points	• Identification via the mobile phone • New collection mechanics	• Participation with every purchase, no need for post-processing • Higher involvement with the program
Tracking points	• Permanent access to the current level of points • Active notification at the reach of thresholds	• Interactive tracking of bonus opportunities leads to stronger use and effect of the program
Spending points	• Use of mobile coupons • Viral marketing through forwarding and invitation mechanisms	• Support of campaigns through mobile coupons • Member-get-Member through forwarding and invitation mechanisms
Receiving Information	• Real-time communication • Cost reduction and higher personalisation	• Short-term influence on purchasing behavior
Program Analytics	• Interaction with traditional media	• Better control of advertising effects

Figure 38: Mobile features as an extension to the existing loyalty program

The element of *preference recording* (D3) was included in the concept as a means to discover specific customer preferences through their interactions with the system. Preferences have been defined in terms of product categories. All recorded transactions are related to specific product categories. By aggregating the transaction data for each customer by the product category, a preference profile of the customer can be created based on the product categories purchased within the regarding period. This customer profile serves as input to various other functions of the concept that are based on preferences of customers in order to conduct value analysis or personalised communication.

The reference model element of *class definition* (M1) is supported in the concept through an administration interface that allows for modelling and refining the rules specified for specific customer categories. The customer classes that are defined via these rules can encompass more than the preferences on products as determined through *preference recording* (D3), but preferences can be a defined selector for the attribution of a specific customer into on defined segment. The rules are executed by the system in regular definable intervals and customers are regrouped according to the specified rules.

The function of *category relations* (M3) is another feature that enables modelling of system behaviour. In the developed concept, relations between different product categories can be defined in terms of whether these categories represent supplementary or complementary goods. Based on the data generated by the *preference recording* (D3) feature, new product categories can be identified that are relevant to the customer and messaging can be triggered based on these category relations. The messaging element that is designed on top of the analytics module is an implementation of the reference model element of *cross category messaging* (C2). Based on the defined category relations, communication content can be specified for certain system states that define the customer's current interaction points and product categories with the department store.

Another major extension to the current program was developed in the course of the design phase for mobile extensions in the *retail industry case study*: The analysis and controlling strategies for purchase pattern identification and reactions to transitions in purchasing patterns and their implementations. Multiple elements of the reference model contribute to this function. *Repurchase cycle analysis* (A1) provides the base functionalities for all dialogue and communication features that are based on its analysis results. Repurchase cycles have been defined as the purchasing frequency within specific product categories or groups of product categories in the course of the development of the concept. The function supporting the identification of changes in purchasing behaviour is provided through an implementation of the reference model's element of *pattern transition* (A2) management. This functionality monitors changes in customer data or specific events as defined in the modelling interface for *repurchase cycle analysis* (A1). When specific events are raised by the underlying layers, or transitions between patterns occur, the element itself can raise events towards the communication layer above it in the architecture. Hence, the *repurchase cycle analysis* (A1) module represents a business logic layer that controls communication based on transitions in purchasing behaviour. The implementation of the *repurchase pattern transition reaction* (MC1) module as defined in the reference model constitute the communication layer for the reactions to transitions in purchasing patterns. Communication messages are defined for possible types of transition and sent to customer based on the events raised in the lower layers representing the business logic for the management of purchasing patterns. The element of *transition management* (MC2) from the reference model supports the proactive reaction to potential positive transitions in purchasing behaviour, as for example the customer's switch to a brand that contributes higher margins. The element therefore needs to be aware of current purchasing behaviours as well as indicators for changes in the transitions. When changes are identified, appropriate communication can be triggered that either defects a potential negative transition, or support a potential positive transition.

6.3.3 System integration

The development of an integration plan for the mobile features was included in the concept that was created in the course of the *retail industry case study*. Two phases led to the development of the integration plan. Firstly, an analysis of the current information technology infrastructure including the identification of relevant data sources, and secondly the design of the interfaces required by the new features in order to access the customer master data and the transactional data that was presently stored and processed in the existing system.

The new features could be segmented into three distinctive categories. The mobile communication features that support the use of the mobile communication channel for the loyalty program, the mobile identification features that support the identification of the customer when interacting with the company or purchasing goods from the company at the point of sale, as well as the analytics functions that provide the step of knowledge extraction from available customer and transactional data in order to actively manage the customer relationship lifecycle.

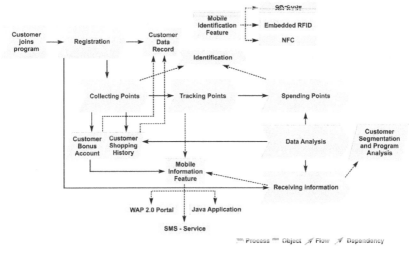

Figure 39: Process model for the loyalty program with mobile features

Figure 39 illustrates how the mobile information feature and the mobile identification feature integrate with the underlying loyalty management process. The analytics features is a core element of the process and generally independent of the mobile communication features. It is, nevertheless, a base requirement in order to provide mobile communication as the content of message via the mobile channel need to be targeted to customer in order as to provide relevant information to the consumer.

The legacy system that was available bundled all transactional information from all outlets in a central data centre. The data was transmitted from the point of sale terminals either in real time when an online connection to the data centre was available, or through a batch transmission at the end of the day. Offline capability of the point of sale terminals was a crucial of the system's architecture, as a missing connection to the data centre should not prevent point of sale checkout terminals from working properly as an effortless and fast checkout constitutes one of the most important measures in the retail industry. All mobile services needed to be adapted in order to work under potential offline conditions of the point of sale terminals, as well as having no negative effect on checkout convenience and speed. The mobile services were therefore designed for use outside the area of the point of sale. Functionalities that needed to interact with the point of sale were designed for offline capability and simplicity and speed of use.

6.3.4 Results from system analysis and design

The concept that was developed based on the analysis of the existing loyalty system in place, the marketing requirements as defined by the retail chain's management responsible for sales and customer loyalty operations, and the architectural limitations of the existing loyalty system. The development of the concept delivered many insights on the applicability of the tested reference model elements within a retail environment. Many specifics of the requirements could be addressed by the system, and the implementation of the elements from the reference model could be achieved in the respective implementations.

The reference model has generally been proven to be adaptable to specific customer requirements. Implementation details must be considered in the course of the design and analysis phase as this has been done within the presented case study. A readily implemented set of features based on the elements of the reference model would certainly be more challenging to adapt to the specific requirements of the implementing company.

Based on the feedback gained within the case study, the reference model was reengineered according to the iterative development of the framework and learnings were incorporated into the model. As no operational implementation of the concept took place during the case study, feedback from users of the system, as gained through the *banking industry case study*, could not be collected. In the case of an implementation at the concerned company, future research can consist in accompanying the implementation process and evaluating system success through user surveys and system performance measures.

6.4 Multi-partner program operator case study

The loyalty program operator company that served as a case in the course of the research follows three distinctive business strategies based on the existing infrastructure and knowledge in the operation of loyalty schemes. As a first segment, the company acts as a full service operator for a multi partner loyalty program in Germany with over 25.000 participating retail outlets including some of the strongest national retail brands in Germany. As a second business segment, the company has specialised in operating loyalty programs for newspaper publishers as a third party service and technology provider. The third business segment also consists of offering third party services and operation of loyalty systems, in this case specialised on the requirements of the tourism industry, specifically regional tourism marketing.

In the course of the *multi-partner program operator case study*, as with the *retail industry case study*, a concept for the application of elements from the reference model was developed. An implementation of the created concept has not been conducted in the course of the case study, but insights on application issues of the reference model could be gained within the processes of analysing application options for the reference model elements and designing a potential solution following a software development process consisting of an analysis and design phase. The insights gained from the analysis and design phases for a mobile extension of the currently offered systems have contributed strongly to the definition and refinement of the elements of the reference model.

The notion of dealing with a third party service provider as the operator of the system to be extended with mobile features leads to a value architecture of higher complexity than within the other two, industry specific case studies. The definition of clear requirements towards mobile features also increased in complexity, as the functions needed to be designed not only to fit one specific company and its customer communication needs, but be deployable to different companies in different industries. Functionalities therefore had to be designed in a highly generic fashion that allowed configuration of the features through the support of modelling the analytics and interaction processes for each specific company.

6.4.1 Applied elements of the reference model

The concept for the mobile customer communication program extension in the *multi-partner program operator case study* is based on a range of selected functionalities defined in the reference model for the mobile loyalty framework as defined in section 4.4. The focus in the development of the concept in the course of this case study was put on functionalities from the communication groups as well as functionalities from the analysis group that went beyond previously conducted analysis in order to provide specific customer information that could be used to personalise mobile communication on a per user base. At the same time the system extensions needed to be kept as generic as possible in order to be adaptable to different circumstances at different companies implementing the program operator's systems.

The reference model's element of *preference extraction* (A7) was selected as a module of the target system. As an analysis module, this element supports the extraction of potential customer preferences through an analysis of customer interactions and transaction histories. The aggregation of customer preferences by product category and communication channel is conducted by the *preference construction* (A6) module. Preferences are attributed to customer based on the extracted information. The update of customer preferences is conducted on a regular basis in a scheduled interval. The function of *message definition* (M2) supports the possibility to define communication content for different channels and assign it to specific events that can be triggered by underlying analytical functions. The management of purchasing patterns is supported in the target system by including the functions of *repurchase pattern transition reaction* (MC1) that supports messaging and dialogue based communication as a reaction to transitions in purchasing behaviour and *transition management* (MC2). The support for multichannel communication is provided by the element of *automated multichannel output* (AC2) that supports flexible selection of communication channels based on customer preferences and the customer's familiarity with the processes and dialogues to be conducted. The messaging layer on top of the *automated multichannel output* (AC2) is provided by an implementation of the function defined as *multichannel output communication* (C4). This functionality supports channel independent output communication based on the results of the underlying analytics layer for the selection of the channel. In order to enhance reporting features, the element of *behaviour patterns* (IA1) was included in the concept. This element supports the monitoring of typical customer behaviour patterns and the domain specific development of customer relationships and the domain's customer relationship lifecycle over time.

The case study consequently encompassed a total of eight elements from the reference model that were developed and refined based on the experiences made within the analysis and design phases. The insight gained within the application has been encompassed into the reference model as assures validity applicability of the presented concepts in accordance with the selected process for the construction of the reference model.

6.4.2 Identification and design of the mobile customer touch points

As the company involved in the *multi-partner program operator case study* was active as a loyalty program operator in three distinctive fields, namely the operation of a nationwide multi-partner loyalty program, the operation of various newspapers publisher's subscriber loyalty programs, and the operation of regional tourism marketing programs, one specific field was selected for the application of mobile elements in the first place. The multi-partner loyalty program was selected as the system that should be enhanced with mobile customer communication features as developed in the reference model. Based on the program's targets and current status, the elements that have been discussed in the previous section have been selected for incorporation into the system. In the course of the case study, a concept has been developed how the selected elements could contribute to the existing system in operation throughout a large number of retail outlets and currently handled through a membership card that is electronically processed at the point of sale at each of the merchants' outlets.

The business model behind the provisioning of a multi-partner loyalty program to retail merchants consists in constructing an efficient marketing channel that is able to generate additional revenue for the retailer. The program operator then receives a share of the revenue generated by the customers taking part in the loyalty program. The program operator thus has strong incentives to attract customers to the retail partners and drive revenue for them. As a means to achieve this, the operator has the ability to provide personalised communication to the consumers and recommend them attractive offers that match the preferences that have been exposed by the card holder through previous purchases and interactions. The aim of using mobile applications for customer communication consists in reducing the cost for personalised communication and providing shorter reaction time to customer exposed preferences of transitions in purchasing behaviour.

Based on the transactional data collected from all participating retailers, the feature of *preference extraction* (A7) as defined in the reference model was incorporated into the concept. Although customer preference analysis was conducted in the existing system based on the customer's transaction, evaluation cycles were adapted to the communication process of paper mailings, and therefore only executed before mailing production not supporting an interactive customer monitoring as required in the context of mobile communications. The *preference extraction* (A7) feature for mobile communi-

cations therefore was designed as an interactive monitoring system of customer transactions that triggers events when preferences can be discovered from the transactional
logs. Based on this feature, the element of *preference construction* (A6) that represents
the aggregation layer for customer preferences defines a representation of the customers' preferences by product category and preferred and most effective communication
channels.

In order to support the modelling of mobile communication processes for defined
events triggered by elements of the underlying analytics layer, the function of *message
definition* (M2) provides the ability to model dialogues and message content with dynamic elements to allow message personalisation. All of the message definitions and
respective processes are administrable through a web interface and can be adapted to
requirements as they evolve.

The conception of the *repurchase pattern transition reaction* (MC1) module as defined
in the reference model implements the communication layer for the reactions to transitions in purchasing patterns. Mobile messages are defined for possible types of pattern
transitions, and sent to customers based on the events raised in the lower analytical
layers. The element of *transition management* (MC2) from the reference model supports the proactive reaction to potential positive transitions in purchasing behaviour, as
for example the customer's switch to a brand that contributes higher margins. The aim
of proactively managing and observing pattern transition is to support the goal of the
program operator and serve customers with relevant offers based on their current needs
in order to raise program participants' spending with the program partners.

As the newly defined mobile features of the concept must integrate with the existing
system, a strategy for multi channel communication was defined based of the reference
model's function for *automated multichannel output* (AC2). In this way, the existing
communication channels to which the program users are accustomed remain un-
touched and can be integrated with the new messaging strategies. The selection of the
channel for communication can be effected by the execution of defined rules that take
into account customer preferences and the urgency of the message to be transmitted.
Based on the results from the *automated multichannel output* (AC2) element, the messaging adaptor for multichannel output implements the reference model's concept of
multichannel output communication (C4). It serves the purpose to select appropriate
message according to the output channel and render the message to the respective

adapted for either sending a paper mail based on the triggered event, sending a mobile message to the customer, or presenting the information at the next customer login into the web interface.

The analysis of customer behaviour through the reference model's element of *behaviour patterns* (IA1) allows the system operator to identify each customer's potential within the program. Defectors can therefore be detected early and marketing spending can be targeted to customers that generate an appropriate return. The feature is based on the reference model's theoretical foundation and represents the customer relationship in terms of breadth and depth as the different product categories the customer is active in, and the frequency of interactions in each category.

An infrastructure integration perspective was not evaluated in the course of the case study as a reengineering of the complete operational system was underway during the conduction of the study. The new system that is being implemented by the program operator is meant to support a flexible architecture in order to be able to extend functionality through connecting modules to standardised interfaces.

6.4.3 Results from system analysis and design

The scope of the concept for the *multi-partner program operator case study* was defined early during the conduction of the case study. From the program operator's different business segments, the multi-partner program was selected to be enhanced with mobile features. Hence, the concept that was developed based on an analysis of the existing multi-partner loyalty system in place. The business model of the program operator, that is based on sharing of revenues generated by program members, leads to target definitions for the mobile customer communication system that differ from those of the other two case studies.

The reference model has generally been proven to be adaptable to specific customer requirements in the other two case studies, also the requirements formulated in the *multi-partner program operator case study* have shown to be supportable through functions of the reference model. As after the conduction of the other case studies, a further design iteration was conducted over the reference model and the reference model was reengineered according to the newly emerged requirements. As no implementation of the concept was conducted, feedback from program members, as gained through the *banking industry case study*, could not be gathered.

The difficulties that arose during the case studies were mainly due to the fact that unlike with a single operator loyalty scheme, the operator of a multi-partner scheme has no access to detailed product data of the partnering retailers. Hence, analyses based on product specifics, including product categories or product margins cannot be accounted for in the same level of detail than in cases of direct system integration of enterprise resource planning or stock keeping systems into the loyalty program. The value created by the use of the mobile channel for communication to customers lies in the ability to communicate personalised messages and information in near to real time at comparably low costs to the customers. In order to realise this value, a number of steps must be accomplished in order to be able to provide relevant personalised content with the correct timing, the discovery of the required information in order to provide this service is conducted by the analytical functions of the reference model. As the case study has shown, these functions need to be adaptable to work based on the available data in each case.

6.5 Overview of evaluated reference model elements

The following table summarises the evaluation process. Due to the constraints of the case studies, not all theory derived elements could be applied in the case studies. Six elements as defined in the first iteration of the reference model based on the theoretical foundations were not tested during the conduction of the case studies. The elements are highlighted in table 17. These elements remain untested in real application environments in the course of this research work. The evaluation of these functions represents potential for further work on the evaluation of the presented reference model.

Requirement ID	Identifier	Case study application
D1	customer event monitoring	retail industry
D2	interaction recording	banking industry
D3	preference recording	retail industry banking industry
D4	customer information collection	banking industry
M1	class definition	retail industry
M2	message definition	multi-partner program operator
M3	category relations	retail industry

MC1	repurchase pattern transition reaction	retail industry multi partner program operator
MC2	transition management	retail industry multi partner program operator
A1	repurchase cycle analysis	retail industry
A2	pattern transitions	retail industry
A3	automated classification	
A4	relationship monitoring	banking industry
A5	interaction category assignment	
A6	preference construction	multi partner program operator
A7	preference extraction	multi partner program operator
AC1	Dynamic pricing	
AC2	automated multichannel output	multi partner program operator
AR1	present customer value	
AR2	customer lifetime value analysis	
I1	service system integration	banking industry
IA1	behaviour patterns	multi partner program operator
IC1	multichannel input	banking industry
C1	communication triggering	
C2	cross category messaging	retail industry banking industry
C3	customer identification	banking industry
C4	multichannel output communication	multi partner program operator

Table 17: List of evaluated reference model elements

7 Results and recommendations

The research presented in this thesis has led to the development of a reference model for the employment of mobile features in the context of relationship marketing and loyalty schemes. The reference model has been constructed based on the requirements derived from the theoretical foundations of relationship marketing, the current tools used in loyalty schemes and from the conception and implementation of the model within three case studies.

The reference model is designed according to a modular approach and can therefore be implemented by companies following an application model by configuration of the elements of the reference model. Based on the conducted case studies, implementation considerations have been included in the description of the reference model and support an adaptation of the model's elements to specific application domains.

The *social penetration theory*, which has been selected as to provide the major theoretical foundation for the reference model, provides the core functionality that has been applied in the case studies. The case studies have shown which of these elements are applicable in a corporate context based on the availability of data and capabilities of the mobile channel. Through the feedback from the case studies, the model has iteratively been re-engineered in order to incorporate the findings from the case studies.

A thorough analysis of the infrastructural capabilities of the mobile communication channel has provided an insight on the technical possibilities to be used within the construction of the reference model and the development of concepts and implementations within the case studies. Existing approaches to mobile and interactive customer communication have been considered in designing the system. Through this approach, previously tested features could be integrated into the reference model and supported the notion of providing a description with a comprehensive perspective.

7.1 The reference model for mobile customer communication

During the iterative construction of the reference model, 27 features have been identified and developed that constitute the singular modules of the model. These features have been classified into five categories: Analysis, communication, data collection, integration, and modelling, where some features serve multiple categories.

By conducting the case studies, 21 features could be tested by being specified within the creation of application concepts for mobile customer communication or being implemented within the construction of the system in the *banking industry case study*.

Besides the description of the functional elements that have been derived from the theoretical foundations and the application within the case studies, implementation approaches have been described for each of the functional categories. For the analysis category, methods have been evaluated to conduct the required segmentation of customer groups and recommendation of products based on purchasing behaviour and other customers' choices. For the communication category, a multichannel communication model has been presented that incorporates all major communication channels, interactive, as well as traditional. For data collection and system integration, a concept based on data warehousing has been presented with special attention to the requirement of being able to provide real time access to the data from other systems in order to use it for the direct communication via the customers' mobile device.

For the application of the reference model in different practical contexts, the section on business models provides insight on how the service must be composed in order to provide value to all required entities along the value chain. A business model for the provisioning of services related to the developed model based on the concept of a third party service provider has been developed and presented.

Through the application of the reference model in three case studies that were conducted in different industries and application domains: *Banking, retail* and *loyalty program operator*, application models have been created that demonstrate the use of the reference model and the configuration process of reference model elements according to the requirements of the implementing company.

7.2 Implications for practitioners

The research provides insight for practitioners from different domains. For marketing practitioners within companies, the presented research results can serve as a reference point in analysing what features of current or planned relationship marketing activities can be supported by mobile communication, and how these can be implemented. The illustrated dependencies among the features allow an insight into the requirements that must be fulfilled in order to be able to implement a specific feature. Based on the reference model, the previous experience from the case studies, and an elicitation of requirements derived from the company's relationship marketing strategy, a concept for the use of mobile technology to support the strategy's relationship marketing goals can be created. The three case studies presented in this work offer examples on how this process can be conducted. The proposed implementation strategies for the elements of the reference model can support the specific implementations at companies. Additionally, the presented implementation strategies provide a suggestion on how the elements can be implemented in real environments. The business model section provides insight on the benefits that can be gained from implementing a successful relationship strategy that achieves to retain customers for the company.

For marketing professionals who offer consulting and software solutions related to the construction of relationship marketing strategies and instruments for companies, the reference model describes a way on how mobile features can be introduced in this domain. A core result from the case studies was the requirement to provide integration into existing systems. The solution proposed in this thesis provides a data aggregation layer that supplies the analysis functions of the model with the required data from various data sources available within the target company's information infrastructure. One case study was specifically targeted to loyalty service providers and demonstrates how the features of the reference model can be applied in this specific domain. The development and discussion of business models has shown that the value of the operation of mobile loyalty features is closely related to the gains that can be leveraged through higher customer retention rates. These differ strongly among industries, which can lead to advantages when specialising the features towards the industries with the highest potential. Concerning the selection of companies for the application of features from the reference model, a model for evaluation of the target group for the mobile loyalty services was developed within the analysis of the business model.

Mobile operators and traditional mobile third party service providers have the advantage of deep knowledge concerning the technological aspects of mobile communications. Their systems are tightly integrated with the mobile communication networks, and they often serve large numbers of customers from which they have important data at hand that can be used in the analytical functions proposed by the reference model. The analysis of the value chain within the section of business model development has shown how important the role of the mobile third party service provider is, and how it can be extended to offer relationship marketing services based on the elements of the reference model. During the conduction of the case studies, lack of knowledge on specific topics of mobile infrastructure and technology has often been a problem within projects. This strengthens the role of the habitual players in this domain, as they can provide technical services and expertise that are required in order to offer relationship supporting mobile services of high quality.

7.3   Opportunities for future research

A foundation has been set through this research for the integration of mobile technology into the operational relationship marketing process. While previous research on the mobile channel as a means to support marketing activities has mostly been campaign oriented or identified mobile stand-alone services that support relationship marketing goals, the results from this work integrate mobile communications into the relationship marketing process.

The proposed model has been derived from a theoretical foundation, the *social penetration theory*, and from the requirements that arouse in three case studies of different industry backgrounds and application scenarios. The description of the elements of the reference model has not yet been formalised, the elements are described as functional requirements, underlying data models have been formalised in order to derive requirements towards a practical implementation.

Future research can therefore consist in the formalisation of the reference model elements by selecting or extending an existent modelling language in order that is able to capture all aspects of the reference model and that supports the implementation in specific application contexts through configuration of the model's elements according to the defined requirements.

Other possible extensions of the presented research can consist in the conduction of further evaluations on how the mobile features contribute to loyalty among participation customers. These experiments should be conducted in real application contexts and require applications of the reference model elements in large environments so that user numbers are sufficient in order to provide data for the analysis of the feature's impact on the buyer-seller relationship.

An application of the reference model in other contexts than those of the three case studies presented in this research could represent another extension of the present research. As has been shown in the discussion of business models for the mobile supported loyalty framework, relationship marketing impact varies strongly among industries. Further, the selection criteria for companies that are suited for the application of the reference model could be tested through an extension of application cases.

Bibliography

Aaker, DA (2001): Strategic market management 6th edition. New York: Wiley & Sons.

Ahlert, D; Kenning, P; Petermann, F (2001): Die Bedeutung von Vertrauen für die Interaktionsbeziehungen zwischen Dienstleistungsanbietern und -nachfragern, in: Bruhn, M; Stauss, B (Eds.): Dienstleistungsmanagement Jahrbuch 2001, S. 279-297. Wiesbaden: Gabler.

Alcatel (2007): Technology Whitepaper: Mobile Network Evolution: From 3G Onwards. http://www.alcatel-lucent.com/wps/portal last accessed 19.09.2007.

Algesheimer, R; Dholakia, U; Herrmann, A (2005): The Social Influence of Brand Community: Evidence from European Car Clubs, Journal of Marketing, No. 69, pp 19-34.

AlShaali, S; Varshney, U (2005); On the usability of mobile commerce. International Journal of Mobile Communications (IJMC), Vol. 3, No. 1.

Altman, I; Taylor, D (1973): Social Penetration: The Development of Interpersonal Relationships. NewYork: Holt, Rinehart and Winston.

Anderson, JC; Narus, JA (1990): A Model of Distributor Firm and Manufacturer Firm Working Partnerships. Journal of Marketing, Vol. 54, January, pp. 42-58.

ARCchart Research (2007): Mobile Operating Systems: The New Generation. http://www.arcchart.com last accessed 24.11.2007.

Aschmoneit, P (2003): Mobile Services für das Beziehungsmarketing - Grundlagen - Einsatzpotenziale - Design , Dissertation, Universität St.Gallen.

Bansal, HS; Voyer, PA (2000): Word-of-Mouth Processes within a Services Purchase Decision Context, Journal of Service Research, Vol. 3, No. 2, pp. 166-177.

Bänsch, A (1995): Käuferverhalten, 6. Auflage, München: Bauer.

Bartels, R (1976): The History of Marketing Thought, Second Edition. USA: Grid Inc.

Barth, K; Hartmann, M; Schröder, H (2002): Betriebswirtschaftslehre des Handels, Wiesbaden: Gabler.

Barwise, P; Strong, C (2002): "Permission-based Mobile Advertising", Journal of Interactive Marketing, vol. 16 (1), pp. 14-24.

Bauer H.H., Martin I., Albrecht C.M., Virales Marketing als Weiterentwicklung des Empfehlungsmarketing, in: Bauer, Große-Leege, Rösger, Interactive Marketing im Web 2.0+, Vahlen, Munich, 2007

Bauer, A., Günzel, H., Data-Warehouse-Systeme, D.Verlag, 2004

Bauer, HH; Reichardt, T; Barnes, SJ; Neumann, MM (2005): Driving Consumer Acceptance of Mobile Marketing: A Theoretical Framework and Empirical Study, Journal of Electronic Commerce Research, vol. 6 (3), pp. 181-192.

Bell, GH; Ledolter, J; Swersey, AJ (2006): Experimental Design on the Front Lines of Marketing: Testing New Ideas to Increase Direct Mail Sales , International Journal of Research in Marketing, Vol. 23, 309-319.

Bergen, M; Dutta, S; Walker, OC (1992): Agency Relationships in Marketing: A Review of the Implications and Applications of Agency and Related Theories. Journal of Marketing, 56(22), pp. 1-24.

Berger, PD; Nasr, NL (1998): Customer Lifetime Value: Marketing Models and Applications, in: Journal of Interactive Marketing, Vol. 12, pp. 17-30.

Blattberg, RC; Deighton, J (1996): Manage Marketing by the Customer Equity Test, in: HBR July - August 1996, pp. 136 - 144.

Bolton, RN; Kannan, PK; Bramlett, MD (2000): Implications of Loyalty Program Membership and Service Experiences for Customer Retention and Value, in: Journal of the Academy of Marketing Science, 28 (1), p. 95–108.

Brännback, M (1997): Is the Internet changing the dominant logic of marketing? European Management Journal Vol. 15 No. 6 pp. 698-707.

Brocke, J; Buddendick, C (2004): Konstruktionstechniken für die Referenzmodellierung - Systematisierung, Sprachgestaltung und Werkzeugunterstützung. pp. 19-49 in Jörg Becker, Patrick Delfmann (Eds.): Referenzmodellierung - Grundlagen, Techniken und domänenbezogene Anwendung. Physika Verlag.

Brown, A (2006): "Subscriptions By Country", Mobile Communications Europe – Strategic Intelligence on Mobile Operators & Markets, Informa Telecoms & Media, UK. Issue 436, p. 20.

Brown, J; Craig, C; Hester, G (2003): Enterprise Java Programming with IBM Web-Sphere (2nd Edition). Addison Wesley

Bruhn, M (2000): Kundenerwartungen – Theoretische Grundlagen, Messung und Managementkonzept, in: Zeitschrift für Betriebswirtschaft, 70. Jg., Nr. 9, S. 1031-1054.

Bruhn, M (2003) Relationship Marketing: Management of Customer Relationships, Pearson Education Limited.

Bruhn, M (2005): Unternehmens- und Marketingkommunikation - Handbuch für ein integriertes Kommunikationsmanagement. München: Vahlen Verlag.

Brumley, CM (2002): Creating Loyalty in Relationship Marketing: A descriptive study of supermarket loyalty programs. Master Thesis at the Perley Isaac Reed School of Journalism, West Virginia University.

Caves, RE; Porter ME (1977): From entry barriers to mobility barriers: Conjectural decisions and continued deterrence to new competition. Quarterly Journal of Economics, 91, pp. 241-262.

Clark, R; Clark, P (2006): The loyalty guide. Ilminster, Somerset, UK: Wise Research Limited.

CMO Counsil (2005): http://www.cmocouncil.org/ last accessed 09.02.2008.

Coase (1937): The Theory of the Firm. Economica, N.S. 4, pp. 386-405.

Cooper, G (2002): The Mutable Mobile: Social Theory in the Wireless World, pp. 19-31 in: Brown, B., Green, N. und Harper, R. (Eds.): Wireless World: Social and Interactional Aspects of the Mobile Age, London.

Cooper, RG; Kleinschmidt, EJ (1986): An Investigation into the New Product Process: Steps, Deficiencies and Impact. Journal of Product Innovation Management, No. 3 pp. 71-85.

Cooper, RG; Kleinschmidt, EJ (1995): Benchmarking the Firm's Critical Success Factors in New Product Development. Journal of Product Innovation Management, 12(5), pp. 374–391.

Cornelsen, J (2000): Kundenwertanalyse im Beziehungsmarketing, Nürnberg.

Crank, T (2007): A New Dimension in Loyalty Programs. Available from: http://www.maritz.com/White-Papers/Loyalty/A-New-Dimension-in-Loyalty-Programs.aspx last accessed: 09.02.2008.

Crosby, LA; Evans, KR; Cowles, D (1990): Relationship Quality in Services Selling: An Interpersonal Influence Perspective, Journal of Marketing. Vol. 52, April, pp. 21-34.

Cundiff, EW (1988): The Evolution of Retailing Institutions across Cultures, in Nevett, T. and Fullerton, R.A. (Eds.), Historical Perspectives in Marketing: Essays in Honor of Stanley C. Hollander. Lexington Books, Lexington, Massachusetts.

Davis, FD (1989): Perceived Usefulness, Perceived Ease of Use, and User Acceptance of Information Technology. MIS Quarterly, Vol. 13, No. 3 (Sep., 1989), pp. 319-340.

de Ruyter, K; Wetzels, M; Kleijnen, M (2001): Customer adoption of e-service: an experimental study. International Journal of Service Industry Management (12:2), 184-207.

de Vriendt J; Laine P; Lerouge C (2002): Mobile network evolution: a revolution on the move, IEEE Communications Magazine, April 2002.

Dickinger A; Haghirian, P; Murphy, J; Scharl, A (2004): An Investigation and Conceptual Model of SMS Marketing, in Proceedings of the 37th Hawaii Int. Conf. on System Sciences, Hawaii, 2004, pp. 31-41.

Dittrich, S (2000): Kundenbindung als Kernaufgabe im Marketing: Kundenpotentiale langfristig ausschöpfen, St. Gallen.

Dowling, GR; Uncles, M (1997): Do Customer Loyalty Programs Really Work? MIT Sloan Managment Review, Vol. 38, No. 4.

Economist (2005): Frequent-flyer miles, In terminal decline? The Economist, Jan 6th 2005.

Eisenhardt, K. (1989): Building Theories from Case Study Research, The Academy of Management Review, Vol. 14, No. 4, pp. 532-550.

Fischer, T; Tewes, M (2001): Vertrauen und Commitment in der Dienstleistungsinteraktion, in: Bruhn, M; Stauss, B.: Jahrbuch für Dienstleistungsmanagement 2001.

Floch, J; Hallsteinsen, S; Lie, A; Myrhaug, HI (2001): A Reference Model for Context-Aware Mobile Services, available from: http://www.nik.no/2001/06-floch.pdf last accessed 09.02.2008.

Flyvbjerg, B (2006): Five Misunderstandings About Case Study Research. Qualitative Inquiry, vol. 12, no. 2, April 2006, pp. 219-245.

Foss, K; Foss, NJ; Klein, PJ; Klein, SK (1997): Resources, Firms and Strategy: A Reader in the Resource-Based Perspective. Oxford: Oxford University Press.

Frank, U (2007): Evaluation of Reference Models, in: Fettke, P. and Loos, P.: Reference Modeling for Business Systems Analysis, Idea Group.

Gamma, E; Helm, R; Johnson, RE (1995): Design Patterns. Elements of Reusable Object-Oriented Software. Addison Wesley.

Gillenson, ML; Sherrell, DL; Chen, L (1999): Information Technology as the Enabler of One-to-One Marketing Communications of AIS Volume 2, Article 18.

Goldberg, D; Nichols, D; Oki, BM; Terry, D (1992): Using collaborative filtering to weave an information tapestry. Communications of the ACM 35, 12, pp. 61-70.

Grönroos, C (1994): Quo Vadis, Marketing? Toward a Relationship Marketing Paradigm, Journal of Marketing Management, Vol. 10, No. 5, pp.347-360

Grönroos, C (2004): The relationship marketing process: communication, interaction, dialogue, value, Journal of Business & Industrial Marketing, Vol.19 No.2, pp 99-113.

GSM Association (2005): European SMS Guide, Internet: http://www.gsmworld.com/documents/index.shtml, last accessed 26.11.2005.

Haig, M (2002) Mobile Marketing: The Message Revolution, London: Kogan Page.

Hargadon, A; Sutton, RI (1997): Technology Brokering and Innovation in a Product Development Firm. Administrative Science Quarterly 42(4), pp. 716–749

Heitmann, M; Aschmoneit, P (2003): Consumer Cognition towards Communities, in: Proceedings of Hawaii International Conference on System Sciences (HICCS-36).

Helyar, H (2002): Usability of Portable Devices: The Case of WAP, in: Brown, B., Green, N. und Harper, R. (Eds.): Wireless World: Social and Interactional Aspects of the Mobile Age, London, pp. 195-206.

Henard, DH; Szymanski DM (2001): Why Some New Products are More Successful than Others. Journal of Marketing Research, 38(August), pp. 362-375.

Hevner, AR; Salvatore TM; Park, J; Ram, S (2004): Design Science in Information Systems Research, MIS Quarterly Vol. 28 No. 1.

Hohmann, L (2003): Beyond Software Architecture: Creating and Sustaining Winning Solutions, New York: Addison Wesley.

Houston, FS; Gassenheimer, JB (1987): Marketing and exchange. Journal of Marketing, 51(October), pp. 3-18.

Hoyer, WD; Brown, SP (1990): Effects of Brand Awareness on Choice for a Common, Repeat Purchase Product, Journal of Consumer Research, vol. 17 (2), pp. 141-148.

Impaq Group (2005) Mobile life 1, Challenging the rules of loyalty. London, UK.

Jaffe, LJ; Jamieson, LF; Berger, PD (1992): Impact of comprehension, positioning, and segmentation on advertising response. Journal of Advertising Research, 32(3), 24–33.

Jain, AK; Murty, MN; Flynn, PJ (1999): Data Clustering: A Review, ACM Computing Surveys, Vol 31, No. 3, pp. 264-323.

Jelassi, T; Enders, A (2004): Leveraging Wireless Technology for Mobile Advertising, in Proceedings of the 12th European Conf. on Information Systems, Turku, Finland, 2004.

Jensen, MC; Meckling, WH (1976): Theory of the firm: Managerial behavior, agency costs and ownership structure. Journal of Financial Economics, Vol. 3, pp. 303-360.

Jupiter Research (2005): The ROI of Email Relevance: Improving Campaign Results through Targeting. Research Report.

Kaas, KP (2000): Alternative Konzepte der Theorieverankerung, in: Backhaus, K. (Ed.): Deutschsprachige Marketingforschung. Bestandsaufnahme und Perspektiven, Stuttgart: Schäffer-Poeschel, pp. 55-78.

Kahan, R (1998): Using database marketing techniques to enhance your one-to-one marketing initiatives, Journal of Consumer Marketing, Vol. 15 No. 5, pp. 491-493.

Kalwani, M; Narayandas, N (1995): Long-Term Manufacturer-Supplier Relationships: Do They Pay Off for Supplier Firms?, Journal of Marketing, Vol. 59, January, pp. 1-16.

Kalyanam, K; Zweben, M (2005): The Perfect Message at the Perfect Moment. Harvard Business Review, November 2005. 83(11):112-20.

Kaplan, LB; Szybillo, GJ; Tocoby, J (1974): Components of perceived risk in product purchase: a cross validation, Journal of Applied Psychology, Vol. 59 No.3, pp. 287-91.

Katz, ML; Shapiro, C (1994): Systems Competition and Network Effects, in: Journal of Economic Perspectives, 8 (2), pp. 93-115.

Kavassalis, PN; Spyropoulou, DD; Mitrokostas, V; Gikas, G; Hatzistamatiou, A (2002): Mobile Permission Marketing - Framing the Market Inquiry, in Proceedings of the 13th Int. Telecommunications Society's (ITS) European Regional Conf., Madrid.

Keller, KL (1993): Conceptualizing, Measuring, and Managing Customer-Based Brand Equity, Journal of Marketing, vol. 57 (1), 1993, pp. 1-22.

Kimball, R; Reeves, L; Thornthwaite, W; Ross, M; Thornwaite, W (1998): The Data Warehouse Lifecycle Toolkit: Expert Methods for Designing, Developing and Deploying Data Warehouses. New York: John Wiley & Sons.

King, P; Tester, J (1999): The landscape of persuasive technologies. Communications of the ACM, 42, 5, pp. 31-38.

Klee, A (2000): Strategisches Beziehungsmanagement. Ein integrativer Ansatz zur strategischen Planung und Implementierung des Beziehungsmanagement. Aachen.

Kopalle, P; Neslin, S (2003): The Economic Viability of Frequency Reward Programs in a Strategic Competitive Environment, Review of Marketing Science, Berkeley Electronic Press, vol. 1(1), pp. 1002-1002.

Kotler, P (1966): A Design for the Firm's Marketing Nerve Center, Business Horizons, Fall 1966, pp. 63-74.

Kotler, P (1972): A Generic Concept of Marketing, Journal of Marketing, Vol. 36, April 1972, pp. 46-54.

Krasner, G (1985): Smalltalk- 80: User Interfaces and Graphical Applications. Addison Wesley.

Krassnig, H; Paier, U (2006): Collaborative support for on-line banking solutions in the financial services industry. WIT Transactions on Modelling and Simulation, Vol 43, pp. 21-32.

Kroeber-Riel, W; Weinberg, P (2003): Konsumentenverhalten, 8. Aufl. München: Vahlen.

Kruchten P (1995): Architectural Blueprints: The 4+1 View Model of Software Architecture. IEEE Software 12 (6).

Kumar N; Scheer, LK; Steenkamp, J (1995): The Effects of Perceived Interdependence on Dealer Attitudes. Journal of Marketing Research, Vol. 32, No. 3, pp. 348-356.

Kumar, V; Reinartz, WJ (2006): Customer Relationship Management : A Databased Approach. Wiley.

Lehner, F; Sperger, EM; Nösekabel, H (2004): Evaluation Framework for a Mobile Marketing Application in 3rd Generation Networks, in Mobile Economy – Transaktionen, Prozesse, Anwendungen und Dienste, Augsburg.

Leppäniemi, M; Karjaluoto, H (2005): Factors Influencing Consumers' Willingness to Accept Mobile Advertising. A Conceptual Model, International Journal of Mobile Communications, vol. 3 (3), pp. 197-213.

Li EY; McLeod, R; Rogers JC (2001): Marketing Information Systems in Fortune 500 companies: a longitudinal analysis of 1980, 1990 , and 2000, Information & Management 38, pp. 307-322.

Mahajan, V; Wind J (1992): New Product Models: Practice, Shortcomings and Desired Improvements. Journal of Product Innovation Management, No. 9, pp. 128-139.

Market (2005): Market Kundenkarten Monitor, 2005, Market Studienblätter 70/05.

McManus; Scornavacca (2005): Mobile Marketing: Killer application or new hype? Proceedings of the International Conference on Mobile Business, ICMB05.

Meyer, C; Schwager, A (2007): Understanding Customer Experience, Harvard Business Review, Harvard Business School Publishing Corporation, Boston, MA, 85 (2), 2007, pp.117-126.

Muniz, AM; O'Guin, TC (2001): Brand Communities, Journal of Consumer Research, No. 27, pp. 412-432.

Neudorfer, R (2004): Analyse der Leistungserstellung und des Leistungsabsatzes von Mobilfunk Geschäftsmodellen, Dissertation, Karl-Franzens-Universität Graz.

Nielsen (1993): Usability Engineering. San Diego: Academic Press.

Nieschlag, R; Dichtl, E; Hörschgen, H (2002): Marketing, 19. Auflage, Berlin.

NTT DoCoMo (2007): History of DoCoMo, Internet: http://www.nttdocomo.com/about/company/history/index.html last accessed 11.08.2007

Olson, JR; Olson, GM (1990): The growth of cognitive modeling in human-computer interaction since GOMS. Human-Computer Interaction, 5, pp. 221-265. Reprinted in Baecker, RM, Grudin, J, Buxton, WAS, Greenberg, S (1995), Readings in human-computer interaction: Toward the year 2000, pp. 603-625. 2nd ed. San Francisco, CA: Morgan Kaufmann Publishers.

Padilla, M (2004): The Requirements Rift, User Experience, 3 (6), Usability Professionals' Association, Bloomingdale, IL, 2004, pp.12-13.

Parasuraman, A; Leonard, LB; Zeithaml,VA (1991): Refinement and Reassessment of the SERVQUAL Scale, Journal of Retailing, No. 67, pp. 420-450.

Petrovic, O; Kittl, C; Teksten, RD (2001): Developing Business Models for eBusiness, International Conference on Electronic Commerce, Wien.

Pousttchi, K; Wiedemann, DG (2006): A Contribution to Theory Building for Mobile Marketing: Categorizing Mobile Marketing Campaigns through Case Study Research. International Conference on Mobile Business (ICMB). Copenhagen, Denmark.

Rafaeli, S (1988): Interactivity: From new media to communication, in Hawkins, RP; Wiemann, JM; Pingree, S (Eds.), Advancing Communication Science: Merging Mass and Interpersonal Processes, Sage, Newbury Park, CA, 1988, pp. 110-134.

Rai, A; Patnayakuni, R; Patnayakuni, N (1997): Technology investment and business performance. Communications of the ACM 40, Jul. 1997, pp. 89-97.

Reichheld FF (1996): The Loyalty Effect, Boston, Massachusetts: Harvard Business School Press.

Research and Consultancy Outsourcing Services (2007): Europe Mobile Handset Market Analysis, http://www.researchandmarkets.com/reportinfo.asp?report_id =337216, last accessed 22.02.2007.

Rogers, E (1995): Diffusion of Innovations. New York: The Free Press.

Room, A (1987): History of Branding, in Murphy, JM (Ed.), Branding: A Key Marketing Tool. UK: The Macmillan Press Ltd.

Rosenberg, LJ; Cziepiel, JA (1984): A Marketing Approach to Customer Retention, Journal of Consumer Marketing, Vol. 1, Spring, pp.45-51.

Rösger, J; Herrmann, A; Heitmann, M (2007): Der Markenareal-Ansatz zur Steuerung von Brand Communities, in: Bauer, Große-Leege, Rösger, Interactive Marketing im Web 2.0+, Munich: Vahlen.

Rudolf, T; Emrich, O; Meise, JN (2007): Einsatzmöglichkeiten von Web 2.0-Instrumenten im Online-Handel und Ihre Nutzung durch Konsumenten, in: Bauer, Große-Leege, Rösger, Interactive Marketing im Web 2.0+, Munich: Vahlen.

Sapia, C; Blaschka, M; Höfling, G; Dinter, B (1999): Extending the E/R Model for the Multidimensional Paradigm. In Proceedings of the Workshops on Data Warehousing and Data Mining: Advances in Database Technologies (November 19 - 20, 1998). Y. Kambayashi, D. L. Lee, E. Lim, M. K. Mohania, and Y. Masunaga, Eds. Lecture Notes In Computer Science, vol. 1552. Springer-Verlag, London, pp. 105-116.

Sarwar, B; Karypis, G; Konstan, J; Reidl, J (2001): Item-based collaborative filtering recommendation algorithms. In Proceedings of the 10th international Conference on World Wide Web (Hong Kong, May 01 - 05, 2001). WWW '01. ACM, pp. 285-295.

Schmid, BF (2000): Elektronische Märkte, in: Weiber, R. (Eds.): Handbuch Electronic Business: Informationstechnologien - Electronic Commerce - Geschäftsprozesse, Wiesbaden, pp. 179-207.

Schmid, BF; Lyczek, B (2006): Unternehmenskommunikation: Kommunikationsmanagement aus Sicht der Unternehmensführung, Wiesbaden: Gabler.

Schütte, R (1998): Grundsätze ordnungsmäßiger Referenzmodellierung : Konstruktion konfigurations- und anpassungsorientierter Modelle. Wiesbaden: Gabler.

Schwarz, T (2001): Permition Marketing im Mobile Commerce, Mobile Commerce, Gabler, Wiesbaden.

Segaran T (2007): Programming Collective Intelligence, Sebastopol, USA: O'Reilly.

Shapiro, BP; Wyman, J (1981): New Ways to Reach Your Customer, Harvard Business Review, (July-August), pp. 103-110.

Shapiro, C; Varian, HR (1999): Information Rules. A Strategic Guide to the Network Economy. Boston.

Sharp, B; Sharp, A (1997): Loyalty Programs and their Impact on Repeat-purchase Loyalty Patterns, International Journal of Research in Marketing, Volume 14, Number 5, pp.473-487.

Sheth, JN; Parvatiyar, A (1995): The evolution of relationship marketing, International Business Review, Vol. 4 No.4, pp.397-418.

Sheth, JN; Sisodia, R (1995): Improving the Marketing Productivity, in Encyclopedia of Marketing for the Year 2000. American Marketing Association - NTC, Chicago.

Simonitsch, K (2003): Mobile Business – Geschäftsmodelle und Kooperationen, Köln: Eul Verlag.

Singh, SS; Dipak, J; Krishnan, T (2007): Customer Loyalty Programs: When Are They Profitable, Work in progress.

Smudde P (2005): Blogging, Ethics and Public Relations: A Proactive and Dialogic Approach, Public Relations Quaterly, No. 50, pp. 34-38.

Spremann, K (1990): Asymmetrische Information. In: Zeitschrift für Betriebswirt-schaft 60 (1990), pp. 561-586.

Staehle, W; Conrad, P; Sydow, J (1999): Management. München: Vahlen.

Stähler, P (2001): Geschäftsmodelle in der digitalen Ökonomie: Merkmale, Strategien und Auswirkungen, Köln-Lohmar: Josef Eul Verlag.

Stake, RE (1995): The art of case study research. Thousand Oaks, CA: Sage.

Statistik Austria (2007a): Umsatzanteil der über E-Commerce abgewickelten Verkäufe von Unternehmen im Jahr 2006. Available from: http://www.statistik.at/web_de/static/umsatzanteil_der_ueber_e-commerce_abgewickelten_verkaeufe_von_unternehmen__022201.pdf last accessed: 09.02.2008,

Statistik Austria (2007b): Unternehmen mit Website im EU-Vergleich 2007. Available from: http://www.statistik.at/web_de/statistiken/informationsgesellschaft/ikteinsatz_in_unternehmen_e-commerce/020544.html last accessed: 09.02.2008.

Steinbock, D (2003) Wireless Horizon – Strategy and competition in the worldwide mobile marketplace, New York: Amacom.

Stewart, K (1998): The customer exit process - a review and research agenda, Journal of Marketing Management, Vol. 14 No.4, pp. 235-50.

Strauss, B; Seidel, W (2005): Beschwerdenmanagement, München und Wien: Carl Hanser-Verlag.

Symbian (2007): Java Support in Symbian OS, http://developer.symbian.com/main/ oslibrary/java_papers/, last accessed 25.11.2007.

Telephia (2007): European Subscriber and Device Report, Q3 2006, http://telephia.com/html/Smartphonepress_release_template.html, accessed 2007-02-22.

Timmers, P (1998): Business Models for Electronic Markets, in: Gadient, Yves; Schmid, Beat F.; Selz, Dorian: EM - Electronic Commerce in Europe. EM - Electronic Markets, Vol. 8, No. 2, 07/98.

Treiblmaier H; Strebinger A (2006): B2C-E-Commerce als Treiber simultaner Veränderungen in IT-Struktur und Markenarchitektur, WIRTSCHAFTSINFORMATIK 48, pp. 87-95.

Trommsdorff, V (1998): Konsumentenverhalten, 3. Auflage, Stuttgart.

Turowski, K; Pousttchi, K (2003): Mobile Commerce – Grundlagen und Techniken, Heidelberg: Springer.

Ulrich, H (1984): Die Betriebswirtschaftslehre als anwendungsorientierte Sozialwissenschaft, in: Ulrich, H., Dyllick, T., Probst, G. (Hrsg.), Management, S. 170-195.

Uncles, M; Dowling, GR; Hammond, K (1997): Customer Loyalty and Customer Loyalty Programs, School of marketing Working Paper, University of new South Wales.

Wamser, C (2000): "Werbung und Electronic Commerce – eine ökonomische Perspektive der Werbeinteraktion", pp. 131-168 in C. Wamser (Ed.), Electronic Commerce - Grundlagen und Perspektiven. München: Vahlen.

Widom, J; Ceri, S (1996): Active Database Systems: Triggers and Rules For Advanced Database Processing. Morgan Kaufmann.

Wieringa, R; de Jonge, W (1991): The identification of objects and roles - object identifiers revisited, Technical Report IR-267, Faculty of Mathematics and Computer Science, Vrije Univeriteit, Amsterdam, December 1991.

Wilke, K; Duscha, A, Hudetz, K (2005): Kundenbindung über das Internet, in: Hudetz, E-Commerce im Handel – Status Quo und Perspectiven, Gernsbach.

Wilkie, WL (1994): Consumer behavior. New York: Wiley.

Williamson, O (1975): Markets and Hierarchies: Analysis and Antitrust Implications. New York: The Free Press.

Wirtz, B; Becker, BD (2002): Geschäftsmodelle und Geschäftsmodellvarianten im Electronic Business, Eine Analyse zu Erscheinungsformen von Geschäftsmodellen, in WiSt, Wirtschaftswissenschaftliches Studium, 2002, 31. Jahrgang, Heft 2, p. 85.

Woolf, B (2001): Loyalty Marketing: The Second Act. Available online: http://www.brianwoolf.com/downloads.

Yin RK (2002): Case Study Research. Design and Methods. Third Edition. Applied social research method series Volume 5. California: Sage Publications.

Yrjänäinen, J; Neuvo, Y (2002): Wireless Meets Multimedia, in: Wireless Communication and Mobile Computing, 2 (6), pp. 553-562.

Zeidler, C (2004), Economics of the Software Industry, Diplomarbeit, Technische Universität Wien.

Zeng, W; Wen, J (2002): 3G Wireless Multimedia: Technologies and Practical Issues, in: Wireless Communication and Mobile Computing, 2 (6), pp. 563-572.

Zuser, W; Grechenig, T; Köhle, M (2001): Software Engineering. Mit UML und dem Unified Process, Pearson Education.

GPSR Compliance
The European Union's (EU) General Product Safety Regulation (GPSR) is a set
of rules that requires consumer products to be safe and our obligations to
ensure this.

If you have any concerns about our products, you can contact us on

ProductSafety@springernature.com

In case Publisher is established outside the EU, the EU authorized
representative is:

Springer Nature Customer Service Center GmbH
Europaplatz 3
69115 Heidelberg, Germany